WORKING WITH CHILDREN, YOUNG PEOPLE AND FAMILIES

To order, please contact our distributor: BEBC Distribution, Albion Close, Parkstone, Poole, BH12 3LL. Telephone: 0845 230 9000, email: learningmatters@bebc.co.uk.

You can also find more information on each of these titles and our other learning resources at www.learningmatters.co.uk

WORKING WITH CHILDREN, YOUNG PEOPLE AND FAMILIES

A course book for
foundation degrees

Editors
**Billie Oliver
and Bob Pitt**

LearningMatters

First published in 2011 by Learning Matters Ltd

© 2011 Billie Oliver, Bob Pitt, Rachel Sales, Maggie Whittle, Richard Kimberlee, Jonathan Coles, Tillie Curran, Shekar Bheenuck, Helen Bovill, Jane Tarr, Adele Gardner and Gill Evans.

The rights of Billie Oliver, Bob Pitt, Rachel Sales, Maggie Whittle, Richard Kimberlee, Jonathan Coles, Tillie Curran, Shekar Bheenuck, Helen Bovill, Jane Tarr, Adele Gardner and Gill Evans to be identified as Authors of this Work (as listed above) have been asserted by them in accordance with the Copyright, Designs and Patents Act 1988.

British Library Cataloguing in Publication Data
A CIP record for this book is available from the British Library.

ISBN: 978 0 85725 421 4

This book is also available in the following ebook formats:

Adobe ebook ISBN: 978 0 85725 423 8
EPUB ebook ISBN: 978 0 85725 422 1
Kindle ISBN: 978 0 85725 424 5

Cover and text design by Topics
Project management by Swales and Willis, Exeter, Devon
Typeset by Kelly Winter
Printed and bound in Great Britain by Short Run Press Ltd, Exeter, Devon

Learning Matters Ltd
20 Cathedral Yard
Exeter EX1 1HB
Tel: 01392 215560

info@learningmatters.co.uk
www.learningmatters.co.uk

Contents

About the authors

Billie Oliver is a Principal Lecturer in Children and Youth Studies in the Department of Health and Applied Social Sciences at the University of the West of England (UWE). Her teaching specialisms include group work, interpersonal skills, community engagement and social policy. She has a practitioner background as a teacher, youth worker and community education worker and has worked extensively with the voluntary and community sector.

Bob Pitt is a Senior Lecturer in the Department of Health and Applied Social Sciences at UWE. He has a practitioner background in community development and lifelong learning. He is Programme Leader for the Foundation Degree, Working with Children, Young People and Families and teaches social policy and engaging with service users across programmes in the Department.

Helen Bovill is a Senior Lecturer in Lifelong Learning in the Department of Education at UWE. She is the Programme Leader for the Foundation Degree Educational Support and is currently researching the issues that non-traditional students face in returning to learn. She has taught widely in college and university, principally with under-represented groups and mature students. Her research interests lie in lifelong learning, non-traditional student identity, widening participation and social justice.

Rachel Sales is Professional Lead for Children's Nursing in the Department of Nursing and Midwifery at UWE. She has a practitioner background as a children's nurse working with children and young people with cancer and head injuries and teaches across a broad range of subjects.

Jane Tarr is Director of Training for the Children and Young People's Workforce in the Department of Education at UWE. She has a practitioner background as a teacher having worked in special, primary and secondary schools. She currently leads programmes for learning support assistants in schools and colleges and teaches on a range of modules designed to enhance inclusive educational provision and encourage students to research their professional practice at all levels. Her current research explores diverse perspectives on inclusive school communities, community cohesion and equalities legislation.

Maggie Whittle has a background as a practising children's nurse and university teacher for undergraduate and postgraduate health care and education students. Her research and teaching interests focus on safeguarding children affected by loss, and death education for professionals caring for children and families living with life limiting and life threatening health care needs.

Gill Evans is an Associate Lecturer at UWE and Chartered Psychologist. She is a former teacher and Principal and Specialist Senior (Child Protection) Psychologist. Gill's works in primary schools on a preventative, personal safety programme resulted in the publication of *Child Protection: A Whole Curriculum Approach* (1992). Gill has been involved in a range of national working parties related to safeguarding and was Chair of the British Psychological Society Child Protection Working Party, resulting in publication of *Child Protection Portfolio* (2007).

Richard Kimberlee is a Senior Research Fellow in the Department of Health and Applied Social Sciences at UWE. He has a background in exploring young people's political disposition and participation and he researches young people's involvement in health and community initiatives in the UK and Europe.

Jonathan Coles is a senior lecturer in Mental Health and Learning Disabilities at UWE. He has a practice background as a special educational needs teacher, developing courses for young people and adults with learning difficulties and/or mental health needs. He currently supports the development of service user and carer involvement in social work education within the faculty.

Adele Gardner is a Senior Lecturer in the Department of Education at UWE. She has a practitioner background as a teacher and has worked within the field of special education in the UK and the United States of America. She currently teaches on a range of modules that engage students in thinking about inclusive education and multiprofessional contexts. She has a particular research interest in the education of children in care.

Shekar Bheenuck is a Principal Lecturer in the Department of Nursing and Midwifery at UWE. His doctoral dissertation explored the lives and experiences of overseas nurses working in the National Health Service. In 2005 he collaborated with colleagues from the University of Bristol and the Peninsula Medical School in producing Different Differences, a curriculum framework for embedding disability equality teaching in medical education. He continues to work on a range of projects concerned with diversity and equality.

Tillie Curran is a Senior Lecturer in social work in the Department of Health and Applied Social Sciences at UWE. She teaches concepts of diversity and equality practices, working with students on a range of professional programmes, and her research is around disabled children's childhoods.

Abbreviations and acronyms

APIR	Assessment, Planning, Implementation and Review
BSL	British Sign Language
CAF	Common Assessment Framework
CBT	Cognitive Behavioural Therapy
CWDC	Children's Workforce Development Council
C4EO	Centre for Excellence and Outcomes in Children and Young People's Services
DAP	developmentally appropriate practice
DCSF	Department for Children, Schools and Families (2007–2010)
DfE	Department for Education (2010–present)
DfEE	Department for Education and Employment (1995–2001)
DfES	Department for Education and Skills (2001–2007)
DH	Department of Health
EWO	education welfare officer
EYFS	Early Years Foundation Stage
EYPS	Early Years Professional Status
GP	general practitioner
GSCC	General Social Care Council
HLTA	higher level teaching assistant
HMSO	Her Majesty's Stationery Office
ICAS	Independent Complaints Advocacy Service
IQF	Integrated Qualifications Framework
ISP	Information Sharing Protocol
KSI	killed or seriously injured
LARSOA	Local Authority Road Safety Officers Association
LGB	lesbian, gay and bisexual
NCAS	National Care Advisory Service
NCB	National Children's Bureau
NCMA	National Childminding Association
NCVYS	National Council for Voluntary Youth Services
NEET	not in education, employment or training
NSPCC	National Society for the Prevention of Cruelty to Children

NVQ	National Vocational Qualification
Ofsted	Office for Standards in Education, Children's Services and Skills
PDP	personal development plan
PEP	personal education plan
Quango	quasi non-governmental organisation
QCG	Qualification in Careers Guidance
QTS	Qualified Teacher Status
SCIE	Social Care Institute for Excellence
SDF	Skills Development Framework
SEAL	Social and Emotional Aspects of Learning
SEN	special educational needs
SENCO	Special Educational Needs Co-ordinator
SEU	Social Exclusion Unit
TIN	Transition Information Network
UKYP	United Kingdom Youth Parliament
UNCRC	United Nations Convention on the Rights of the Child
UNESCO	United Nations Educational, Scientific and Cultural Organization
UNICEF	United Nations International Children's Emergency Fund
UWE	University of the West of England
YJB	Youth Justice Board
YOT	Youth Offending Team

1 AN INTRODUCTION TO INTEGRATED WORKING AND THE CHILDREN'S WORKFORCE

Billie Oliver and Bob Pitt

COMMON CORE OF SKILLS AND KNOWLEDGE FOR
THE CHILDREN'S WORKFORCE

- The Common Core describes the skills and knowledge that everyone who works with children and young people is expected to have.

- The six areas of expertise in the Common Core offer a single framework to underpin multi-agency and integrated working, professional standards, training and qualifications across the children and young people's workforce.

- The Common Core reflects a set of common values for practitioners that promote equality, respect diversity and challenge stereotypes. It helps to improve life chances for all children and young people, including those who have disabilities and those who are most vulnerable.

- The six areas of expertise in the Common Core work as a whole – so it will be important for individuals and organisations to consider the Common Core in the round.

(CWDC, 2010a)

CHAPTER OBJECTIVES

By the end of this chapter you should have an understanding of:

- key developments in policy and legislation that have led to the emergence of the children's workforce;

- key terminology associated with this policy agenda;

- theories and approaches underpinning integrated practice;

- guidance on how to make effective use of this book;

- useful resources to improve knowledge and practice.

Introduction

The aim of this chapter is to set out the framework for the rest of the book. Firstly the chapter will offer a discussion of the Common Core of Skills and Knowledge for the Children's Workforce and an overview of the variety of initiatives that have led to the Children's Workforce Reform Strategy and to the need for this book. Secondly, the chapter will explain the structure and thinking behind the way that each chapter has been constructed and suggest ways in which you might use the book to develop your knowledge and understanding.

The book is separated into nine chapters. The government has set out the basic skills and knowledge needed by people whose work brings them into regular contact with children, young people and their families (CWDC, 2010a). The book is built around this Common Core. It aims to help students and practitioners understand the theory behind these issues and to develop strategies for embedding them within their own practice.

Each chapter will focus on a different element of the Common Core of Skills and Knowledge for the Children's Workforce (CWDC, 2010a). As you will note when you read each chapter, there is frequently considerable overlap and connection between these different elements. By breaking them down into separate chapters we offer a *starting point* to begin to engage with some quite complex ideas. Each chapter will also offer you a range of activities and further resources to help you move beyond this starting point and begin to engage with the complexity and with the elements *in the round* (CWDC, 2010a).

This is a practical book. Written by a team of experienced practitioners and educators from a range of professional backgrounds, it is built around case studies and activities that will help you to deepen your understanding and skills. However, it is not possible to explore every facet of the lives of children and young people within the scope of this book. This book is an introductory text for those wanting to enter the world of work with children and young people and for those who, with some experience of work already, desire to strengthen their theoretical understanding of practice in order to move forward in their career.

Policy and legislation

In 2003 an inquiry was led by Lord Laming into what could be learned from the tragic death of a little girl called Victoria Climbié, who had been killed by those who were meant to take care of her. That inquiry resulted in a series of recommendations that led to the publication of a key government document: *Every Child Matters* (DfES, 2003).

> **ACTIVITY 1.1**
>
> There have been further tragic cases, since 2003, where children have died at the hands of those who were supposed to care for them. Some of these cases have received media publicity and have led to changes in practice (for example: Peter Connelly, Holly Wells and Jessica Chapman, and Khyra Ishaq).
>
> See if you can find out about any of these. What was learned from these cases? What recommendations for changing practice were made?

Laming concluded that children's needs were being neglected or overlooked through a lack of *joined-up working*, poor systems for information sharing and too great a reliance on professional and agency boundaries. As a result, *Every Child Matters* was characterised by calls for the creation of new services and new working practices that emphasise the integration of services that deal with children and young people. These new practices included multi-agency working and partnerships between the voluntary, community and statutory sectors; common assessments; information sharing; and joint training. The strategic aim behind this policy agenda was that those working with children and young people should be enabled to work across professional boundaries and to understand how their role fits in with the work of others.

The Common Core of Skills and Knowledge for the Children's Workforce

As a result of *Every Child Matters*, the government proposed a radical workforce reform strategy that aimed to overhaul the organisational and professional structures affecting all those working with children and young people. *The Children's Workforce Reform Strategy* (DfES, 2005a) set out the six areas of the Common Core of Skills and Knowledge for the Children's Workforce that outlines the basic skills and knowledge needed by people whose work brings them into regular contact with children, young people and their families – including volunteers. The six areas of expertise in the Common Core offer a single framework to underpin multi-agency and integrated working, professional standards, training and qualifications across the children and young people's workforce.

The Common Core was *refreshed* in 2010 and it is the updated version that is referred to throughout this book (CWDC, 2010a).

The six areas of the Common Core of Skills and Knowledge for the Children's Workforce are:

1   effective communication and engagement with children, young people and families;
2   child and young person development;
3   safeguarding children and promoting welfare of children;
4   supporting transitions;
5   multi-agency and integrated working;
6   information sharing.

Building Brighter Futures: Next Steps for the Children's Workforce (DCSF, 2008a) further committed government to ensuring that *services are integrated and personalised* through a ten-year workforce reform strategy. These commitments were affirmed in the government's *2020 Children and Young People's Workforce Strategy* (DCSF, 2008b) published in December 2008. In 2009, *The Children's Plan Two Years On* (DCSF, 2009a) summarised progress that had been made and set some further objectives for the continuing development of a *highly skilled and professional workforce across all our services for children and young people* and for improved partnerships within and between schools and children's services.

One of the aims of the Workforce Reform Strategy was to develop an Integrated Qualifications Framework (IQF) that would include a set of approved qualifications allowing progression, continuing professional development and mobility across the children and young people's workforce. For a qualification to be included in the IQF it would need to have been nationally accredited and to reflect the Common Core of Skills and Knowledge for the children and young people's workforce. The vision was that the qualifications would have credibility with employers and be understood and accepted across the whole of the children and young people's workforce. It was hoped that, in time, the IQF would become a valuable resource, enabling employers, careers advisers and individual practitioners to map out career progression across the workforce and showing how qualifications link to one another.

Progress with launching the IQF was, however, delayed by the general election in May 2010 and the subsequent change of government. In November 2009, the Young People's Workforce Reform Programme was launched with the aim of developing a skilled and confident workforce to deliver the best possible outcomes for young people. This programme also included a common platform of skills and competences and the development of a common foundation degree. The Skills Development Framework (SDF) was launched in September 2010 (CWDC, 2010b). The SDF aims to support employers across the workforce to cultivate integrated working skills within their organisations. It focuses on the shared skills that underpin integrated working practice and that complement the professional and specialist skills that workers already have (see 'Useful resources' at the end of this chapter for a link to download a copy of these documents).

ACTIVITY 1.2

In November 2010 it was announced that the government would no longer fund workforce development activity through the CWDC as a separate organisation. Instead, *ongoing key functions* would be integrated into the Department for Education (DfE).

Visit the DfE website (www.education.gov.uk) to see if there have been any further developments with integrated working since this book was written.

The children's workforce

The children's and young people's workforce is broad and diverse. It includes paid staff and volunteers who work with children and young people. Many practitioners combine work with young people with a specialism such as sport, health or the arts.

ACTIVITY 1.3

Pick a role within the children's workforce diagram (Figure 1.1) with which you are unfamiliar. Search the internet to identify some useful sources that tell you more about the role.

Being a part of *the children's workforce* does not mean that everyone has the same disciplinary expertise or professional knowledge base. The aim of developing an integrated workforce was not to make everyone *the same*. Rather the aim was to enable practitioners from different disciplinary backgrounds to be able to work together, supporting each other to ensure the best outcomes for each child. It is important to recognise different professional approaches as being complementary to each other rather than in competition.

Understanding terms and definitions

Key terms in the policy agenda outlined so far are set out below. We acknowledge that there are few single, all-encompassing definitions for most terms and that some are problematic; however the aim is to offer some explanation to aid understanding and avoid confusion with similar words or phrases.

- *Common Core*: refers to a set of common values, skills and knowledge that those working with children and young people (including volunteers) are expected to have.
- *Children and young people's workforce*: all those who work in paid employment or voluntary work with children or young people (usually defined as aged 0 to 18).
- *Workforce reform strategy*: government policy setting out a series of principles and initiatives aiming to change and improve the current workforce.
- *Joined-up working*: describes working together across organisational or professional boundaries to tackle shared issues or to provide services jointly.
- *Integrated working*: where everyone supporting children and young people work together effectively to put the child at the centre, meet their needs and improve their lives (source: www.cwdcouncil.org.uk/integrated-working).
- *Professional boundaries*: these define the limits of competence and behaviour within an individual's professional practice, usually set out in codes of conduct or ethical guidelines on the principles of good practice.
- *Agency boundaries*: these define the limits of competence and behaviour of the agency or organisation in the service it provides, usually set out in mission statements and policy documents.
- *Personalised services*: public services in health, education, care and welfare that are tailored to meet the personal needs of an individual.
- *Multi-agency working*: where professionals or staff from different organisations work together to provide services to meet the needs of children, young people and their families.
- *Voluntary, community and statutory sector partnerships*: an arrangement or agreement between independent organisations, operating as not-for-profit, within a single local community or established by law, to work together to achieve common aims or objectives.
- *Common assessments*: a standard approach adopted by different organisations and services to identify the needs of a child or young person in order to decide how those needs should be met.
- *Information sharing*: where practitioners use their professional judgment and experience on a case-by-case basis to decide whether and what personal information to share with other practitioners in order to meet the needs of a child (source: www.cwdcouncil.org.uk/information-sharing).

See 'abbreviations and acronyms' on page ix for explanations of other terms commonly found within the field of working with children, young people and their families.

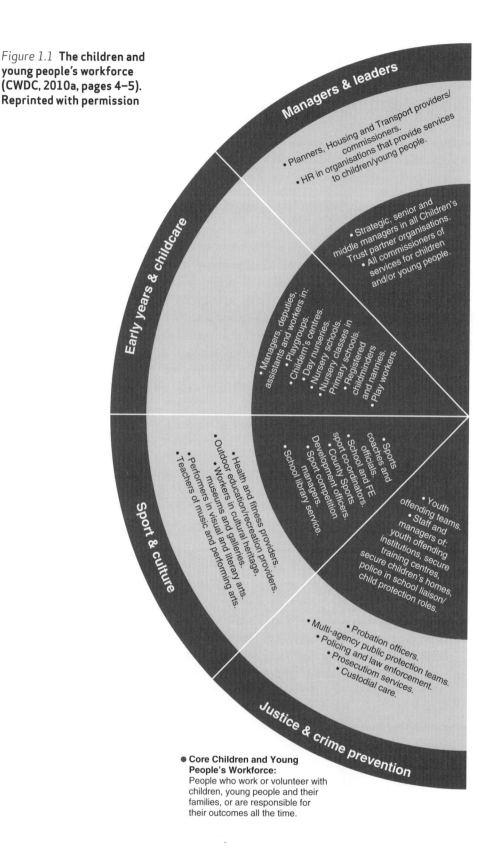

Figure 1.1 **The children and young people's workforce (CWDC, 2010a, pages 4–5). Reprinted with permission**

Managers & leaders

- Planners, Housing and Transport providers/ commissioners.
- HR in organisations that provide services to children/young people.

- Strategic, senior and middle managers in all Children's Trust partner organisations.
- All commissioners of services for children and/or young people.

Early years & childcare

- Managers, deputies, assistants and workers in:
- Playgroups.
- Children's centres.
- Day nurseries.
- Nursery schools.
- Nursery classes in Primary schools.
- Registered childminders and nannies.
- Play workers.

- Sports coaches and officials.
- School and FE sport co-ordinators.
- County Sports Development officers.
- Sport competition managers.
- School library service.

Sport & culture

- Health and fitness providers.
- Outdoor education/recreation providers.
- Workers in cultural heritage, museums and galleries.
- Performers in visual and literary arts.
- Teachers of music and performing arts.

- Youth offending teams.
- Staff and managers of: youth offending institutions, secure training centres, secure children's homes, police in school liaison/ child protection roles.

- Probation officers.
- Multi-agency public protection teams.
- Policing and law enforcement.
- Prosecutiom services.
- Custodial care.

Justice & crime prevention

- **Core Children and Young People's Workforce:**
  People who work or volunteer with children, young people and their families, or are responsible for their outcomes all the time.

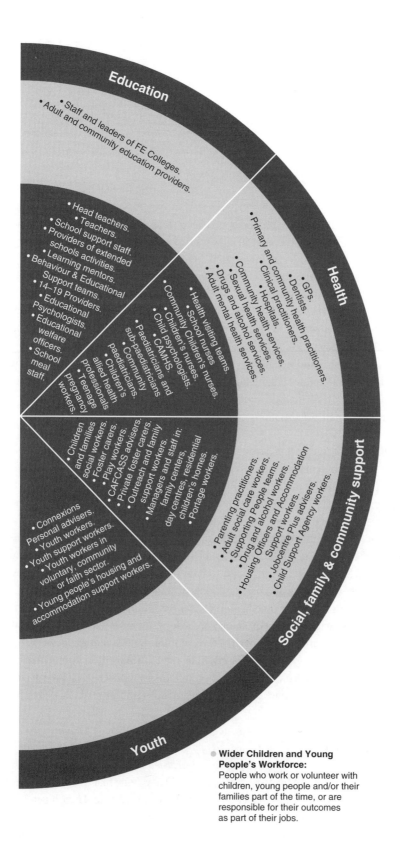

Education

- Staff and leaders of FE Colleges.
- Adult and community education providers.

- Head teachers.
- Teachers.
- School support staff.
- Providers of extended schools activities.
- Learning mentors.
- Behaviour & Educational Support teams.
- 14–19 Providers.
- Educational Psychologists.
- Educational welfare officers.
- School meal staff.

Health

- GPs.
- Dentists.
- Primary and community health practitioners.
- Clinical practitioners.
- Hospitals.
- Community health services.
- Sexual health services.
- Drugs and alcohol services.
- Adult mental health services.

- Health visiting teams.
- School nurses.
- Community Children's nurses.
- Children's nurses.
- Child psychologists.
- CAMHS.
- Paediatricians sub-paediatricians.
- Community paediatricians.
- Children's allied health professionals.
- Teenage pregnancy workers.

- Children and families social workers.
- Foster carers.
- Play workers.
- CAFCASS advisers.
- Private foster carers.
- Outreach and family support workers.
- Managers and staff in: family centers, residential day centres, residential children's homes.
- Portage workers.

Social, family & community support

- Parenting practitioners.
- Adult social care workers.
- Supporting People teams.
- Drug and alcohol workers.
- Housing Officers and Accommodation Support Workers.
- Jobcentre Plus advisers.
- Child Support Agency workers.

- Connexions Personal advisers.
- Youth workers.
- Youth support workers.
- Youth workers in voluntary, community or faith sector.
- Young people's housing and accommodation support workers.

Youth

- **Wider Children and Young People's Workforce:**
  People who work or volunteer with children, young people and/or their families part of the time, or are responsible for their outcomes as part of their jobs.

Theories and approaches underpinning integrated practice

Cunningham declared a commitment to joined-up government in his introduction to the White Paper *Modernising Government* (Cabinet Office, 1999):

> *To improve the way we provide services, we need all parts of government to work together better. We need joined-up government. We need integrated government.*
>
> (Cabinet Office, 1999, page 5)

The goal of *integrated government* was extended to policies and programmes at local and national levels in order to tackle issues and problems facing society, for example child poverty and neighbourhood renewal. Frameworks for integration, joined-up multi-agency working and collaboration are described in a number of academic texts and government documents.

Stewart et al. observe that *different models of integrated working can be located on a spectrum, ranging from limited collaboration on specific issues to full integration as represented by pooled resources and a single set of objectives* (2003, page 336). Horwath and Morrison (2007) describe five levels of collaborative arrangements in child welfare services on a continuum from *Communication* with individuals from different disciplines talking together, through *Co-operation* on a case-by-case basis, *Co-ordination* with more formalized joint working, *Coalition* with joint organisational structures, to *Integration* where organisations merge under a new joint identity.

Anning et al. (2010) present integration as four layers of an onion: *governance, strategy, processes and front-line delivery*, with outcomes for children, young people and their families at the centre. At a national level under New Labour in 2007, government departments responsible for children and young people services were reorganised into the Department for Children, Schools and Families to reflect an integrated services approach. Inter-agency governance was demonstrated by, for example, incorporating inspection of childcare and youth services into national inspection of children's services carried out by the Office for Standards in Education, Children's Services and Skills (Ofsted). Integrated strategy involved reallocation of resources from different departments to create new organisational arrangements, for example establishing Children's Trusts to bring together all services for children and young people in an area. Integrated processes include setting up shared procedures for assessment and information sharing, for example the standardised approach of the Common Assessment Framework. Integrated front-line delivery may be seen in, for example, the Sure Start programme that targeted whole communities and drew on a range of professional support to seek improvements *in health, education, social welfare, family support and employability* (Anning et al., 2010, page 128).

While some writers acknowledge advantages to integrating services with *unified management system, pooled funds, common governance, whole systems approach to training, information and finance, single assessment and shared targets* there are also likely to be *tensions, conflicts and dilemmas for partnership members* (Horwath and Morrison, 2007, page 58). They argue that working practices are likely to be affected by collaborations that emphasise systems, structure and funding rather than working relationships and outcomes for those receiving the services. Such *tensions, conflicts and dilemmas* arise from complexities in theoretical approaches, policy intentions and working practices that will be explored in chapters that follow, for example in Chapter 7.

How to use this book

This book is separated into nine chapters. The title of each chapter clearly indicates its focus.

Chapter 2 compares perspectives on childhood, youth and families from different time periods and countries to demonstrate the social construction of these terms. It highlights contemporary debates such as childhood in crisis, moral panics, age of consent and the rights of children and young people.

Chapter 3 introduces major theories and concepts on child and adolescent development that often contradict each other. It critically discusses how emotional, physical, intellectual, social and moral development can impact on the development of children and young people.

Chapter 4 explores safeguarding in the context of children and young people's services. The chapter outlines key legal and policy procedures for child protection, underpinned by he importance of sharing information. It considers the needs of vulnerable children, young people and their families in different situations and the roles of a range of professionals.

Chapter 5 advocates for improved practitioner communication skills that support and encourage children and young people to participate. An emphasis is placed on the importance of listening skills as a tool to develop trust and encourage participation. Practical examples illustrate ways of empowering children and young people to be involved in decision-making and present methods to facilitate their voices being heard.

Chapter 6 considers transitions experienced by children and young people throughout their lives from early years and on into adulthood accompanied by greater independence and more responsibilities. The chapter outlines effective and appropriate support offered by a range of professionals and agencies that address particular, as well as contested, and increasingly complex, transitions.

Chapter 7 examines the range of agencies involved within children's services to emphasise the importance of organisations and professionals working in a collaborative integrated manner. Key professional roles are described and theoretical models of partnership working are explored. The Common Assessment Framework is examined as a tool to encourage collaborative interprofessional communication.

Chapter 8 recognises the richness, possibilities and challenges for those working with children and young people arising from living and working in a world that is increasingly diverse. The chapter explores key concepts in diversity such as age, gender, disability, class, sexuality, culture and race, and manifestations of oppression. It introduces a number of models and frameworks to assist practitioner development.

Chapter 9 concludes with an exploration of a range of new roles that have emerged as a result of the Children's Workforce Strategy. It outlines developments in professional training, the IQF and the Children's Workforce Reform Strategy. The chapter invites the reader to reflect on their future career pathways and personal development.

This first chapter and the final chapter adopt a slightly different structure to the other seven chapters. Chapters 2–8 cover the skills and knowledge contained within the Common Core. The chapter authors have structured their content in such a way as to introduce you to the key policy and theoretical ideas behind their chapter topic. In addition they have gone on to illustrate the practical application of those ideas through illustrative case studies, reference to resources that you might use and a series of activities to help you to extend your theoretical and practical understanding. In each chapter you are encouraged to consider how you might progress your learning further and to reflect on your progress and development. The final chapter aims to provide an overview of some of the new roles and practice contexts that have emerged, and are still emerging, as a result of the policy agenda outlined in this first chapter. In that final chapter you are encouraged to consider job and career opportunities and to produce a personal development plan that sets out your goals and aspirations and how these may be achieved.

Each chapter ends with a summary of the key messages that you should have received from reading that chapter, followed by suggestions of further resources to extend your learning.

ACTIVITY 1.4

Choose a chapter of particular interest to you. Skim read the chapter to make brief notes to identify the following:

- a key policy or piece of legislation behind the chapter topic;
- a theory or model presented that you will return to for a closer reading;
- an idea or example of practice that you could apply to your own practice setting;
- a useful resource and an item of additional reading for further research and note-taking.

CHAPTER SUMMARY

This chapter has set out the overall aim of the book as an introductory text. It is structured to mirror the presentation of each chapter by including uniform headings, activities and useful resources. It has outlined key developments in policy and legislation to establish the Common Core of Skills and Knowledge for the Children's Workforce and the Children's Workforce Reform Strategy. It has listed and explained some key terms used within the policy agenda that has developed since the late 1990s. It has introduced models and approaches underpinning the concept of integrated practice.

This chapter has briefly outlined the content of the chapters while indicating how to make effective use of the book. The chapter concludes with an activity aimed at getting the reader to engage with the content in a practical and useful manner to develop their knowledge and understanding.

USEFUL RESOURCES

www.education.gov.uk This is the website address for the DfE. Look here for updates on government policy in relation to children and young people.

www.cwdcouncil.org.uk/common-core Use this link to find information about the Common Core and to download the most recent version.

www.cypnow.co.uk The on-line version of the magazine *Children and Young People Now* regularly contains discussion and news about changes to policy in children and young people's services.

www.cwdcouncil.org.uk/assets/0001/0487/Skills_Development_Framework_phase_one_24_August_2010.pdf Use this link to access a copy of the Skills Development Framework.

www.tda.gov.uk/teacher/developing-career/integrated-qualifications-framework.aspx This site offers some information on progress with the IQF.

http://cwdcouncil.blogspot.com Children's Workforce Matters blog about issues affecting those who work with children and young people in England.

FURTHER READING

Barker, R (ed) (2009) *Making Sense of Every Child Matters*. Bristol: Policy Press. This book contains detailed analysis of the practice implications of the *Every Child Matters* approach to policy.

Barrett, G, Sellman, D and Thomas, J (2005) *Interprofessional Working in Health and Social Care.* London: Palgrave. This book presents a helpful overview of the range of roles and perspectives of delivering integrated health and social care practice.

Knowles, G (2009) *Ensuring Every Child Matters,* London: Sage. This book explores the impact of *Every Child Matters* on practitioners' attitudes, beliefs and values.

2 CONSTRUCTIONS OF CHILDHOOD, YOUTH AND FAMILIES

Helen Bovill

COMMON CORE OF SKILLS AND KNOWLEDGE FOR
THE CHILDREN'S WORKFORCE

- Understand that babies, children and young people see and experience the world in different ways.

- Know and recognise the child or young person's position in their family or caring network, as well as a wider social context. Appreciate the diversity of these networks.

- Understand how the balance of influence from parents, peers, authority figures and others alters as the child or young person develops.

- Understand and take into account the effects of different parenting approaches, family structures and composition, backgrounds and routines.

- Understand the principles that dictate when young people are considered sufficiently mature to give or refuse consent to their information being shared.

- Understand the use that children and young people make of new technologies to understand the implications of risks of harm.

(CWDC, 2010a)

CHAPTER OBJECTIVES

By the end of this chapter you will have explored the following in relation to the constructs of childhood, youth and family:

- the multiple meanings of these constructs – and approaches that may help you understand them;

- how these constructs evolve and change over time and space;

- post-modern concerns regarding childhood, youth and families.

Introduction

The way in which we make sense of the world around us is shaped by our experiences of childhood, youth and family. The way that we interact as professionals with children, youth and families is heavily influenced by our own backgrounds. Aspects such as generation, gender, ethnicity and class impact upon our understandings of these concepts. Our ideas of these concepts are contested both in terms of time (historical emergence) and space (local, national and global). Consensus upon what childhood, youth and family actually are remains difficult; they are different things to different people throughout time and space. Exploration of the multiple meanings of these constructs is explored throughout this chapter.

What is a construct?

A construct can be said to be an idea, situation or event that has been 'invented' or 'made-up' by individuals and groups in a particular culture or society, in a particular time. A construct comes to exist because individuals and groups agree to behave as if it exists and they follow certain rules and conventions that may become the taken for granted 'norm' in a particular society at a particular time. A construct may become established because it is useful as a mechanism of social, economic and political organisation or control. A strong view of what particular constructs should look like may be held at a given time and in a given place, but if we look more deeply, a range of variations of constructs exists within all times and spaces. Childhood, youth and family have not always existed, they have not always existed as they do today, and they continue to exist very differently throughout the world.

How might we approach the study of childhood, youth and family?

ACTIVITY 2.1

Think about terms used to describe aspects of childhood, youth and family, such as:

- 'Victorian childhood', 'child of the 60s', 'child soldiers';
- 'debutant', 'hoodie', 'gang member';
- 'civil partnership', 'living together', 'arranged marriage';
- 'suburbia', 'kibbutz', 'inner-city living';
- 'lone parent', 'same sex parents', 'two-parent family';
- 'extended family', 'nuclear family', 'reconstituted family'.

What images do these terms conjure up? Do they suggest similar stages or rites of passage?

'Life cycle' or 'life course'?

To explain experiences of childhood, youth and family sometimes the idea of a *life cycle* (Allat and Keil, 1987) is used. A life cycle approach emphasises how we pass through similar stages (e.g. babyhood/childhood/youth/adulthood/age/death) and 'rites of passage' (e.g. education/work/marriage/childbearing or rearing/retirement).

There is merit in this approach as many of us go through these stages in one way or another; however a biological and social inevitability is implied that emphasises sameness in terms of when, how and if we go through these stages and rites of passage.

Another approach, which emphasises diversity and difference in terms of change throughout life, is the *life course* (Hockey and James, 1993). The life course approach emphasises how we are different; how we experience life differently; that we do not move through distinct stages of life at the same time; and that we may not experience particular rites of passage or that we may experience them differently.

Examples of the life course approach applied to childhood, youth and family might be:

- to recognise that childhood, youth and family as we know it has not always existed and that these concepts are 'lived out' in diverse ways;
- to consider and explore when and if constructs begin and end;
- to resist characterising a particular construct of childhood, youth or family as an 'ideal type';
- to explore how, when, where and why different types of childhood, youth and family operate without seeking to suggest preference for a particular type.

ACTIVITY 2.2

Use a long sheet of paper to map the major events, changes and occurrences in your own life. This might include:

- birth, attendance at pre-school, school starting age, transition to secondary school, age you finished secondary school.

Also include whether/when/if you:

- attended college or university, married, worked, had children. (If you are a younger student consider potential future plans.)

Now map a parent's, carer's or an older significant person's life that you are familiar with, in a different colour against your own. What are the similarities or differences and what might have influenced these? Think about generation, class, gender, ethnicity, culture and policy.

This section has demonstrated the dynamic rather than fixed nature of the social constructs of childhood, youth and family. This next section gives some detail regarding the debates over the emergence, definition and merit of these constructs.

Childhood

Is modern childhood, as we variously conceptualise it today, an invention? This debate started to emerge around the 1960s and prominent theorists offer competing discourses. They consider various arguments which explore when this particular 'stage' in life originated as a distinct and separate period in our lives.

Ariès (1962) investigated the construct of childhood and argued that babies and infants were cared for in terms of their biological needs, but once they were able to look after themselves they were very quickly treated in the same way that adults were. He uses the depiction, in art and literature, of children as small adults to support his argument. He further states that words such as 'child' would be used for any age and that terms such as 'adolescent' did not exist in pre-modern times. He argues that if words did not exist to describe childhood, then childhood could not exist. Within this argument childhood is not viewed as a separate and distinct stage; rather that it developed from the modern period.

De Mause (1974) would concur with this arguing that levels of childcare can be seen as progressively worse the further you look back in history. He discusses stages such as a period of *infanticide* followed by *abandonment* then *ambivalence* toward children. Stone (1977) offers further support for this argument exploring the rationality of parents' lack of emotional investment in their offspring in pre-modern times. Because of high mortality rates, he argued, parents did not risk the emotional damage that may occur as a result of so many infants and babies dying young; instead they were *emotionally neutral*.

Both Ariès and De Mause have been criticised for not taking account of gender, social class, status and national and local variations in child-rearing. Their evidence relied, almost solely, upon elite sources of art and literature. Pollock (1983) further adds that Ariès concentrated only upon children's education, therefore omitting to assess the period of life before the age of seven. Shahar (1990) offers a powerful counter argument to Ariès and De Mause. She assesses an abundance of art and literature devoted to a specific stage of childhood that also depicts love, care and attention. Hanawalt (2002, pages 440–460) offers a summary of these arguments and draws attention to the literature surrounding childhood in the late Middle Ages in the form of manuals such as: *The Babees' Book* and *How the Good Wife Taught Her Daughter* (page 443) and the rise of 'miracle stories' (pages 446–447) that depicted children being cured, saved or raised from the dead by saints. This would counter Stone's claim of emotional neutrality and offer an argument that parents were, indeed, affected by the mortality rates of their children.

None of these theorists is suggesting that childhood was thought of in the same way in medieval times, the Middle Ages or Victorian times as it is today, but there is a strong argument that childhood as a distinct and separate stage before adulthood was seen as existing in some form. To follow up some of these ideas in more detail you might like to look at books by Jenks (1996), Madge (2006), Mayall (2002) and Zwozdiak-Myers (2007).

ACTIVITY 2.3

Choose one of the following tasks to explore the experience of children from the beginning of the nineteenth century to the end of the Second World War.

Find legislation that was passed in the areas of labour and work for children (e.g. Factory Acts, Chimney Sweep Acts, Hours of Labour Acts); educational changes (e.g. Education Acts, establishment of state and charity schools); and the emergence of child protection and rights (e.g. establishment of children's societies and charities, provision of care for children outside of the family, and acts establishing rights or offering protection from cruelty, abuse or neglect).

Plot your findings on a timeline and consider the effects these changes may have had upon the construct of childhood; how this might have further established or prolonged the 'stage'; the effect this may have had upon the lives of children; how children began to be offered protection and rights, and the balance between these.

Useful sources of information

Look at some of the books in the reference list. Some of them have timelines. Look at some history books and websites that schools might use such as:

www.spartacus.schoolnet.co.uk/REVhistory.htm
www.schoolhistory.co.uk/
www.bbc.co.uk/history/

Youth

Just as the emergence, meaning and duration of childhood is debated, the same can be said of youth. Trying to define what youth is and which terms exemplify this stage remains difficult. When does the stage between childhood and adulthood begin and end? What characterises this stage? Is it the same or different now and in different places throughout the world? Do other constructs such as class, gender, ethnicity, generation and disability affect our understandings and experiences of youth? First it is useful to understand how different societies in different times describe this period.

ACTIVITY 2.4

Think about all the words you know that describe the period of youth.

For example, a news report on a National Children's Bureau survey of young people's attitudes, demonstrated that young people *resent* the way that they are often stereo-typically depicted (BBC News, 2009). Gardner (2009) gives more information on the way that the media tends to portray this period of time in his article: 'Hoodies, louts, scum...'.

Consider stereotypes and prejudices behind some terms describing youth.

Terms in common usage within British society today to describe those passing through this time of life are: *adolescent, teenager* or *youth*. Though these terms seem familiar to many today their origins give us a clue as to how this period of life was characterised and seen as distinct from childhood and adulthood in some modern, western cultures.

What characterises this period of life?

Biological

From the point of view of biological development, a span of time starting with puberty and concluding with maturity is used to judge when this time period begins and ends. Chronologically, this is often considered to begin around the ages of 12 or 13 and to conclude around 18 or 19 years of age, consequently the terms *teen* years or *teenager* apply though there is much debate about the meaning of these terms. As discussed in Chapter 3, some children may commence puberty much earlier than 12 and some young people continue developing into biological maturity after the age of 20.

Identity and anxiety

Another way of characterising this period is the time in which children begin to demonstrate a desire for a distinct, separate and chosen identity. This discourse is often coupled with consideration of the anxiety that some teenagers may experience, terms such as 'teen angst' may be used to explore this or: *[a] time of storm and stress* (Arnett, cited in Zwozdiak-Myers, 2007, page 93) is another way of constructing adolescence.

Responsibility

This period can also be viewed as the time in which increasing independence from parents or carers is achieved. The concept of *storm and stress* might be applied here as the balance of power shifts between adult and young person. This is coupled with an extension of rights for young people and debates over 'ages of consent' are useful in exploring the complexity of when this time of life begins and ends within different times and spaces. The Children's Legal Centre is a useful resource for information on law and policy that affects children and young people. Claridge (2008) provides a useful edited information guide on ages of consent.

ACTIVITY 2.5

Think about key milestones in your life such as at what age:

1 you were given consent to walk to school independently;
2 you were allowed to stay home on your own or had a 'key to the door';
3 you learned to drive, left school, left home;
4 you began to socialise more with friends outside the family.

ACTIVITY 2.6

Use the internet to explore the different ages of consent for different countries such as:

- voting age/marriage age/adult age/alcoholic drinking age;
- age of criminal responsibility/age of sexual consent (note differences in heterosexual versus gay and lesbian ages of consent);
- age when it is considered appropriate to engage in and serve your country in war.

Consider possible explanations for differences in ages of consent and levels of responsibility in different parts of the world. How do these age boundaries apply to young people that you know? To what extent do the life cycle or life course approaches help us understand the construct of youth?

In modern Britain age seems to determine many events. It could be argued that there has always been a pre-occupation with age. However, age can also be demonstrated to be a construct. The English calendar, as we know it today, was developed around 1750 and in much European society, prior to the sixteenth century, time, date and age had much less significance than today. Many people knew very little about how old they were. Women had babies in the spring, summer, autumn or winter rather than a specified date; people went to bed and got up with the sun and farmed with the cycles of the season and the weather.

Theories about the emergence of adolescence and youth

Stanley Hall (1844–1924), a pioneering American psychologist, who focussed on child development, is seen as having defined the term *storm and stress* as conflict with parents, mood disruptions and risky behaviour.

He stated that the development of the defined period of time, characterised by the term *adolescence*, came about with the extension of education as this extended the period between childhood and adulthood. The rise of youth employment opportunities alongside the development of rights in work, such as legislation on when young people could work, provided both a time of protection and disposable income for young people. These changes began to occur around the industrial revolution and continue to evolve to the present day.

Hall also considered aspects of class and gender within his analysis. For example, he stated that prior to the distinctive characterisation of a period of adolescence, the working classes were sent to work as soon as they were considered to be old enough as their income was needed by the family. Girls often looked after siblings and helped in the home from a very early age so they moved quickly from child to adult. The middle and upper classes were educated from a young age for their adult purpose in life before quickly becoming copies of their parents. Girls might be taught music and the arts, and boys educated for business or would receive a more classical education.

Osgerby (1998) explored the concept of a *youthquake* where he describes a stronger emergence of youth as a distinct and separate phase from around the 1950s. He attributed this to the emergence of 'rock 'n' roll', coffee bars, fashion trends targeted at young people, access to jobs and a greater disposable income. He argued that at this time young people began to find an image of themselves as separate to their parents. Other evidence identifies a stronger sense of a separate and distinct youth identity from earlier periods than Osgerby identifies. For example, there is evidence of youth subcultures from the late nineteenth century such as 'scuttlers', 'ikey lads' and 'peaky blinders' who wore distinct clothing and had particular hairstyles to distinguish themselves from adults of the time. As with the discussion about childhood, none of these theorists is suggesting that these periods of youth are the same as today but that this concept has existed in one form or another for some time and that it is a contested area that cannot be homogenised and to which generalisations do not apply.

There are significant changes occurring today in the UK that may cause us to reflect once more upon when the period of adolescence or youth begins and ends. The period of compulsory education and training is set to change again and legislation regarding working hours has made early youth employment increasingly difficult. Combined with a volatile housing market, rising cost of living and extensions in the numbers of young people going to university this may result in many young people seeking security from parents and carers for longer, once again extending this period of life in a particular time and space.

ACTIVITY 2.7

Carry out some research on what life for young people might have been like during the following periods of history. Imagine that you were living during this period. What might you have written in your diary if you were:

- a 14-year-old working-class girl recently sent out to 'service' in 1920;
- a 16-year-old boy just about to leave school in a Welsh mining village in 1960;
- a 15-year-old girl whose family has recently been settled on a permanent traveller site, who is attending her local secondary school for the first time in 2010.

What do your diary entries tell you about similarities and differences in young people's lives over time?

Youth and 'moral panics'

When we think about constructs such as youth, it is often coupled with a discussion that explores this period as a time of heightened risk and threat around which 'moral panics' may emerge. Cohen (1978, page 9) defines the occurrence of a moral panic as: *A condition, episode, person or group of persons (who) emerges to become defined as a threat to societal values and interests.* Cohen is not saying here that a particular issue, risk or threat does not exist but that it may be exaggerated out of proportion by those he describes as *moral entrepreneurs* such as the media, politicians, or others viewed as in authority or as 'experts'. Feelings around a particular issue become heightened, and 'solutions' to problems abound in ways that are disproportionate to the actual issue. He goes on to discuss how the panic may disappear, linger almost as *folklore*, or lead to change in policy and law. All of this revolves around the emergence of new panics to replace the old. This can result in an issue being exaggerated to such an extent that it becomes more difficult to debate and discuss it. It becomes surrounded by myth and misinformation. The issue itself can sometimes become a taboo subject, which may lead to misinterpretation and individuals and groups can become uninformed or misinformed about the facts. This can lead to the creation of stereotypes and prejudices that result in what is often termed *knee-jerk* policy reactions or overly disproportionate initiatives to tackle the issue. Thompson (1998) is a further useful source of information regarding 'moral panics'.

ACTIVITY 2.8

Spend a few minutes writing down all the *negative* things that you have heard regarding young people today. For example think of how young people are depicted in terms of violent activity, involvement in gangs, teenage pregnancy, binge drinking etc.

Then write a list of all the *positive* things that you have heard regarding young people today.

Compare your two lists. Was one easier to put together than the other? Do you have more or less on your negative or positive list? If so, why do you think this is? Have your own thoughts and feelings regarding young people been challenged or confirmed during this activity?

'Moral panics': folklore or fact?

Cohen (1978) is particularly well known for his work on 'mods and rockers' and the panic, moral outrage and reaction to this youth phenomena from the 1960s. The period after the Second World War is often characterised in modern western culture as a time when youth subcultures and anxiety around youth emerged (Osgerby, 1998). In contemporary political and media discourses the portrayal of a *breakdown of society* has emerged. In January 2010, the leader of the Opposition Conservative Party, David Cameron, gave a speech about *mending our broken society* and this has remained a strong theme throughout the first months of the coalition government since May 2010. This discourse is strongly related to issues such as rising crime, workless households, family breakdown, loss of community, increasing teenage pregnancy, school exclusions and a lack of power for teachers to discipline in school. The government has extended the powers of teachers to search young people in schools and there is increasing emphasis being placed on discipline and the power to punish in general. This is in response to what Cameron (2010) describes as an *irresponsible society*.

ACTIVITY 2.9

Reflecting on claims against some youth, do you think that this suggests a genuine change in the character of youth or does it mirror similar patterns of panic from past generations?

To what extent is youth constructed and reconstructed as a scapegoat for moral outrage? How far is expressed moral outrage based on a real and increasing threat? Who expresses that moral outrage?

There are many areas that could be examined to ascertain whether panics around youth are modern phenomena and to what extent they are exaggerated or proportionately represented. Current debates might involve adolescent health anxieties such as self-harm, drug abuse or eating disorders; earlier and more excessive sexual behaviour; increased criminal activity; involvement in gang culture and carrying weapons. Given the rise in availability of different forms of media and the widespread access to media outlets, such as the internet, it is interesting to investigate some of these areas further. This will give insight into the recurring nature of 'moral panics' such as a concern over exposing young minds to influential material. We could hypothesise that because there were fewer media outlets available to youth in the past then a 'moral panic' linking media exposure to criminal behaviour of youth did not exist in previous generations. An exploration of similar Victorian arguments (Sutter, 2003) may counter this.

Sutter cites many instances of similar concerns regarding criminal youth behaviour after exposure to what was termed in Victorian times as *penny dreadfuls* or *cheap, serialised literature* (Sutter, 2003, page 163). In particular *highwayman genres* were cited as being the cause of much youth crime. In the cycle of Cohen's (1978) moral panic Sutter describes how a link was made between this cheap literature and increasing youth crime though the evidence for the connection was not convincing. As today, the press exaggerated the issue and 'moral campaigners' called for the abolition of such literature. Sutter further relates this to the 'moral panics' surrounding youth access to internet porn today and similar calls for censure and regulation. He traces similar concerns as far back as Greek civilisation around the time of Plato where the *dramatic poets* of the time were seen to influence the minds of the young (Sutter, 2003, page 163).

Sutter (2003) states, as does Cohen (1978), that it is not that the issue does not exist, but that it is exaggerated, seized upon and becomes difficult to be debated rationally. Over exaggeration and unreliable evidence that connects youth and internet access to increased exposure to pornography, bullying, violence and paedophilia belies that overwhelmingly these media outlets are used responsibly and that pornography and violence makes up only a very small proportion of what is available on the internet. It also evades the fact that access to material such as this is accessible in many forms. Young people, therefore, need to learn how to assess the risks for themselves and make sensible choices. Informed use of such media can lead to promoting good self-regulatory behaviour. Bullying, violent behaviour, access to pornography and instances of paedophilia are not new phenomena for youth brought about by the advent of the internet. The 'moral panic' around youth usage of the internet ignores the fact that the internet may also provide a useful source of information to overcome and report such behaviour. This may actually help young people to escape such situations of abuse, whereas in past generations some youth may have had to suffer in silence.

Countering 'moral panics': young people as citizens

As this chapter has highlighted, much of the debate around young people tends to focus on negative images and behaviour. Young people are often portrayed by the media, politics and society in general as troubled and troublesome, politically apathetic, risk takers and as self-interested. In actual fact many young people are actively engaged as citizens in their local, national and international communities in positive action for change working towards better rights and an improved way of life for themselves and others. There are a range of examples of this and this section will draw on just a few. Further resources establishing young people as motivated citizens can be found in the 'Useful resources' and 'Further reading' sections.

The UK Youth Parliament (UKYP)

UKYP is an organisation encouraging political engagement for young people between the ages of 11 and 18. It has 600 elected members between the ages of 11–18 and more than one million young people have exercised their right to vote within UKYP over the last two years. Their campaigns are wide and varied. Further information can be found at: www.ukyouthparliament.org.uk/.

Headliners

This is a UK-based charity that trains young people in journalism and encourages them to research and report upon the issues which affect them. Further information can be found at: www.headliners.org/.

Youth 2 Youth

A UK-based confidential helpline offering trained support and advice by young people and for young people. It has identified the four most common areas for young people today as: sexuality; emotional well being; sexual relationships; and self-image. Further information can be found at: www.youth2youth.co.uk

Tony Jeffs and Mark Smith have published widely on issues of youth (see 2006, 2010). Their work has highlighted the role of young people as active citizens in society. Jeffs and Smith's work might be the sort of research that underlies current government initiatives seeking to draw upon the reserves of young people in helping to build Cameron's (2009) vision of the *Big Society*. The principle of the *Big Society* is that the state has become too big and power needs to be redistributed back to society.

Since the coalition government took office in 2010 Prime Minister Cameron has officially launched the National Citizen Service (NCS) (Cabinet Office, 2010). The aim of this programme is that all 16 year olds will be given the opportunity to gain new skills and to take part in community volunteer work. This initiative is seen as potentially having a substantial impact upon the *Big Society*. Cameron stated in this launch that:

> *There is a tragic waste of potential in this country today. The young people of this country are as passionate and idealistic as any generation before – perhaps more passionate. But too many teenagers appear lost and feel their lives lack shape and direction.*
>
> (Cabinet Office, 2010, page 1)

Views upon this programme are divided. Some young people view the scheme as a type of enforced *boot camp* or a form of social control (Children and Young People Now, 2010, page 1). The programme has been criticised for constructing young people as a social *problem* and for diverting attention from an economic crisis for which they have no responsibility. It is feared that funds will be less, as a result of this programme, for existing youth work with already *highly engaged* young people and that the programme amounts to a *costly error* (Children and Young People Now, 2010, page 1). Alongside these criticisms, whether such a scheme has the potential to reconstruct views regarding youth stereotypes is yet to be seen.

This section has begun to draw out some of the issues around constructions of youth. Definition of terms alongside explorations of when and how to identify this period as distinct and separate have been considered. Importantly this section has asked that you think about the perceived anxiety that accompanies the period of youth. Such anxiety may be surrounded by myth, exaggeration and misinformation that has a long history in the form of 'moral panic' and can make informed debates around youth issues hard to achieve.

Family

> *Some argue that the family is the foundation of society, indeed of civilisation itself. Others maintain it is the source of most of our problems and unhappiness.*
>
> (Gittins, 1993, page 1)

Just as childhood and youth can be seen to have changed, evolved and been constructed and reconstructed across time and space so can the family. Both the left and right of politics in modern western society have seized upon the family as both the cause of societal disorder and the cure to bring harmony once more.

Family has often been connected in the past to tradition, community ties, strong connections between family members and a sense of order. Recent discourse might suggest that this has given way to a more chaotic, directionless family structure without value or morality. In this section we will examine the construct of the family within different periods of time – medieval, Middle Ages, Victorian, modern and post-modern.

The structure of the traditional family

In the UK a range of family structures are evidenced as existing in pre-modern times as they do today. Whether you lived in urban or rural surroundings, your occupation, gender, class, family size – all these factors would have an impact. Before industrialisation it is often assumed that families were extended and that the nuclear family arose with the needs of industrialisation. As this chapter will now highlight research has led us to believe this is false and that a variety of family types has always existed.

Laslett and Wall (1972) demonstrate that families before industrialisation were often smaller than thought. Wilmot and Young (1962) conversely demonstrated an 'extended' type of family in 1950 in a study carried out in East London. Stone (1977) has traced the family and theorised about a range of family types. The *open lineage family* in medieval times is characterised by the importance of lineage (ancestors) and all living family. Relationships towards one another were formal and marriages based upon property and land arrangements in a business-like manner. The *restricted patriarchal nuclear family* is said to have arisen around the sixteenth to the mid-seventeenth century and is identified more by companionship within marriage and compatibility. Immediate relatives are said to have taken on more importance at this time with lineage being less important. The patriarchal power of the father remained.

From around 1640 the *closed domesticated nuclear family* is identified by Stone and a decline in patriarchy and the establishment of marriage based more on love is said to arise. Grief is shown in relation to the death of relatives and children begin to be shown more affection. In the earlier section on childhood we have already contested research such as that by Stone, finding evidence from other theorists such as Hanawalt's (2002) summary to suggest that such neutrality towards family members and children was open to question. The same can be said here of Stone's theories of family structures where it is likely that a range of relationship types existed.

To oversimplify family type within given periods often associated with pre-industrial and industrial time is not very helpful. Other factors, such as changes in mortality rates for infants and adults, time given to the bearing of children, wealth and income changes, technological change, social mobility and changes in laws and rights have had more of an impact upon family structure.

Other factors that brought about changes in family structures were the demise of the peasant class who existed by farming the land, which began from around the time of the plague in the late fourteenth century. Increases in literacy as technological changes such as the printing press occurred meant that the written word became more widely available from the fifteenth century. Therefore knowledge of the wider world and 'alternative' ways of being began to be more widely circulated.

The movement from rural to urban areas with industrialisation in the eighteenth and nineteenth centuries brought about other changes such as keeping children in the family home for longer as a source of waged labour. The changes brought about with industrialisation and the move to working outside of the home posed many family issues. In the nineteenth century most working-class households needed two wages to survive, so women faced the dilemma of what to do with their children. Many took them to work in factories with them or used informal childcare calling on relatives, friends and neighbours.

In the Victorian era (1837–1901) it can be argued that the middle classes were responsible for the dominant ideology that *a woman's place was in the home*. It was not until the late eighteenth century that the gendered division of labour between a waged male breadwinner and a female housewife and mother arose in such a distinct manner; previously men and women often worked together in cottage industries. This was largely a result of middle-class values that served the needs of the new industrial classes that required a waged male workforce to be reproduced, fed and cared for by mothers and wives at home. For many working-class women this was simply not possible as their secondary wage was often required to make ends meet. It was around this time that the modern dilemma facing many women of today about whether to go out to work or stay at home began to prevail. This emerging ideology became the dominant point of view and today's society still battles with this.

Anxiety over the family structure of the working classes can be explored as another 'moral panic'. Dyhouse (1977) reports on the social anxieties surrounding the working classes between 1890–1920 and how poverty, squalor, high infant mortality, malnutrition, feckless husbands and unsanitary living conditions were blamed upon the *ignorance* and *incompetence* (Dyhouse, 1977, pages 22–23) of working-class women whose place should be in the home. Less attention was paid to the inequality that may bring about these issues or to the organisation, battles against adversity and resourcefulness of a vast majority of working-class families. This period saw a rise in the number of reports drawn up, and in monitoring of working-classes families. There was a surge in domestic training within schools for working-class girls, along with *Schools for Mothers* later to become *Infant Welfare Centres* (Dyhouse, 1977, page 28). At this time there was a rise in working-class consciousness of their inequality, a drop in the number of girls going into service and an increase in securing of more rights for this class, which is likely to have contributed to the outbreak of this social 'moral panic'. From the early to mid part of the twentieth century concern over the capacity of working housewives and mothers continued.

This ideology became particularly prevalent once more after the Second World War. In the two previous World Wars women had been needed to work outside of the home whilst men were fighting in war; childcare services were set up for this purpose. After the Second World War a fierce ideology arose of women needing to return to the home because of a 'moral panic' around infant attachment (Bowlby, 1957, 1969; Bowlby et al., 1965). It might also be viewed as a way of rebuilding society or a way of returning to the ideology of a gendered division of labour.

ACTIVITY 2.10

Think about how family was portrayed in the 1950s and 1960s. Consider what you know about your own family history:

- How many people lived in the home?
- How many people went out to work and who were they? What sort of work did they do?
- Did people stay together or separate/divorce?
- When did young people leave home and what did they leave home for?

Compare some of this to your own life. What key changes do you notice?

In more recent times the image of the family can be seen to have been used in attempts to structure, organise and control society. Politicians in particular have called upon particular images of the family for this purpose. In much of the western world the image of the family has diversified over time so that prevalent and powerful perceptions of 'typical' or 'preferred' family types have come to be challenged. Images of mono-cultural, heterosexual, able-bodied, two-parent families headed by a powerful male figure and organised through a gendered division of labour, have begun to give way to a celebration of greater family diversity.

This part of the chapter has highlighted the historical diversity of the family and tells us that, whilst family is held in high esteem, there is little consensus upon what constitutes family. Yet its image is used to entertain us, sell products to us, launch and destroy political careers, and is presented as both a reason for social decline and a cure for societal ills at the same time. We can easily trace a pattern of 'moral panic' surrounding the family. It is a powerful tool used as a means of social control and organisation; a 'smokescreen' for other societal issues such as economic downturn; a haven of safety and a place of fear and distress; a means for independence and freedom and a restrictive and stifling place from which there seems no escape. One thing that family is not is a simple, straightforward unit that is similar across time and space; it is a complex and dynamic institution invested with enormous power.

ACTIVITY 2.11

Consider the ways in which politics utilises family image. The following are some well-known statements or political platforms that politicians have used:

- What do you think Margaret Thatcher meant about the family when she said: *[T]here is no such thing as society. There are individual men and women, and there are families?* (Woman's Own Magazine, 1987, pages 8–10).
- What do you think John Major's campaign of *back to basics* said about 'family values' and what sort of family type was this referring to?
- Tony Blair also utilised the family as a platform for New Labour's campaign stating: *[T]he family was the starting place for combating crime* (Brown, 1993, page 1). What sort of family did New Labour mean?
- What do you think David Cameron means by family when he talks of *family values as the key to responsible society?* (Prince, 2009, page 1).

Now consider:

- What changes have occurred in society to account for family diversity (e.g. legislation, work, migration)?
- The range of family types that exist today – for example, lone parent; gay, lesbian, bisexual and transgender; step; dual heritage; traveller and service families.

Add to this list and note down various issues and difficulties each family type may face. Do some family types have greater protection in law, status and acceptability? If so, why do you think this is? Do you hold particular views of certain family types? How might this affect your professional and personal interactions with them?

CHAPTER SUMMARY

This chapter has covered a wide range of issues that has explored the contested constructs of childhood, youth and family. By the end of this chapter you should have gained some knowledge of how and why childhood, youth and family have been constructed in the past and present. You should have developed an understanding of the role of the media and of politics in constructing and reconstructing these concepts. You should have considered how the idea of 'moral panic' is used to organise, structure and control society, and also have gained insights into some of the stereotypes, prejudices and myths within these concepts.

Above all this chapter has offered an introduction that brings all of these constructs into question and demonstrates the dynamic and complex nature of what it is to be a child, youth or family.

USEFUL RESOURCES

www.headliners.org.uk UK-based charity training young people in journalism.

www.ukyouthparliament.org.uk Parliament for young people encouraging political engagement between the ages of 11 and 18.

www.youth2youth.co.uk A UK helpline run for and by young people.

www.ukyouth.org UK Youth is a national youth work charity supporting young people to raise aspirations and realise their potential.

www.suttontrust.com A trust that aims to promote social mobility through education.

www.unicef.org/voy/explore/explore.php The United Nations International Children's Emergency Fund (UNICEF) 'Voices of Youth' is a web-based resource that looks at the issues and rights of young people across the globe.

www.yjb.gov.uk/en-gb The Youth Justice Board oversees the youth justice system in England and Wales.

www.childrenscommissioner.gov.uk A web-based resource promoting the views and interests of children and young people in England with many useful links to publications.

www.creative-partnerships.com/about A programme that brings together creative workers to inspire young people. Links to many useful research and other resources.

www.barnardos.org.uk Barnardo's children's charity.

www.ncb.org.uk National Children's Bureau, a leading charity working on behalf of children, young people and families.

www.cypnow.co.uk Children and Young People Now, a web-based resource for all those working with children, young people and families.

www.childrenslegalcentre.com The Children's Legal Centre, a national charity that gives information on law and policy affecting children and young people.

www.invo.org.uk/pdfs/Involving_Young_People_in_Research_151104_FINAL. pdf Kirby, P (2004) *A Guide to Actively Involving Young People in Research*. INVOLVE and PK Research. A guide about how and why you would involve young people in research, which covers ethical issues and offers useful other publications in this area.

FURTHER READING

Jones, P and Welch, S (2010) *Rethinking Children's Rights: Attitudes in Contemporary Society*. London: Continuum Books.

Kellet, M (2010) *Rethinking Children and Research: Attitudes in Contemporary Society*. London: Continuum Books.

These two books are both very accessibly written and contain some helpful activities to help you engage further with some of the ideas discussed in this chapter. They also have companion websites containing further resources,

Lowe, RJ (2010) Children deconstructing childhood, in *Children & Society*, no. doi: 10.1111/j.1099-0860.2010.00344.x. The *Children & Society* journal contains many interesting and relevant articles that explore constructions of childhood and youth in more depth. This article attempts to address the question 'what is childhood?' by consulting the primary source – children. Perspectives of childhood such as the 'playful child', the 'unknowing child', the 'needful child' and the 'unauthorised child' are identified.

UNICEF (2007) *Child Poverty in Perspective: An Overview of Child Well-Being in Rich Countries*. Innocenti Report Card 7. This research report identifies a range of indicators measuring child and adolescent well-being in a range of economically advanced countries. Available at: www.unicef-irc.org/publications/pdf/rc7_eng.pdf.

UNICEF (2008) *The Child Care Transition: A League Table of Early Childhood Education and Care in Economically Advanced Countries*. Innocenti Report Card 8. This research report analyses the effects of spending increasing amounts of time in out-of-home child care from the early years stage. Available at: www.unicef-irc.org/publications/pdf/rc8_eng.pdf.

3 THE DEVELOPING CHILD AND YOUNG PERSON

Rachel Sales and Billie Oliver

COMMON CORE OF SKILLS AND KNOWLEDGE FOR THE CHILDREN'S WORKFORCE: CHILD AND YOUNG PERSON DEVELOPMENT

- Understand how babies, children and young people develop.

- Know that development includes emotional, physical, sexual, intellectual, social, moral and character growth, and that these can all affect one another.

- Understand that babies, children and young people see and experience the world in different ways.

- Be able to recognise the signs of possible developmental delay and/or regression in the behaviour of children and young people.

- Support children and young people with developmental difficulties or disabilities.

- Understand the different ways in which babies and children form attachments and how these might change.

- Understand that play and recreation that is directed by babies, children and young people – rather than by adults – has a major role in helping them to understand themselves and the world.

- Understand the effects of different parenting approaches, family structures and composition, backgrounds and routines.

- Know how to use theory and experience to reflect upon, think about and improve practice.

(CWDC, 2010a)

Introduction

The Common Core (CWDC, 2010a) covers the physical, intellectual, linguistic, social and emotional growth and development of babies, children and young people. It emphasises the importance of recognising and understanding developmental changes and the effect such changes can have on behaviour. Smidt (2006, page 2) has described the discipline of child development as *holistic* in that it aims to *identify, to describe and to predict patterns* in children's growth. She goes on to explain that this approach assumes that *all aspects of development are interrelated,* so that *children who fail to thrive physically are sometimes expected to fail in other areas of development.* It is clear that a number of factors influence children's physical growth and development. These factors include diet, housing, environment, access to healthcare, and poverty. Children's centres and schools and extended school activities can play an important role in supporting children's physical activity, healthy eating and emotional development. However, a recent study (Save the Children, 2010) has indicated that nearly two-thirds of parents with at least one child aged 4 to 18 cannot afford to send their children to after-school activities.

It can be difficult to determine specific times when developmental change occurs, as they differ from person to person. Furthermore, theories on child and adolescent development often differ and contradict each other. This chapter offers an introduction to major theories and concepts surrounding childhood development and the transition into adulthood. It critically explores how emotional, physical, intellectual, social and moral development can impact on the development of children and young people. Family context and structure, familial position and sibling influence are explored through the use of case studies that examine the impact of delayed or atypical development.

The aim is to provide an overview rather than explore every aspect of physical, cognitive and emotional development in children. Further links, texts and resources are suggested at the end of the chapter to help you explore these aspects more fully.

Policy and legislation

Every Child Matters (DfES, 2003) built on previously existing plans to strengthen preventative services by putting the spotlight on supporting families and carers and by focusing on early intervention strategies to safeguard and protect children. *Early intervention* was seen as key to promoting the physical, intellectual and social development of babies and young children to enable them to flourish at home and when they get to school. The Childcare Act 2006 and *Choice for Parents, The Best Start for Children* (DfES, 2004a) introduced a range of measures to foster improvements in the provision of childcare and early years learning including enhanced access to Sure Start children's centres, flexible childcare for families with children aged up to 14, and 15 hours a week free early education for all 3 and 4 year olds.

Since May 2010, the coalition government has indicated its continuing commitment to an early intervention strategy and to continued support for early years provision (Teather, 2010). *Healthy Lives, Healthy People* (DH, 2010) emphasised their support for Sure Start children's centres, family intervention projects and parenting support projects. It also pledged support for the continuation of the Healthy Child Programme and the role of schools in promoting children and young people's health and well being through, for example, the Healthy Child Programme 5–19 and additional access to talking therapies for young people.

The Early Years Foundation Stage (EYFS), a framework for assessing young children's development, was introduced in September 2008. A review of the EYFS commenced in July 2010, to evaluate how best to protect young children's safety and welfare, and support their development and learning. The review considered the need for regulation through a single framework for all early years providers; looked at the latest evidence about children's development and what is needed to give them the best start at school; considered whether young children's development should be formally assessed and what this should cover; and considered the minimum standards to support healthy development (Tickell, 2011).

An independent review on poverty and life chances (Field, 2010) set out a new strategy to prevent poor children from becoming poor adults. The report proposed the establishment of a *set of life chance indicators*. This recommendation is based on evidence from the review that children's life chances are most heavily predicated on their development in the first five years of life and that family background, parental education, good parenting and the opportunities for learning and development in those early years matter more to children than money in determining their potential in later life. The review proposed offering parenting classes throughout school life; annual monitoring of *life chances* measuring progress on a range of factors in young children which are predictive of children's future outcomes; a strategic focus on foundation years similar to that in primary and secondary schools including the *kite marking* of children's TV programmes to help speech development.

A recent report *Born Creative* (Timms, 2010) has found evidence to support early years intervention, arguing that *exposing children to creative learning in the early years is key to equipping them with the right skills for a modern economy.* Key recommendations include the importance for children's long-term development of bridging the gap between home and school and creatively involving parents in their children's education; and the importance of breaking down barriers to parents' engagement in their children's education by addressing poor educational experiences and limited knowledge of the importance of games, rhymes and stories in the development of children's learning.

Major theories of child development

Child development theory can be broadly divided into three distinct, but complementary areas:

- physical development;
- cognitive development;
- social and emotional development.

Theories of child development can be traced as far back as the Greek philosopher Plato (427–347 BC) who argued that individual differences are genetically based. However, it was not until the industrial revolution and the changing concepts of childhood in the 1800s that the view of children as miniature adults, with all their adult skills, knowledge and ability present at birth, began to be challenged and, as Doherty and Hughes (2009) observe, child development became an academic area of study through scientific enquiry. Systematic studies of child development began in the first half of the twentieth century along with a thirst for information about how children learn best. There was a decline of interest in the late 1930s and 1940s but in the 1950s a new period of growth and expansion occurred, highlighting important changes in psychological functioning that occur between birth and maturity.

The growth in developmental biology, embryology and genetic discoveries during the past 30 years have all informed the ongoing debates surrounding the nativist (nature) versus empiricist (nurture) debate. This debate explores the extent to which innate skills such as intelligence and personality are genetically inherited. Those advocating the nurture argument suggest that we are products of all the experiences that we have had as we grow up and that we can change (and be changed) in response to our experience and environment (see Spencer et al., 2009 and Rutter, 2002 for further reading). Macgregor captures the two sides of the Nature versus Nurture debate when using height as an example. She states that *adult height is achieved through the interaction of the inherited potential from both parents and the child growing in an optimum environment, where they receive adequate nutrition and are free from disease* (2008, page 4).

ACTIVITY 3.1

Read what some theorists have said about the nature versus nurture debate. The further reading section for this chapter suggests sources that include summaries of key child development theories and theorists of the twentieth century. Use these, and any resources that you have access to, to read about and research the following theorists and their theories of development:

- Sigmund Freud (1856–1939);
- Urie Bronfenbrenner (1917–2005);
- Erik Erikson (1902–1994);
- Jean Piaget (1896–1980);
- John Watson (1878–1958);

- Lawrence Kohlberg (1927–1987);
- John Bowlby (1907–1990);
- Lev Vygotsky (1896–1934);
- Margaret Donaldson (1926–).

Where would you place these theories on the nature versus nurture continuum?

Nature ←————————————————————————————————→ **Nurture**

Reviewing some of this work in the above activity offers a wide perspective on a range of child development theories. However, we need to also maintain an awareness of more recent evidence. Alexander (2009) provides a review of research evidence about children's cognitive development and learning. He also highlights current controversies in the field of child development. Key findings in the review are that Piaget's view of active learning and Vygotsky's theories about the role of language continue to be sound interpretations of how children learn. It also outlines a growing evidence base that challenges Piaget's previously accepted stages of development, and Bowlby's assertions that the mother should be considered the primary attachment figure for effective child development.

Physical development

There is ongoing debate amongst theorists about how physical development and growth is understood, assessed and measured. This issue of how far childhood development can be predicted or expected to follow standardised milestones remains a contentious issue. Nevertheless, all those working with children and young people need to have a thorough understanding of *normative* development in order to be able to recognize and support *atypical* development and *childhood disorders*. The EYFS (DfES, 2008) guidance advocates seeing the developing child as a *Unique Child* and argues that all children *develop and learn in different ways and at different rates*. The EYFS also stresses the importance of *positive relationships* asserting that *children learn to be strong and independent from a base of loving and secure relationships with parents and/or a key person*; and *enabling environments* that *support and extend* children's development and learning.

The first two years of life are times of rapid physical development. During this stage a child's growth and development is often compared against developmental milestones. These milestones use average ages as examples. It is important to remember that not all children develop and grow at the same rate. However, the degree of growth and the order in which new skills are mastered are generally consistent. Doctors have compiled charts that indicate the *ideal* height and weight for children from birth to adulthood and pre-school check-ups include assessment against these measures. It is possible to predict how tall each child will be once fully grown and, to some extent, whether growth is occurring at the expected rate. It has been calculated that children at birth are approximately a third of their adult height and by age 2, this rises to a half (Doherty and Hughes, 2009, page 187).

The early childhood years (2–6 years) are characterised by continued development of both physical and cognitive capabilities. After the age of two, most children gain about 2.3 kg per year and grow at a steady rate of 5–6 cm per year. They begin to challenge and explore the world around them through testing their abilities such as running and jumping. Their coordination and motor skills advance as they begin to master the ability to run and jump, play catch and throw, ride a bicycle, dress and feed themselves. The child's body shapes and proportions continue to change during this stage. For example, the infant's protruding abdomen becomes less noticeable and by the age of three most children will have a complete set (20) of milk teeth.

In the middle and late childhood years children begin to develop their proficiency in activities such as sports and dancing. However, physical growth, during these years tends to slow down as though to prepare the body for the tumult of *puberty* that is to follow (Doherty and Hughes, 2009, page 185).

At puberty major hormones released by the pituitary gland trigger the onset of puberty, which is the collective name given to a series of physical milestones that culminate in human reproductive ability (Bee and Boyd, 2009). Puberty as a term is derived from the Latin word *puberatum* (age of maturity, manhood). It is at this stage that the physical rate of development of boys and girls differs, due to the gender differences of when puberty commences. Pubertal changes can occur in boys from around ten years of age but this can be as late as 16, with girls tending to start puberty two years earlier than boys (Macgregor, 2008). Puberty is often seen as the beginning of adolescence, which comes from the Latin word *adolescere* meaning *to grow into maturity*. Traditionally this stage has been regarded as a prelude to adulthood, and the transitional period between immaturity and maturity.

ACTIVITY 3.2

Look up one of the many on-line development calendars such as www.mumsnet.com/devcal, www.kidsdevelopment.co.uk or www.bemyparent.org.uk. What do you think are some of the positive things about development calendars such as this?

What do you think could be some of the dangers with such on-line guidance?

Media representations of young people as *adolescents* tends to stereotype them as *spotty, stroppy and hungry* young people who sleep all day and stay awake into the night (such as the television characterisation of Harry Enfield's *Kevin the teenager)*. Adolescent spots and acne are seen by some as a phase that all young people go through. It is estimated that 85 per cent of the population suffer from acne at some time (Shaw and Kennedy, 2008) as it is related to rising androgens in puberty that increase the size of oil glands that then become infected with bacteria (Macgregor, 2008). Magin et al. (2005) discuss the many myths and misconceptions that exist in the treatment of acne. However, acne has been shown to cause severe negative psychological effects such as depression (Mallon et al., 1999; Hassan et al., 2009; Joseph and Sterling, 2010), and often related to self-image and appearance, highlighting a need to consider the emotional and mental health of young people with acne rather than considering acne as a rite of passage.

The rapid developmental changes that occur in this stage of physical development as the body matures also mirrors an increasing metabolism, which is fuelled by an increasing appetite (Macgregor, 2008), as the body needs more energy. This natural increase in appetite, when paired with growing concerns about the rising number of overweight and obese children and young people in the UK (Kipping et al., 2008), has brought concerns about the quality of adolescent diets under the spotlight (Johnson et al., 2002) and in particular the meals available when personal food choices are made at school or when out with peers. Through initiatives such as Jamie Oliver's school dinners the School Food Trust (www.schoolfoodtrust.org.uk) has attempted to raise the profile of healthy eating amongst children and young people, in an attempt to prevent poor eating habits and choices that can have long-term health effects into adulthood.

ACTIVITY 3.3

According to the Healthy Schools Initiative (http://home.healthyschools.gov.uk/), it is believed that quality school food can improve children's health, behaviour and performance.

Research and plan a school menu for a Year 11 class.

The biological changes in this age group can also affect sleep and wakefulness (Noland et al., 2009) resulting in changing sleep patterns and disturbances, and a need for more sleep (Laberge et al., 2001). Before entering adolescence sleep patterns on school and non-school days tend to be constant. However, for young adolescents these sleep patterns change. Wolfson and Carskadon state that *the way adolescents sleep critically influences their ability to think, behave, and feel during daytime hours* (1998, page 875). Changes in adolescent sleep patterns are thought to be due to hormonal fluctuations that change the circadian rhythms guiding a person's sleep–wake cycle. Given these changes in appearance, appetite, disturbed sleep patterns and the ongoing physical changes and changes in the brain's development causing the release of pubertal hormones (Dahl, 2003), it is not surprising that these years are seen as turbulent as children make the transitions from childhood into being young adults.

Motor development

The development of motor skills includes skills such as hand–eye co-ordination, the ability to feed oneself, hold a spoon, hold a pencil, ride a bike and so on. Doherty and Hughes (2009, pages 204–205) describe the four phases of motor development as being:

1 *The reflexive movement phase* – this covers the first year of life and describes spontaneous responses to stimulation.
2 *The rudimentary movement phase* – from birth to age 2. This phase includes learning to sit up, stand, crawl and walk as well as fine motor skills such as reaching out to touch and picking up objects with thumb and finger.
3 *The fundamental movement phase* – between the ages of 2 and 7 children learn to throw, catch, hop, run and climb as well as fine motor skills such as using scissors or holding a crayon.
4 *The specialised movement phase* – from age 6 to 11 the fundamental skills are usually well established and children are more eager to test out their capabilities in challenging situations.

As with other aspects of child development there are established milestones in motor development and *motor milestones* are one tool that professionals use to assess whether or not a child is developing 'normally'. However, as with other such charts we must remember that there will be considerable individual variation between children.

A recent report by Ofsted (2010) found that around 1.7 million children in England (just over one in five pupils) had been identified as having special educational needs ranging from physical disability to emotional problems. The report recommended that schools should stop identifying children as having special needs when what was needed was more effective teaching and pastoral care. Ofsted inspectors found that labelling or *statementing* a child as *special needs* did not reliably lead to the appropriate support being put in place for that child. The report also found that children identified as having special educational needs were disproportionately from disadvantaged backgrounds and were much more likely to be absent or excluded from school.

The Common Assessment Framework (CAF)

The CAF is a shared assessment and planning framework for use across all children's services. It aims to help the early identification of children's additional needs and promote co-ordinated service provision to meet them. The CAF is a standardised approach to conducting an assessment of a child's additional needs and deciding how those needs should be met.

The CAF advocates a form of assessment that follows the *non-deficit* or *strengths/needs* model, where the focus is placed on a child or young person's strengths and needs, rather than their weaknesses. The assessment process should be a positive experience and practitioners should work *with* a child or young person, their parents/carers and other agencies to gather information to establish the issues that need to be addressed and assess the most suitable responses.

The CAF advocates that all assessments should be guided by the following principles: assessments should be: child/young person centred, transparent, not discriminatory, consensual, collaborative, current, continuous, sufficient and formative, progressive, sound.

ACTIVITY 3.4

Find out what the established motor milestones are for the age group of children with whom you work.

If you observe that a child you work with has delayed development in motor skills, such as an 18 month old who is not crawling or a two year old who is not able to hold a spoon, how would you apply the principles outlined above by the CAF guidance?

Cognitive development

Cognitive development focuses on the underlying processes that contribute to how individuals begin to process information, develop conceptual understanding, the ability to reason and to problem solve. Piaget conceived of the developing child, not as an empty vessel but as curious and actively involved in trying to understand the objects, people and experiences around them. Piaget viewed developmental change as sequential – occurring through a series of stages – and his thinking has been very influential. Development is, therefore, generally conceived to be *continuous and cumulative* (Smidt, 2006) with the early years seen as crucial to the development that takes place in the later years. Piaget also, however, viewed development as essentially an individual activity and he has been criticised by later theorists for overlooking social and group factors and their influence on the developing child (Dunn, 1988).

Vygotsky, another key theorist, believed that the role of others in a child's learning and development was essential. Vygotsky introduced the notion of *socialisation* – interacting with others – into the study of child development. Through interacting with others the child grows to internalise the norms and behaviours of their cultural group. However, for Vygotsky, the *other* could be other children as well as adults.

Bruner developed this idea further, introducing the idea of an *educator* who could provide the *scaffolding* to help the child make the necessary steps to progress developmentally. Crucial to the idea of *scaffolding* is the progressive withdrawal of support as the child's own competence increases.

Developmentally appropriate practice (DAP)

DAP draws on western research and is often presented as *the manual of current knowledge about young children* (Smidt, 2006, page 51).

DAP (Bredekamp and Copple, 1997) takes an age and stage approach and attempts to prescribe to parents and educators what sorts of play activities they should be providing for their child. DAP promotes self-directed play as being the most effective way of learning and suggests activities and resources to support this.

The approach has been criticised by Smidt (2006) and others as ignoring social, cultural and economic differences. Critics argue that stage theories such as this work to a *deficit* model of assessment and can lead to some children being viewed as *lacking something* or as being *behind*.

In the middle years of childhood (5–13), some of the most significant areas of cognitive, emotional and moral development can be observed. By the time they reach school age, children are beginning to assert their ability to be responsible and independent as well as their ability to act co-operatively. The challenge for adults during this period is often that of knowing how much freedom to allow children to work things out for themselves. Finding the right balance is important for supporting children to take steps towards emotional maturity. The Children Act 2004 and the Mental Capacity Act 2005 set out the rights of children and young people and ensure there is respect for a young person's autonomy when choices over their own health and care are needed. Lord Fraser's ruling of competence (known as the Fraser guidelines) can be used when children's and young people's ability to consent needs to be assessed to ensure that they are *sufficiently mature and sufficiently understanding of the nature of the matter requiring a decision* (NSPCC, 2007, page 5). The guidelines follow from a legal case (for further information see *Gillick v. West Norfolk & Wisbech Area Health Authority* [1985] UKHL 7 [17 October 1985] www.bailii.org/uk/cases/UKHL/1985/7.html).

Between the ages of 7 and 12 children are often coming to terms with issues of self-concept and identity. This stage of development is important for building healthy relationships with peers. This period of life is a very active one for children, who are often keen to engage in many activities. Children in this age group are eager learners and respond well to advice about safety, healthy lifestyles and avoidance of high-risk behaviours.

The Social and Emotional Aspects of Learning (SEAL) is a national voluntary programme promoted by the government, designed to develop the social and emotional skills of children in primary and secondary schools. The materials that the programme offers aim to support a whole-school approach that allows skills to be practised and consolidated. The skill areas in the programme include self-awareness; managing feelings; empathy; motivation; and social skills.

The Children's Society has developed a *Good Childhood Index* (see 'Useful resources' section) for measuring children's well being. The aim is to look at a wide range of factors that affect a child's sense of well being and give a more personal perspective of satisfaction levels. Issues covered include school, home life, money and appearance. The tool aims to help ensure problems such as mental health issues are picked up at an early stage.

Language development

social interaction can add on.

Human infants demonstrate the ability to communicate from very early on. From a young age babies imitate sounds and words used by adults in an attempt to share communication. Bruner (1977) believed that a lot of learning about communication takes place during familiar routines. Therefore, it is important for those caring for babies and young children to be aware of their vocalisations and gestures and to respond as though in conversation.

From sounds, infants generally progress to using names or nouns. Later, they begin to combine nouns with other words to create phrases. The process of language acquisition is complex and theorists do not agree on how this process works. However, what is agreed is that being able to use language to communicate is a milestone in development that usually occurs in the first year. After 12 months the child has an expanding repertoire of words and by age 3 can usually be expected to be putting words together to form short phrases and short sentences.

By the ages of 3 to 4 the child will frequently be asking 'why' questions. They will be able to talk about the past and speculate about the future. Between the ages of 3 to 5 children can generally be understood by adults and peers and they are more confident at speaking using increasingly complex sentences. Children from age 5 onwards become increasingly aware of the need to adjust their language to the listener and to view communication as a two-way process.

Theories about how children learn to read are numerous and contentious. What can generally be agreed is that children actively seek to make sense of the written word. Young children will readily explore books, and books aimed at this age group actively encourage exploration through the use of colour, pictures, interactive devices such as flaps, holes and textures. When children start to read they often begin by re-telling the story from the pictures or from memory. They progress from there to trying to make sense of the codes, such as letters or shapes of words, on the page.

Social and emotional development

Every Child Matters: Change for Children (DfES, 2004b, page 9) asserted that all children and young people should be supported to *make a positive contribution* in order to *develop self-confidence and successfully deal with significant life changes and challenges.*

One of the most influential theories in relation to social and emotional development of children and young people is *attachment theory*. The key elements of attachment theory are that a human child will seek a relationship with a carer or carers who will provide security and support while the child learns about the world. Where there is an *insecure attachment* the child will experience anxiety. These *selective attachments* (Beckett, 2006, page 49) start to form at about the age of five or six months and they form a template for the child's relationship with others. Babies begin to demonstrate *separation protest* during the second half of their first year of life. This onset of *separation protest* is widely believed to indicate that the young child has formed *emotional attachments* to a parent or care-giver (Woodhead and Montgomery, 2003, page 103).

As they grow older, children become increasingly capable of spending time away from their secure attachment, but the need for attachment figures is lifelong. It is claimed that *early attachment relationships can affect many aspects of development including mental health, parental ability, the ability to form friendships and to establish satisfactory sexual relationships* (Beckett, 2006, page 49).

The roots of this theory lie in the work of John Bowlby (1953) who wrote about the importance of the bond between the mother and the child in early childhood. The significance of attachment and attachment type relationships is not, generally, disputed and it has been very influential on practice for a number of years. However, many theorists have sought to build on Bowlby's ideas in order to overcome what is seen as its central weakness – that there may be other significant people in a child's life to whom they can form attachments: *It may be concluded that attachment is an important, perhaps crucial, aspect of the mother–child relationship, but equally it is a characteristic shared with other relationships* (Rutter, 1972, page 25).

The National Children's Bureau has produced a booklet (NCB, 2010) that includes suggestions of behaviour to look out for in children who might be experiencing attachment difficulties. It offers case examples and suggestions for how to help children overcome these difficulties. Please see the Useful resources section at the end of this chapter

PRACTICE EXAMPLE: USING SONGS AND RHYMES TO SUPPORT SOCIAL, COGNITIVE AND LANGUAGE DEVELOPMENT

Go to the website www.c4eo.org.uk/themes/earlyyears/vlpdetails.aspx?lpeid=43 to view a video presentation by early years' practitioners in a reception class. They introduced a Songs and Rhymes Programme because they had found that there were a lot of children coming into school with under-developed speech and language. They noticed that as children came into school they seemed to have a smaller repertoire of nursery rhymes, and maybe had had less exposure to pattern, rhythm and rhyme in language. They also had concerns about the time it was taking for some children to make a smooth transition from home to school.

The programme invites children and their families to take part in eight 'twilight sessions' during the term before they enter school. The programme is delivered in areas where there is evidence of gaps in communication, language and literacy, and social and emotional development.

They start each session with a welcome song to help facilitate social belonging. The programme involves children, parents, childcare and school staff sharing songs and rhymes together. The programme aims to support home learning by empowering parents as co-educators:

> *The hardest thing for a child coming into Reception class is probably that separation from their primary carer and then forming a new relationship with somebody new. . . there's more understanding now about attachment theory and the importance of transitions. We have a Key Person system so during the Rhyme and Song project, the child is going to find out who their key person is for the next year, and be able to make a relationship.*

> *About twenty-five percent of our families do not speak English as a first language. We needed to respect the first language but also to introduce the new language that children were going to be using within school. If you don't have good language skills you're not going to access the rest of the curriculum well.*

Reflecting on our practice and articulating the *how and why* of what we do, is an important part of becoming a skilled practitioner. The practice example outlined above illustrates how practitioners in this setting are working creatively with parents and carers to support children's development in order to ensure the best possible access to education and ongoing developmental opportunity. There are many other practice examples on the same website and on some of the other websites listed in the useful resources section.

ACTIVITY 3.5

Visit some of the websites that offer examples of good practice listed in the useful resources section. Try to identify examples of practice with children or young people that are informed by a commitment to support delayed development. What sorts of strategies or activities do the practitioners use?

Do you have other examples of practice to support delayed development? Reflect on some of the strategies or activities that you (or a practitioner that you observe) use to extend children's social, emotional or language development.

The importance of play

There is a general consensus amongst child development theorists that play is an extremely significant feature of childhood and that it is an important route to learning and development. Daniel et al. (1999, page 179) have argued that watching the way in which a child plays can inform us about their developmental progress.

Play is seen as important because it is the way in which children are able to reflect on and make use of their experiences. It is also seen by many as an important way for children to make sense of their emotions. Play allows children to problem solve, engage in abstract thinking and develop communication skills. Play is currently regarded as the primary mode of learning in the Foundation Stage part of the National Curriculum in the UK (DfE, 2010a). The philosophy underpinning the Foundation Stage curriculum is that learning should be carefully planned and structured, with an emphasis on activities that are fun, relevant and motivating for each child. Practitioners delivering the Foundation Stage curriculum therefore support children's learning through planned play and through extending and developing children's spontaneous play. Knowledge of child development is considered to be crucial in order to support practitioners in assessing the most appropriate activities to support children's development.

ACTIVITY 3.6

Observe a child or group of children at play. In what ways do you think they could be said to be *actively exploring their own environment?* How are they doing this? Can you identify any resources that have been provided to encourage this exploration? What sorts of resources are they?

There are a number of different theoretical perspectives on play. The box below summarises a range of types of play that are currently discussed by theorists.

Types of play

Free-flow play – the spontaneous, un-directed play that children engage in. Children are solving problems, and symbolically representing their experiences, in creative and spontaneous ways. Adults only need to ensure there is sufficient time, space, opportunity and safety (Bruce, 1991).

Directed play – structured activities led by an adult often with rules, such as games (Moyles, 1998).

Epistemic play – within which children learn and explore the world and its properties. This type of play primarily involves the search for meaning through skills and knowledge acquisition (Hutt, 1989) and is generally thought of as needing the presence of adults who can support, encourage and question the activity.

Ludic play – more creative and 'playful' and only really requires adults to recognise its place in a child's development. It does not require particular adult intervention. In ludic play children are using their imaginations and play as entertainment (Hutt, 1989).

Heuristic play – associated with the play of pre-school aged children (Goldschmied and Jackson, 1994) such as the filling and emptying of containers. This type of play requires adults to provide the varied resources needed to encourage exploration. Goldschmied and Jackson advocate a variety of different materials be provided but that none of them should be bought toys. In *heuristic play* learners solve problems or find out things for themselves.

High/Scope approach– the philosophy behind the High/Scope approach (Holt, 2007) is that children should be involved actively in their own learning. They 'learn by doing', carrying out projects of their own choosing. The adults working with the children are seen as facilitators or partners in the process supporting and extending children's learning. An important part of the High/Scope approach is the plan–do–review sequence. Only once they have made a plan can they go and do it. Afterwards the children discuss what they have been doing and whether it was successful.

Guidance for early years settings (DCSF, 2009b, page 5) stresses that all opportunities for development *must be delivered through planned, purposeful play, with a balance of adult-led and child-initiated activities* and that settings need to provide *individualised opportunities based on each child's needs*. The guidance suggests that the best outcomes for children's learning occur where most of the activity within a child's day is a mixture of *child-initiated play, actively supported by adults and focused learning, with adults guiding the learning through playful, rich experiential activities*. The guidance suggests a *continuum of approaches* should be used:

Unstructured	Child-initiated	Focused learning	Highly structured
Play without adult support	Adult support for an enabling environment	Adult-guided experiential activities	Adult-directed activity

By combining child-initiated play and playful adult-led opportunities, the guidance suggests that *confident and reflective practitioners will select the approach that is best for the developmental stage of the children.* There are recurrent debates about whether boys and girls should be encouraged to play with toys that are perceived as *gendered*, such as dolls for girls and cars for boys. Owen-Blakemore and Centers (2005) suggest that it is toys that are described as *gender neutral or moderately gendered* that have been found to support children's physical and cognitive development more than toys that are perceived as *overtly gendered*.

ACTIVITY 3.7

Choose a toy or a piece of play equipment. This could be something that is used in a children's setting where you work, it could be something in your home or it could be something you have seen advertised in a catalogue/magazine or in a shop.

Think about the type of play/games/activities that children might engage in with this piece of equipment. What age group do you think could use it? How would they use it? Is it gender neutral?

Do you think that the toy/game/equipment that you have chosen has an impact on development? What sort of impact might this be? Which aspects of the child's development might be influenced by this equipment?

Can you identify an object that costs nothing (something from the home or garden) that could stimulate development in similar ways?

The impact of siblings and family position

A recent report called *The State of Play: Back to Basics* (Byron, 2010) found that:

- One in five parents in the UK admit to forgetting how to play with their children, blaming a lack of inspiration, confused messaging and a shortage of time.
- Parents should consider a 'back to basics' approach to remember their own childhoods and the games enjoyed when they were young and use these activities to connect to their own children.
- A third of parents think that playing with their children is boring.
- Half of parents surveyed blame work and chores as barriers to the amount of quality time they spend with their children.
- Sibling rivalry is a cause of tension for family play with nearly a third of parents citing this as the biggest problem when they try and play with their children.

The concepts of traditional and non-traditional families explored in Chapter 2 highlight the diverse, complex and contested nature of family on today's society. Reviewing these discussions in relation to their potential effect upon child development, two concepts need further exploration: childcare in the family and the effect of siblings. These are seen by some theorists as having a significant impact. Whilst childcare is often seen as predominantly the mother's responsibility, the Office for National Statistics recently reported that the number of men who are staying at home to care for young children has risen since 1995 as more women are becoming the main financial earner in the family (Office for National Statistics, 2010). In current society more children than before experience non-maternal childcare (Gregg et al., 2005; Crosby and Hawkes, 2007; Hansen and Hawkes, 2009) as women respond to changes in the labour markets. The effect that such care has on the cognitive, emotional and behavioural development of children is contested with evidence often simplistically represented within the media.

Comparisons have been made between formal childcare arrangements, such as through pre-schools and nurseries, and informal arrangements with friends, relatives and neighbours. These studies have concluded that it is the quality of the care and the communication between parents and carers that influences the child development (Belsky et al., 2007; Leach et al., 2007; Hansen and Hawkes, 2009). A recent study that explored childcare and socio-emotional development at 36 months (Barnes et al., 2010) reported no effect from the amount or type of childcare on behaviour.

In the past decades there has been a downward trend in the average household size in Great Britain that has seen a fall from 3.1 people per household in 1961 to 2.4 people in 2009. This has led to smaller family units and large families (with more than 3 children) being seen as against the normal trend. Black et al. (2005) suggest that within larger families there can be a negative effect on children's development through diluted resources.

ACTIVITY 3.9

Compare two families: one that has four children Beth (8), Bradley (7), Jack (5) and Maddie (3) and one that has one child called Victoria (6). Think about the types of play and activity that may occur in these families and list these under two columns:

Small family (one child)   *Large family (four children)*

What do you notice when comparing these lists? Is there a difference? Why do you think this is?

Approximately 80 per cent of western children have at least one sibling (Howe and Recchia, 2006) with siblings described by White (2001, page 555) as *those with whom one most closely shares genetic, family, social class and historical background and to whom one is tied for a lifetime by a network of interlocking family relationships*. Reports such as the recent Netmums Gender Survey have also suggested that children with siblings of a different gender are treated differently by their parents as mothers may praise their sons for being 'funny', 'cheeky' and 'playful', whilst criticising their daughters as 'stroppy' and 'argumentative' for the same behaviour (Netmums, 2010).

Edwards et al. (2005) found that for most children having a sibling meant that they felt there was always someone there for them and that this protected them from a sense of being alone. However if one sibling experiences long-term illness or care needs, then they or other siblings can often feel isolated or different because of the sibling's ill health or needs – a feeling that is repeatedly captured in books, such as Strohm (2002), which portrays sibling experiences of living with a brother or sister whom society views as different:

I felt completely isolated. Thought I couldn't share any of that part of my life with my friends. They didn't understand and I felt alienated from them. Other kids never had the same responsibility. (Meagan)

(Strohm, 2002, page 19)

At what point do I get to cry over it. The answer has been, never. (Tara)

(Strohm, 2002, page 61)

I just wanted to be a kid and not have all those responsibilities. (Meagan)

(Strohm, 2002, page 74)

However, sibling attachment and relationships are also shown to be important in the development of a child's understanding of their social, emotional, moral and cognitive worlds as this relationship tends to be the longest relationship that we can experience (Pike et al., 2009). Kramer (2010) challenges the assumption that sibling rivalry and conflict needs to be reduced or prevented in order to improve sibling relationships when he suggests that the absence of such conflicts will not ensure positive relationships are built with siblings and others.

ACTIVITY 3.10

Read the summary of a Joseph Rowntree Foundation-funded research project (Edwards et al., 2005) *Children's Understanding of their Sibling Relationships*, available at www.jrf. org.uk/publications/childrens-understanding-their-sibling-relationships.

What insights into children's feelings about being close to their siblings does this research give us? What can we learn about how children learn to cope with their brothers and sisters?

Siblings and the effect of birth order on personality has a large evidence base in the literature building on 75 years of research (Healey and Ellis, 2007) into personality traits that result from competitions between children for parental investment and time. Table 3.1 summarises some personality traits that have been associated with the birth order of children (first born (eldest), middle born, last born (youngest).

FIRST BORN	MIDDLE BORN	LAST BORN
Achievement orientated (Claxton, 1994)	Socially adept (Claxton, 1994)	Confident as free from competition from younger siblings (Salmon and Daly, 1998)
Act as surrogate parent (Sulloway, 1996)	Feeling of neglect persisting into adulthood (Salmon, 1999)	Resist authority. Tend to be the rebel in the family (Healey and Ellis, 2007)
Engage in leadership and teaching roles (Howe and Recchia, 2006)	Report negative family relationships (Pollet and Nettle, 2007)	
Conventional (Jefferson et al., 1998) and conservative (Sulloway, 1996)		

Table 3.1 **Personality traits that have been associated with the birth order**

CHAPTER SUMMARY

This chapter has explored a range of theoretical perspectives that have attempted to explain how babies, children and young people develop. Understandably the literature on this topic is large and many of the theories have been vigorously contested. We have attempted in this chapter to give you a flavour of some of these debates and hope that you will follow up some of the suggestions for further reading, as well as reflect on your own observations of children and young people that you know to develop your own critical perspective.

In this chapter we have considered the development of children and young people from the perspectives of physical, cognitive, social and emotional development, as well as considering the impact on development of the family context and structure, position in the family and sibling influence.

We have argued throughout this chapter that all those working with children and young people need to have a thorough understanding of *normative* development in order to be able to recognise and support *atypical* development and *childhood disorders*. We have stressed the importance of viewing children and young people as unique individuals who all develop and learn in different ways and at different rates.

USEFUL RESOURCES

www.primaryreview.org.uk/themes/overview.php This is the official site for the Cambridge Primary Review. It contains a wealth of resources based on the *Cambridge Primary Review Research Surveys* – England's biggest inquiry into primary education for over 40 years. It covers ten themes including children's development, learning, diversity and needs.

http://nationalstrategies.standards.dcsf.gov.uk/inclusion/behaviourattendance andseal/seal This is the official site for the SEAL programme and contains more information about SEAL in primary and secondary schools, including downloadable resources.

http://nationalstrategies.standards.dcsf.gov.uk/node/157774 The EYFS is a comprehensive framework that sets the standards for learning, development and care of children from birth to 5. All registered early years providers are required to use the EYFS as of September 2008.

http://home.healthyschools.gov.uk The government's Healthy Schools Initiative website contains links to a number of useful resources and case studies.

www.jrf.org.uk/publications/childrens-understanding-their-sibling-relationships Summary of the full report by Edwards, R, Hadfield, L and Mauthner, M (2005) *Exploring Children's Understanding of their Sibling Relationships*.

http://wps.pearsoned.co.uk/ema_uk_he_doherty_childdev_1/117/30099/7705 569.cw/index.html This website accompanies the book Doherty, J and Hughes, M (2009) *Child Development: Theory and Practice 0–11* and contains helpful study materials and interactive exercises.

www.nhs.uk/Tools/Pages/birthtofive.aspx This link is to an interactive guide to early child development milestones.

www.mumsnet.com/devcal This links to the Mumsnet website which contains a developmental calendar and other useful resources.

http://open2.net/healtheducation/family_childdevelopment/index.html Open2.net is the on-line learning portal from The Open University and the BBC and contains many useful, accessible resources.

www.cdc.gov/ncbddd/child/middlechildhood.htm A website with helpful suggestions for supporting different stages of development.

http://openlearn.open.ac.uk The OpenLearn website gives free access to Open University study materials.

www.c4eo.org.uk The Centre for Excellence in Outcomes for Children and Young People's Services (C4EO) aims to help those working in children's services improve the life chances of all children and young people, in particular those who are most vulnerable. Its website contains many practice examples and on-line resources.

www.childrenssociety.org.uk all_about_us/what_we_do/Well-being/19903.asp The Good Childhood Index for measuring well being.

www.peal.org.uk Parents, Early Years and Learning (PEAL) aims to support the early home learning environment and enhance parents confidence as educators. The website contains links to useful resources.

FURTHER READING

Aldgate, J, Jones, D, Rose, W and Jeffery, C (2005) *The Developing World of the Child*. London: Jessica Kingsley Publishers. This book covers the range of theoretical perspectives that have been introduced in this chapter, in more depth. It contains an extended grid on what might be expected in children's development at different ages.

Doherty, J and Hughes, M (2009) *Child Development: Theory and Practice 0–11*. Harlow: Pearson. This book contains a very full and thorough exploration of differing theoretical perspectives on child development. It has a companion website with further resources to help you engage with some of the ideas.

Lindon, J (2010) *Understanding Child Development: Linking Theory and Practice* 2nd Edition, Oxon: Hodder Education. This very accessible and easy to read book explains the differing perspectives on child development. It has a helpful chapter on 'nature versus nurture' that will help you with Activity 3.1 in this chapter.

Open University, Department for Children, Schools and Families, Royal Holloway University of London and NSPCC (2007) *The Developing World of the Child: Resource Pack*. Leicester: NSPCC. A child development resource pack for practitioners working with children and their families. It includes diverse perspectives on child development and makes links with practice. It offers guidance on making assessments of the developmental needs of children and young people.

Pound, L (2009) *How Children Learn: Contemporary Thinking and Theorists*. London: Step Forward Publishing Ltd. This book is part of a series of reference books that provide brief, but informative synopses of the main theories and theorists referred to in this chapter.

Strohm, K (2002) *Siblings Coming Unstuck and Putting Back the Pieces. Stories of Everyday Life with Children Who Are Different*. London: David Fulton Publishers. This book contains the stories of the experiences of children growing up with a disabled sibling.

4 SAFEGUARDING CHILDREN AND YOUNG PEOPLE

Jane Tarr, Maggie Whittle and Gill Evans

COMMON CORE OF SKILLS AND KNOWLEDGE FOR THE CHILDREN'S WORKFORCE: SAFEGUARDING AND PROMOTING THE WELFARE OF THE CHILD OR YOUNG PERSON

Knowledge of legal and procedural frameworks

- Understand what is meant by safeguarding and the different ways in which children and young people can be harmed. This includes by other children and young people, by a single event or ongoing maltreatment, through the internet and other media, or by their own risk-taking behaviour.

- Have awareness and basic knowledge, where appropriate, of the laws and policy areas relevant to your role that relate to safeguarding children and young people, including in the online world.

- Have awareness and sufficient knowledge of current legislation and the common law duty of confidentiality.

- Know how to find information about the risk factors that may impair a child or young person's health or development. Know what the triggers are for reporting incidents or unexpected behaviour.

- Understand that signs of abuse or neglect can be subtle and be expressed in play, artwork or online activities, as well as behaviour and the way children and young people approach relationships with other children and adults.

- Understand the use that children and young people make of new technologies to understand the implications of risks of harm.

- Understand the principles that dictate when young people are considered sufficiently mature to give or refuse consent to their information being shared.

Relate, recognise and take appropriate action

- Recognise the factors that can affect parenting and increase the likelihood of a child being neglected or abused, for example domestic violence or parental substance misuse.

- Recognise the range of possible behaviours that may harm children and young people. Know how to address them.

- Support children and young people to develop resilience and build mental, physical, emotional and social well being.

- Be able to recognise when a child or young person's life is in danger, or when they are likely to suffer harm, and take action to protect them.

(CWDC, 2010a)

CHAPTER OBJECTIVES

By the end of this chapter you should have an understanding of:

- the concepts of safeguarding and child protection in the context of children and young people's services;

- key legal and policy procedures for child protection;

- issues to consider to help identify children and young people at risk;

- some strategies to support vulnerable children and young people.

Introduction

The responsibilities of all practitioners working with children, young people and their families have been highlighted following a series of significant safeguarding reviews (Laming, 2003; Bichard, 2004; Laming, 2009). The concept has received much media and government attention over the past 20 years as concerns over the safety of some more vulnerable children has grown. Child protection and safeguarding are challenging aspects of both personal and professional work with children, young people and their families. There are demanding intellectual and emotional dimensions that need to be considered and reflected upon. The maltreatment of children is always highly distressing. All practitioners working with children, young people and their families need to feel supported and enabled to protect and keep safe children with whom they work. The capacity to discuss concerns you might have is essential. It is, therefore, important to be familiar with the child protection procedures in your organisation and with whom you should raise your concerns.

ACTIVITY 4.1
Read the policy document concerned with child protection for your workplace. Make notes about these issues:

- Who is responsible for child protection concerns in your workplace?
- What is the agreed procedure for raising concerns?
- Who would you contact if you had concerns?
- What does the policy/procedure have to say about confidentiality issues in your workplace?

Talk about these issues with a colleague and make sure you are aware of the procedures in your workplace.

Cronin and Smith (2010, page 97) point out how the *focus of work with children and families* over the past 20 years has shifted away from an emphasis on *the management of risk* in order to make greater use of *preventative strategies to support early intervention in circumstances where children may be vulnerable.* We, therefore start this chapter with an introduction to the conceptual understandings behind the terminology of *safeguarding* and *child protection.*

Safeguarding has been defined as*:*

- protecting children from maltreatment;
- preventing impairment of children's health and development;
- ensuring children grow up in circumstances consistent with safe, effective care.

(DCSF, 2010, page 34)

It is expected that everyone working with children and young people would adhere to these principles. However there are some aspects of vulnerability that hold the potential to cause *significant harm.*

Significant harm has been defined as the *threshold that justifies compulsory intervention in family life in the best interests of a child* according to the Children Act 1989. It can be indicated by one traumatic event but in many cases it is attributed to an accumulation of events that damage a child's physical and/or psychological development. The Children Act 1989 goes on to suggest that *significant harm* is the *ill-treatment or the impairment of health and development* (section 31). If practitioners judge a situation to be causing a child *significant harm* then they are required to initiate a formal process of child protection.

Child protection has been defined as *a part of safeguarding and promoting welfare and refers to activities which protect those suffering or at risk of significant harm* (DCSF, 2010, page 35). All practitioners who work with children and young people should be trained in child protection procedures by their employer.

This chapter is concerned with the wider concept of safeguarding in the context of children and young people's services. Integrated children's services require an approach that involves all workers in strategically building children's capacity to resist dangerous situations and to be resilient. This chapter will outline the key legal and policy frameworks for safeguarding and protecting children, underpinned by the importance of sharing information. We will explore the needs of vulnerable children, young people and their families across a range of different situations including bullying, bereavement, disability, children as carers and children of drug and alcohol mis-users.

Theoretical perspectives on safeguarding

Theoretical perspectives on safeguarding have developed over the years and include a range of different themes and perspectives. Munro (2007, page 14) refers to these as *running themes* and urges practitioners to reflect on them in relation to our work with children, young people and their families. These *running themes* include:

- the autonomy and voice of the child;
- working with parents as partners or as suspects;

- working with other professionals from different agencies;
- understanding our own professional code of ethics in balancing rights and responsibilities;
- engaging in anti-discriminatory practice to ensure all persons get fair treatment;
- acknowledging the emotional impact of such work.

The degree to which children and young people have been seen as having *autonomy* has changed over time, as we have seen in Chapter 2. Whereas in the eighteenth century children might have been viewed as *possessions* of the family, or as being reliant on adults to care for them, more recent constructions view children and young people as *participants*, able to participate in decision making and as *citizens* who hold rights and responsibilities and are able to act autonomously in some instances (Tarr, 2000). This changing view of children and young people has led to a current expectation that adults should listen to children and take notice of their viewpoints. However, there is little evidence of this always occurring in relation to child protection investigations (Gough, 1996), despite the United Nations Convention on the Rights of the Child (UNCRC) stating (in article 12) that children should be able to *say what [they] think and be listened to by adults when they make decisions that affect [them]* (UNCRC, 1989).

ACTIVITY 4.2

Reflect upon a child or young person who you know well. This could be a child within your workplace or a child you know personally.

In your view, how do the adults around the child or young person treat him/her? As a possession, as a subject, as a participant, as a citizen? Reflect upon a range of different contexts where the adult and child or young person are together, if possible.

What are the behaviours or actions of the adults that lead you to form your opinion?

Do you feel that the behaviour towards the child or young person is an appropriate approach, given the environmental context, the age or developmental stage of the child? Explain your reasoning.

Practitioners working with children and young people face dilemmas today about the *context of family life* and whether they have the right to intervene. Family life varies considerably across different people, and one of the main concerns of practitioners is to avoid being judgemental and opinionated about different approaches to parenting. Parents may approach their parenting from particular cultural or religious backgrounds that may contrast with that of a practitioner. Coming to the decision that a child is at risk can be highly complex in some cases and yet very clear in others. For example, health practitioners might have views that differ from those of a parent about the appropriateness of issuing contraception to a young person under 16 years of age; a teacher might wish to encourage a young person to apply for and continue their studies at a residential college when the parents wish their child to remain at home. Their decisions may reflect some of the different viewpoints about the culture and structure of the family that were discussed in Chapter 2. *Every Child Matters* (DfES, 2003) policy and legislation has placed the family at the core of provision and resulted in encouragement for all professionals to build partnerships with parents in order to support them. This practice is important as strong relationships can enable development to take place in a trusting, supportive and caring environment.

The concern within society in relation to child abuse has grown over the past 100 years. In the UK the National Society for the Prevention of Cruelty to Children (NSPCC) was established in 1887 following concerns about children living in industrialised towns and experiencing parental violence. In the USA, the first prosecution for child abuse took place in 1874 before any relevant legislation was in place. The social worker at the time had to argue that the human child was an animal in order that they would be covered by the law against cruelty to animals and gain safety for the child:

> At that time there were laws protecting animals, but no local, state, or federal laws protected children. Consequently, Wheeler turned to the American Society for the Prevention of Cruelty to Animals (ASPCA) for help. The case was presented to the court on the theory that the child was a member of the animal kingdom and therefore entitled to the same protection from abuse that the law gave to animals. The court agreed, and the child, because she was considered an animal, was taken from her brutal foster mother.
>
> (Child Abuse – A History Website – see Further Reading)

Today much of society react vehemently to the tragic outcomes of child abuse, and yet the high value given to the autonomy of the family means that under *Common Assessment Framework* (CAF) (CWDC, 2009a) procedures, interventions, even those intended to be supportive ones, can only be instigated with parental agreement unless child protection procedures are invoked. This frequently leads to a confrontational approach (Henricson, 2003).

Since the Education Act (1981) professionals from health, social services and education have been encouraged to work together in support of children and families. The Children Act (1989) and *Every Child Matters* (2003) enhanced the requirement for and further encouraged such practice. The Children Act (2004) clarified the *duty to cooperate and to safeguard and promote the welfare of children* and took a further step that brought social services and education departments together in newly formed children and young people's services. While there are many examples of good practice emerging, such integrated working practice has been very challenging for some. One of the main barriers to successful *interprofessional collaboration* has been the judgement about when and how to share information about a child or family (Daly, 2004).

CASE STUDY 4.1   TOM

Tom is 7 years old and frequently comes to school tired and late. He does not have many friends and is rarely invited to birthday celebrations. He experiences some difficulties with reading and has been assessed as achieving at 'below age appropriate' in numeracy as well. He is prone to sudden outbursts of anger for no apparent reason. His mum rarely meets him at the end of the day and he walks home alone. It can be challenging attempting to discuss concerns with his mother as she can be very abrupt with staff and Tom seems nervous when she is with him.

Reflect upon this case study. If you were a practitioner working with Tom, what would you do about any concerns you might have from these observations? With whom might you share information?

Different agencies and professional groups may have conflicting thresholds for intervening in family life where safeguarding is concerned. It is therefore necessary to be very clear about your own professional values and roles in relation to child protection. Front-line workers such as health and education practitioners might be the first to observe a concern. The observations recorded in the case study above may not mean anything very serious or they might be the initial indication of serious concerns. In this kind of position practitioners hold a responsibility to pass on the information to a more experienced colleague as this might be a case where professional judgement is required. If deemed necessary then the information will be shared with a professional in the investigative agencies such as police or social workers. They have a role to find out about each case and take actions as appropriate.

Information sharing is the term used to describe the situation where practitioners use their professional judgement and experience on a case-by-case basis to decide whether and what personal information to share with other practitioners in order to meet the needs of a child (CWDC, 2010a). All practitioners need to be familiar with the importance of information sharing in maintaining the safety and well being of children and young people and with the current legislation, guidance and protocol governing the sharing of information. Each organisation will have its own policy and guidance that will help practitioners understand when information may be shared and whether or not consent needs to be obtained.

ACTIVITY 4.3

Read the information sharing and confidentiality guidance that applies to your own workplace. What are the circumstances when you might be able to share information about children, young people and their families, or work colleagues without gaining their consent to do so?

The Department for Education (DfE) and the Department of Health have both produced tools, advice and guidance to help promote good practice in information sharing. If you do not have workplace guidance to refer to, look up the guidance on the DfE website (www.education.gov.uk). This guidance provides information on relevant legislation and is designed to help practitioners who have to make decisions about sharing personal information on a case-by-case basis, whether they are working in the public, private or voluntary sectors.

There are clear structures, systems and guidelines about how to approach a family or a child if you suspect that the child might be at risk of abuse. It is important to always maintain the centrality of the interests of the child when sharing information. It is also crucial that you demonstrate a willingness to share information and to explore challenges that you face rather than to ignore your concerns. As your experience grows you will feel more confident in these kinds of challenging situations. As you will see from your reading of Chapter 8, your working practice can be susceptible to assumptions and prejudice. In relation to safeguarding we need to ensure that we do not treat children or families unfairly because of their economic situation, religion, ethnicity, abilities, gender or sexual orientation. The new Equalities Act (2010) clarifies areas of responsibility for practitioners when working with families to ensure they do not make judgements about a parent because of *prejudice, stereotyping or discrimination.*

Munro (2007) reminds us of the highly emotional nature of this area of work. It is therefore important that all involved are respectful of the *emotional impact* on children, families and practitioners, and that we develop capacities to deal with emotions sensitively and in a way that maintains the dignity of all concerned, as far as is possible. This is challenging and requires high levels of personal awareness alongside professional skills and the capacity to share one's own responses with others through supervision and collegial support.

ACTIVITY 4.4

Think about an example from practice in relation to safeguarding or child protection that has worried or upset you in some way. This could be a case that you have read about or something that has occurred in your own practice setting:

- How does it make you feel?
- What, in your opinion, are some of the reasons that you feel this way?
- Who could you talk to about these feelings and concerns?
- How would you approach them to ask for this support? Think about the most appropriate time and place and what you would do if they seem busy or preoccupied.

Policy and legislation

The maltreatment of children is an issue that is of concern to governments across the world. Many countries have attempted to address these concerns through legislation and in 2005, the Council of Europe committed member states to eradicate all forms of violence against children. You can read about some of the different approaches to child protection across Europe in Hetherington et al. (1997).

Cronin and Smith (2010, page 115) have noted that in the UK in recent years there has been a change in policy away from *the management of risk* to a greater use of *preventative strategies*, which they describe as *a shift from child protection to safeguarding*. Table 4.1 covers some key UK events and related policy documents that illustrate this shift over the past 35 years. This list is intended to support your developing understanding of the place of child protection and safeguarding in the UK.

This series of policies in Table 4.1 highlights the tendency of government to create increasingly tighter rules and procedures for workers to follow and organisations to abide by. The media response to child maltreatment is understandable, but can frequently result in a blame culture and enhanced performance management systems which can disempower the very practitioners who need to feel more confident (Munro, 2010). In 2010, a further review of child protection (Munro, 2010) was initiated with the aim of creating *better frontline services to protect children*. This most recent review, due to report in 2011, is underpinned by three principles: *Early intervention; trusting professionals and removing bureaucracy so they can spend more time on the frontline; and greater transparency and accountability* (Gove, 2010). In an earlier review Munro (2007) called for a renewed focus on the professional knowledge and skills of front-line workers who require support and advice in dealing with complex assessment processes, building effective relationships with families, and making professional judgements and decisions in highly emotive contexts.

All people who work with children and young people have responsibilities to safeguard and promote their welfare. This is an important responsibility and requires careful attention. It

DATE	DOCUMENT	COMMENT
1974	*Report into Death of Maria Colwell* by Secretary of State for Social Services (Fisher, 1974)	Concluded that the system was to blame and led to focus on professionals' skills in identification of abuse, sharing of information and coordination between professions and across different agencies.
1988	*Cleveland Inquiry* by Secretary of State for Social Services (Butler-Schloss, 1988)	Led to discussions about the balance between family autonomy and state intervention in family life.
1989	Children Act (1989)	Defined *child in need* (section 17) and introduced concept of *significant harm* (section 47). Introduced the concept of the role of the state in supporting parents to care for their children.
1994	*Seen But Not Heard* by Audit Commission (1994)	Recommended a move towards family support and closer working partnerships between education, health and social services.
1995	*Messages from Research* by Department of Health (DH, 1995)	Described a threshold for most interventions only taking place around concept of *significant harm*.
1999	*Quality Protects* (DH, 1999) by Department of Health and Department for Education and Employment	Raised the importance of effective assessment processes linking recognition of *need* to provision of services.
1999	*Sure Start* early years multi-agency programme of provision	Introduction of *one-stop shops* where all agencies operated to support most disadvantaged families to tackle child poverty and social exclusion.
1999	*Working together to Safeguard Children* (DCSF, 1999) by Department of Health, Home Office and Department for Education and Employment	Designed to stimulate closer working partnerships across agencies of health, social services and education.
2000	*Framework for Assessment of Children in Need* (DH, 2000) by Department of Health and Department for Education and Employment	A tool introduced to draw professionals together as they engage in a multi-agency approach to assessment.
2001	*The Children Act 1989 Now: Messages from Research* (Aldgate, 2001) by Department of Health	Broad ranging study with findings stating that resources were focused on high-risk families to the detriment of overall family support services with goal of prevention or early intervention.

Year	Document	Description
2002	Education Act (2002)	Incorporated the role of schools into child protection and safeguarding.
2003	Report of an Inquiry into the Death of Victoria Climbié (Laming, 2003)	Some 108 recommendations to improve communication and bring all agencies to work together effectively.
2003	Every Child Matters Green Paper (DfES, 2003)	Established the importance of the centrality of children, young people and their families with proactive early intervention and support from all children's agencies to achieve the five outcomes for children and prevent significant harm taking place.
2004	Children Act (2004)	Creation of local authority Children's Services merging education and social services; local safeguarding boards introduced; common language through five outcomes for children.
2004	Extended Schools programme	Schools in disadvantaged communities encouraged to build partnerships with other agencies – social services, health, police, voluntary sector – and provide service from 8.00 am to 6.00 pm throughout the year.
2006	Working Together to Safeguard Children by Department of Health, Home Office and Department for Education and Skills	Updated the 1999 document with greater advice for interagency working practice, role definitions, sharing information and joined-up practices.
2006	Common Assessment Framework (CAF) (CWDC, 2009a)	A new tool to draw multi-agency children's services together to create effective assessment of children and families in need.
2007	The Children's Plan (DCSF, 2007b) by Department for Children, Schools and Families	Focus on all children's agencies to work collaboratively together with children, young people and their families.
2008	Safer Children in a Digital World: The Report of the Byron Review (Byron, 2008)	Review found a need for a child-centred approach, better regulation of the internet, education about e-safety; more classifications of video games to ensure age appropriateness; information sharing guidance for children.
2009	Protection of Children in England: a Progress Report (Laming, 2009)	Report followed death of baby Peter Connelly and made recommendation to review the training of social workers.
2010	Working Together to Safeguard Children: A Guide to Inter-agency Working to Safeguard and Promote the Welfare of Children (2010) by Department for Children, Schools and Families	Further updating of 2006 document to support how organisations and individuals should work together to safeguard and promote the welfare of children and young people.

Table 4.1 **Government policy and legislation related to child protection and safeguarding**

means being able to recognise when a child or young person is not achieving their developmental potential, or when their physical or mental health is impaired. It means recognising when a child is displaying risky or harmful behaviour, or is being neglected or abused. It also means being able to identify sources of help for them and their families. Sometimes more than one risk factor may be affecting a child or young person and it may be necessary to work with others to address them (CWDC, 2010a).

Safeguarding and promoting the welfare of children – and in particular protecting them from significant harm – depends on effective joint working between agencies and professionals that have different roles and expertise. Individual children, especially some of the most vulnerable children and those at greatest risk of suffering harm and social exclusion, will need co-ordinated help from health, education, early years, children's social care, the voluntary sector and other agencies, including youth justice services.

Identifying vulnerable children and young people

All children and young people are vulnerable at some stage of their life. However, some contexts and environments are more risky than others. As professionals we seek to safeguard children and young people from any form of experience that might lead to their feeling unsafe. Awareness of factors and environments where children are more at risk of harm is, therefore, important in safeguarding their well being. In order to achieve this we need to be aware of different kinds of abuse and neglect.

Abuse and neglect

Abuse and neglect have been defined as forms of maltreatment of a child. Somebody may abuse or neglect a child by inflicting harm, or by failing to act to prevent harm. Children may be abused in a family or in an institutional or community setting, by those known to them or, more rarely, by a stranger for example, via the internet. They may be abused by an adult or adults, or another child or children.

Physical abuse – may involve hitting, shaking, throwing, poisoning, burning or scalding, drowning, suffocating, or otherwise causing physical harm to a child.

Emotional abuse – the persistent emotional maltreatment of a child such as to cause severe and persistent adverse effects on the child's emotional development.

Sexual abuse – involves forcing or enticing a child or young person to take part in sexual activities, not necessarily involving a high level of violence, whether or not the child is aware of what is happening.

Neglect – is the persistent failure to meet a child's basic physical and/or psychological needs, likely to result in the serious impairment of the child's health or development.

(DCSF, 2010, pages 38–39)

When we are talking about child abuse we are normally referring to adult behaviour. Adults may be the parents or carers or any other person who may have contact with the child. In most cases of child abuse the adult is known to the child and is in a position of trust or authority with respect to the child. It is usually the result of direct acts towards the child – *doing*, for example beating the child, or *not doing*, for example failure to provide adequate food or safety measures appropriate to the age/stage of development of the child.

The identification of a child who may be experiencing such treatment or being neglected requires us to understand children's behaviour in different contexts and at different ages and stages of development. In this way we will be able to identify changes in a child's behaviour that might be an indication that they are at risk of harm.

ACTIVITY 4.5

From the examples of abuse outlined above, choose three behaviours that you feel could be viewed in different ways in different contexts.

Make some notes about what you believe might be construed as reasonable or caring behaviour in some contexts and why, and in what contexts, it might be construed as maltreatment.

How might you ensure that your professional judgement is in the best interests of the child? What strategies might you employ?

Anyone who works with children and young people needs to be able to identify when a child is being harmed or is at risk of being harmed and be capable of intervening to protect them. This may require a holistic understanding of the child and their family. The causes of harm or neglect of children are highly complex and will involve awareness of interacting factors across the following aspects – the individual, the family, the community and society. These four aspects need to be considered when practitioners identify anything that might be construed as having the potential to cause harm to the child. Such consideration is achieved through interaction and information sharing where appropriate with other adults and professionals in the child's life.

The decision to share a piece of information is itself an aspect of professional judgement. On its own the knowledge may not appear too worrying but when collated with other pieces of knowledge the overall picture may indicate a more significant level of concern and risk. All practitioners need to recognise the importance of building and sustaining good relations with parents and families as then one will be more able to address the causes rather than the symptoms of neglect and abuse. Through a positive relationship parents can be helped to understand, learn from and ultimately if necessary, change their responses to their children.

It may be helpful to consider some of the following possible signs of abuse and neglect in children. These are not intended to be comprehensive but may serve to heighten awareness of some areas of concern. They may help you to begin thinking about the behaviour of children and young people and to consider potential reasons for such behaviour. It is important to acknowledge that signs of abuse in babies and very small children may vary.

Possible signs of physical abuse

This may include unexplained injuries, bruising or burns particularly if they are recurrent or the child gives improbable excuses to explain injuries or refuses to discuss them; admission of punishment that appears excessive; fear of parents being contacted or of returning home; withdrawal from physical contact, flinching at sudden movements; withdrawal and detachment from others; arms and legs kept covered even in hot weather; fear of medical help; self-destructive tendencies; aggressive behaviour towards others and chronic running away.

Possible signs of emotional abuse

This may be recognised with a child or young person in physical, mental and emotional developmental delay or disturbance; over-reaction to mistakes; sudden speech disorders; fear of new situations; inappropriate emotional responses to stressful situations; neurotic behaviours e.g. rocking, hair twisting, thumb-sucking; self-mutilation; extremes of passivity or aggression; fear of parents being contacted; chronic running away; scavenging for food or clothes, compulsive stealing; drug/solvent abuse and bed-wetting.

Possible signs of sexual abuse

This will differ for children at different ages and phases of development. Many of the above signs could be included so we have added here a few of the most commonly displayed responses. These include genital injuries, soreness, infection; explicit sexual drawings, stories, poems; sexualized play, exposing themselves, contextually abnormal masturbation; nightmares; fear of being washed, changed, put to bed; obsessive washing; depression or psychosomatic conditions.

Possible signs of neglect

This may be recognised through constant hunger, emaciation; poor personal hygiene, constant tiredness, poor state of clothing, untreated medical problems; poor supervision, persistent lateness and poor school attendance, low self-esteem; destructive tendencies, neurotic behaviours, lack of social relationships, chronic running away, scavenging for food and clothes and compulsive stealing.

Approaches and strategies for supporting vulnerable children and young people

The Common Assessment Framework (CAF)

The CAF (CWDC, 2009a), see also Chapter 7, was first introduced in 2001 and revised in 2005. The CAF aims to support an integrated approach for all professionals working with children, young people and their families. It is designed to facilitate an understanding of any additional needs a child might have that require consideration. The CAF assessment process can be initiated by any professional or family member. The CAF was developed from combining the underlying model of the Framework for the Assessment of Children in Need and their Families with the main elements used in other assessment frameworks. Nineteen elements are covered in three domains:

- development of baby, child or young person, including health and learning;
- parents and carers;
- family and environmental factors.

The following table (Table 4.2) is a summary of the framework that might help you understand the range of considerations that need to be addressed in the assessment process, when working with others to evaluate when a child might require additional support.

The CAF is a shared assessment and planning framework for use across all children's services and all local areas in England. It aims to help the early identification of children's additional needs and promote co-ordinated service provision to meet them. The CAF consists of a simple pre-assessment checklist to help practitioners identify children who would benefit from a common assessment. The checklist can be used on its own or alongside specialist universal assessments. There is also a standardised process for undertaking a common assessment, to help practitioners gather and understand information about the needs and strengths of the child, based on discussions with the child, their family and other practitioners as appropriate. Finally the CAF consists of a standard form designed to help practitioners record, and, where appropriate, share with others, the findings from the assessment in terms that are helpful in working with the family to find a response to unmet needs.

DEVELOPMENT OF THE INFANT, CHILD OR YOUNG PERSON			
Health			
General health	Physical development	Speech, language and communication development	Emotional and social development
Behavioural development			
Identity, including self-esteem, self-image and social presentation			
Family and social relationships		Self-care skills and independence	
Learning			
Understanding, reasoning and problem solving	Participation in learning, education and employment	Progress and achievement in learning	Aspirations
Parents and carers			
Basic care, ensuring safety and protection	Emotional warmth and stability	Guidance, boundaries and stimulation	
Family and environmental			
Family history, functioning and well being		Wider family	
Housing, employment and financial considerations		Social and community elements and resources including education	

Table 4.2 **Common Assessment Framework**

The CAF is a standardised approach to conducting an assessment of a child's additional needs and deciding how those needs should be met. The DfE has produced a range of tools, advice and guidance to assist practitioners in working with the CAF. The most recent guidance (CWDC, 2009a) takes people through the CAF process and includes case studies to help build understanding.

> **ACTIVITY 4.6**
>
> Visit the website www.cwdcouncil.org.uk/integrated-working/integrated-working-guidance.
>
> On that website you will find a set of guides that explain the CAF process. The guides are also available online as an interactive tool. Choose the guide that appears to be most appropriate to your role and experience and familiarise yourself with the CAF process.
>
> You might also like to visit the website www.cwdcouncil.org.uk/integrated-working/sector-case-studies.
>
> On that website you will find a set of six case studies that demonstrate how practitioners from diverse sectors in the children and young people's workforce are using the CAF to support integrated working.

All practitioners working with children, young people and their families need to be trained in how to use the CAF. It is used as a tool to bring practitioners from different agencies and disciplines together and to support them in meeting the needs of more vulnerable children. It is worth noting the centrality of the parent and the family in the assessment process that emphasises the importance placed upon professionals being able to build supportive relationships with parents.

The most recent guidance (CWDC, 2009a) advises that the CAF has replaced other assessment frameworks such as the Connexions Framework for Assessment, Planning, Implementation and Review (APIR) and that while other assessments, such as universal checks and specialist assessments for children in need, remain in place, the CAF may appropriately be used before, after or in conjunction with these assessments to help understand and articulate the full range of a child or young person's needs. Other specialised assessment frameworks include the Framework for Children in Need and their Families (the Assessment Framework) that has a much more specific purpose to determine whether a child or young person is a 'child in need' under section 17 of the Children Act (1989); Onset or Asset where the main purpose is to assess the child or young person's risk of offending; the developmental checks undertaken by health professionals as part of the Healthy Child Programme; or progress checks against the national curriculum conducted in schools, such as the Foundation Stage Profile. These types of specialist assessment framework are usually undertaken only by staff of a particular occupational or professional group. The most recent CAF guidance (CWDC, 2009a) offers examples of how these more specialist assessments might complement a CAF assessment. However, while you may use the CAF to inform your specialist assessment, it is also important to check that the information is accurate and up-to-date.

Children and young people at risk

All children and young people may be at risk of abuse or neglect but there are some contexts and characteristics that render children to be more at risk. As practitioners working in the field of children's services there will be challenging situations where children and young people need to be supported to develop levels of resilience to enable them to resist dangerous situations and walk away from abusive contexts. Daniel and Wassell (2002) have identified three fundamental building blocks that underpin the development of resilience in children and young people:

- A secure base that offers a child/young person a sense of belonging e.g. within the home, school and wider community.
- Positive self-esteem where a child feels valued and has an intact sense of their self-worth.
- Self-efficacy where a child is confident and displays a sense of mastery with a realistic appraisal of their own ability to contribute to and exert age appropriate control and influence on their life. To demonstrate a sense of empowerment: 'I can do' rather than a sense of hopelessness or failure that 'I can't do', 'I'm no good'.

This section identifies a range of specific areas of concern for children and families, where professionals are required to be more sensitised to protection and safeguarding concerns. Some examples are used here to illustrate levels of risk and vulnerability with suggestions as to how you might support such children.

Bullying

Bullying is very common in contexts where groups of children and young people come together – nursery, playgrounds, leisure centres, schools and colleges. It is important that adults are able to protect children and young people from being bullied and ensure they feel safe in all contexts. All schools should have anti-bullying policies that recognise that both the bully and the victim are vulnerable in different ways. Ensuring that children are aware that bullying is unacceptable, that they can report it and be assured that change will happen as a result is important. Adults need to be clear about the repercussions of bullying and to monitor environments where children feel more vulnerable – for example toilets and spaces within the playground. The anti-bullying alliance has a range of useful resources to support children and young people in learning about the impact of bullying and provides strategies for adults to build a positive ethos of friendship within the inclusive school community (see useful resources section at the end of this chapter).

Disability and learning difficulties

Policies advocating inclusive education (for example UNESCO, 2009) have enabled children with disabilities and learning difficulties to be educated alongside their peers. This has led to a higher level of awareness and understanding of such differences between children. Disabled children can be more vulnerable in this environment where they may rely on others to guide and support them in social interactions. This means that in relation to both adults and peers they are more at risk of being abused in some manner. Practitioners can address this concern through a process of education about individual differences; learning how peers can support and befriend each other; and through enhancing skills of communication and advocacy.

Children with disabilities often require high levels of personal care that can leave them vulnerable to the risk of abuse. Practitioners within the children's workforce need to be alert and aware of this area of vulnerability and ensure respect and responsibility for individual differences. Practitioners need to have good insight to the family life of a child with disability and have knowledge of the network of services that the family might be able to access. Such support has the potential to reduce the stress on the family and broaden the range of people they meet who can support them in caring for their child.

Children experiencing loss and bereavement

The children's workforce has an essential role in safeguarding and supporting children who are experiencing loss. These can range from minor day to day loss, such as through an argument with friends, failing a test, not being picked for a school or club team, through to more serious and long-lasting loss, such as the death of a parent, sibling or close friend, domestic abuse or family breakdown. Whatever their loss, children require time and space to grieve and recover, and to learn constructive and consistent coping strategies. Supporting children to manage their loss is an important aspect of developing emotional literacy and resilience and is the responsibility of all those working in the children's workforce. Children will learn how to manage their losses from the examples of the adults around them, and from the messages that they are given about how their losses are resolved. They will use these as building blocks to construct their own coping strategies as they develop into adulthood.

Grief refers to the feelings that emerge from a loss, whereas *bereavement* refers to the ongoing path towards recovery following a loss. Children tend to respond to loss in similar emotional and behavioural ways although these will vary according to a child's age and developmental stage. Worden (1996) suggests that children can take a minimum of two years to begin to recover from the death of a parent. Klass et al. (1996) argue that when someone close to a child dies, the child will not *forget* the person, and that it is important that the adults around them help them to remain connected with the deceased person. They describe this as *continuing bonds*. This model can also apply to children when a family breaks up. Children need to remain connected to an absent parent although the nature of the connection will vary according to the individual circumstances.

ACTIVITY 4.7

In order to gain some further insight into how children can be affected by loss it is suggested that you undertake this short activity.

Recall a minor personal loss from your childhood and note the following:

- What was the loss, and how old were you at the time?
- What was the context of the loss?
- How did you feel about it at the time?
- How do you feel about it now?
- Who or what helped you to be able to cope with this loss?
- What can you learn from reflection upon this experience that might benefit others experiencing loss?

You will probably note that your initial feelings about your loss included a range of emotions, for example disbelief, denial, shock, upset, anger. However over time your feelings may have changed and you may have overcome and even accepted the loss. You may have used your experience to develop resilience, learning positive strategies that have helped you to manage similar losses.

It is important that you have knowledge of a range of responses and strategies to use when working with children and young people experiencing loss. A level of sensitivity about language is valuable. For example, when talking to children about death, to avoid confusion never use euphemisms and always use the correct vocabulary. Say '*dead*' or '*died*', and don't say '*passed away*' or '*fell asleep*'. Also avoid unhelpful remarks such as '*I know how you feel*' or '*it doesn't matter*', as this devalues the child's experience. A further strategy is to reassure a child that there are people nearby who can support them. Bowlby (1988) recommended an activity called Trust Circles where one encourages the child to identify those adults and peers who are close and trusted by them through drawing circles around their image.

Looked-after children

The Children Act (2004) raised awareness of the specific needs of children looked after by social services. Local authorities were encouraged to place children in stable family units through long-term foster care and adoption. However, the legislation also sought to bring the needs of looked-after children to the attention of all professionals and required each school to appoint a designated person responsible for looked-after children. Such children and young people may be vulnerable to bullying and they may also have attachment or other emotional development needs due to the levels of parenting they have experienced in the past. Practitioners need sensitive language and to be wary of changes in behaviour or possible signs of abuse as listed earlier.

Children as carers

A BBC survey (BBC News, 2010) reported that there are over 700,000 children and young people who are young carers, caring for the physical and emotional needs of adults such as parent(s), siblings, or family members on an ongoing basis often over extended periods of time. These young people may, themselves, be vulnerable and in some cases in need of protection and safeguarding. Many young carers undertake inappropriate levels of emotional and personal care such as bathing and dressing relatives, giving medications and managing the household finances. There may be insufficient support from outside agencies in meeting the needs of, for example, an elderly relative, a parent who is disabled, mentally ill or misusing drugs or alcohol.

ACTIVITY 4.8

Visit the website www.youngcarers.net and identify some aspects which you should be aware of and need to consider in relation to the practice setting where you work.

What would you need to do to support a young carer in the context of your work?

Asylum-seekers and refugees

As people move around the world so do children and young people either with their parents or, in some cases, alone. Children or young people who are refugees and asylum-seekers need to be considered as children first and foremost. In 2008 the NSPCC recommended that the government should adhere to the UNCRC (1989) for all children seeking asylum and suggested that procedures in the UK were compromising their proper care, protection and development. Particular concern was raised that separated children have a thorough needs assessment to ensure that their health, emotional well being and support needs are identified and met. Asylum-seeking children are frequently suffering from bereavement and post-traumatic stress disorders. In December 2010, the UK government announced that they would end the practice of asylum-seeker children being held in immigration detention centres, the first steps in reform of such practice in the UK.

Children whose parents have mental health issues or abuse alcohol or drugs

Children and young people whose parents live with them, but have impaired capacity to care for them, due to, for example, mental illness or alcohol or drug misuse, may be at risk in terms of the adverse impact upon their health and development. Understanding why some children cope with adversity and difficult situations better than others has been the focus of considerable research. Some protective factors that can contribute to a child's resilience in situations where they may be exposed to vulnerable experiences have been identified as:

- strong bonds with family, friends and teachers;
- healthy standards set by parents, teachers and community leaders;
- * opportunities for involvement in families, schools and the community;
- * social and learning skills to enable participation;
- * recognition and praise for positive behaviour.

*These factors operate together as a 'protective process'.

(Beinart et al., 2002)

These factors relate to gender as boys are more at risk in the short term, but girls are equally at risk should the situation endure over a long period of time. Children under five years old and those with complex disabilities are more at risk as their dependence is greater. If only one parent is misusing or ill the other can care for the child and maintain the family unit. If the adversity is relatively mild and/or of short duration and does not result in family stress or dysfunction then impact on the child can be reduced. More resilient children are better able to cope and are often more proactive in seeking ways to problem solve or shield themselves from the impact of poor parenting by seeking support from alternative positive adults, for example grandparents, friends or the wider extended family. The level of risk is increased and the impact upon the child or young person likely to be more severe where domestic violence occurs alongside parental mental illness and/or drug or alcohol misuse.

The world of electronic media

Concerns about protecting children and young people in the world of electronic media have come to the fore as children and young people increasingly use the internet, social networking, mobile phones, video games, and many other electronic modes of communication. Safeguarding carries the same requirements as in other contexts, although the electronic world can have complex codes for social interaction that children may find hard to manage.

The Byron Review (Byron, 2008) recommended government, industry and public services – education particularly – should ensure that children and young people are safe in digital environments. Byron paid particular attention to the use of the internet and video games and launched the UK Council for Child Internet Safety. She advocated a child-friendly approach to ensuring safety, recognising that the electronic world is a new environment that children need to learn to navigate safely, rather than be banned from using.

ACTIVITY 4.9

Find out what policies and practices operate within your workplace to protect children and young people from the dangers of the electronic environment.

You might find an e-safety policy. Make notes about how your practice can protect children and young people from the risks of electronic media.

Safeguarding children and young people is an important aspect of the professional work of all those working in children's services. The best approach to ensuring children are protected from adverse experiences and harm is through building their capacity for resilience, ensuring they have a good level of emotional literacy and providing them with sources of support which they are able to access independently when they feel they require it. The SEAL (Social and Emotional Aspects to Learning) initiative that is delivered in schools has been developed as a pastoral approach to address some of these issues.

ACTIVITY 4.10

SEAL focuses on five social and emotional aspects of learning: self-awareness, managing feelings, motivation, empathy and social skills.

Visit the website http://nationalstrategies.standards.dcsf.gov.uk/primary/publications/banda/seal and explore some of the resources identified.

Which resources might you find useful to help children or young people with whom you work develop their social and emotional skills?

What examples from your own practice can you find of activities that support these skills?

Confidentiality

When considering issues of safeguarding and child protection all practitioners need to have a well-developed understanding of current legislation and the common law duty in relation to confidentiality. Furthermore, all practitioners working with children and young people need to understand the principles that dictate when young people are considered sufficiently mature to give or refuse consent to their information being shared. There is often confusion and uncertainty about when, how and with whom concerns about the welfare or safety of children may be shared.

Making It Happen (DfES, 2006a) provides clear, practical advice for people working with children and young people in the public, private and voluntary sectors and sets out six key principles to help guide practitioners:

- Explain openly and honestly at the outset what information will or could be shared, and why, and seek agreement except where doing so puts the child or others at risk of significant harm.
- The child's safety and welfare must be the overriding consideration when making decisions on whether to share information about them.
- Ensure information is accurate, up-to-date, necessary for the purpose for which you are sharing it, and shared only with those who need it and shared securely.
- Respect the wishes of children or families who do not consent to share confidential information unless in your judgement there is sufficient need to override that lack of consent.
- Seek advice when in doubt.
- Always record the reasons for your decision whether it is to share or not to share information.

Where information given by a young person is shared with those who hold parental responsibility for them, consent of the young person should be obtained wherever possible. Where the young person declines to give consent, the 'Fraser Ruling' should be used as a basis for making a professional decision on whether to share the information without their permission. In every situation, if in doubt about your decision, you should seek advice from a manager.

ACTIVITY 4.11

When deciding whether a child is mature enough to make decisions, people often talk about whether a child is 'Gillick competent' or whether they meet the 'Fraser guidelines'. Gillick competency and Fraser guidelines refer to a legal case that looked specifically at whether doctors should be able to give contraceptive advice or treatment to under 16-year-olds without parental consent. Since then, they have been more widely used to help assess whether a child has the maturity to make their own decisions and to understand the implications of those decisions.

Look up the Fraser guidelines by searching online. For example you might look at the NSPCC website where you will find an easy-to-read fact sheet and guidance: www.nspcc.org.uk/inform/research/questions/gillick_wda61289.html.

CHAPTER SUMMARY

This chapter has provided an introduction to the concept of safeguarding for children and young people and some background to the current policy position in the UK regarding approaches to the protection of children and young people. The chapter has provided an overview of a range of behaviours that we might witness when working with children and young people that could hold potential for concern. This chapter has emphasised the importance of sharing information and concerns about children and young people. It has also encouraged practitioners to explore the nature of professional judgement and to recognise that safeguarding is the responsibility of us all.

The chapter has included sections highlighting areas where there might be particular concerns regarding aspects of vulnerability and specific children who might be at risk. The chapter concludes with reference to some examples of strategies which practitioners might explore to develop emotionally aware, well-networked and resilient children and young people ready to cope with the challenges that life might present them.

Useful resources

There are many websites that offer support to children and young people and also those to support practitioners and parents to develop skills and resources to support children and young people at risk. The following are a small sample of such websites for you to start your explorations:

www.nspcc.org.uk The website of the NSPCC contains a wealth of advice and guidance on warning signs of child abuse, what to do if you suspect abuse and resources and practical advice for practitioners, volunteer workers, parents or carers.

www.winstonswish.org.uk This website offers support to bereaved children.

www.anti-bullyingalliance.org.uk The Anti-Bullying Alliance aims to develop a consensus around how to stop and prevent bullying. They work to develop and disseminate best practice and offer resources to support this.

www.ncb.org.uk/arc ARC – the Asylum Seeking and Refugee Children – Developing Good Practice Project website is an online resource for those working with separated or unaccompanied refugee children and young people.

www.direct.gov.uk/en/Parents/Yourchildshealthandsafety/Internetsafety/ DG_071138 A government website offering advice on how to keep children and young people safe online.

www.protecting-children-update.com This website contains information on research, legislation and resources to support child protection.

www.thinkuknow.co.uk The Child Exploitation and Online Protection website contains resources and advice on keeping children and young people safe online. It also has links to freely downloadable videos.

www.childnet.com Childnet International, a non-profit organisation working with others to *help make the Internet a great and safe place for children.*

www.netsmartz.org/index.aspx An American site with some useful films and quizzes for young people.

www.digizen.org The Digizen website provides information for educators, parents, carers and young people. It is used to strengthen their awareness and understanding of what digital citizenship is and encourages users of technology to be and become responsible *digizens* (*digital* citiz*ens*). It shares specific advice and resources on issues such as social networking and cyberbullying.

www.c4eo.org.uk/themes/safeguarding The Centre for Excellence and Outcomes for Children (C4EO) contains resources to support safeguarding including an interactive e-learning resource.

www.scie.org.uk/children/childprotection.asp Social Care Institute for Excellence (SCIE) contains a suite of resources on safeguarding and child protection.

FURTHER READING

Hetherington, R, Cooper, A, Smith, P and Wilford, G (1997) *Protecting Children: Messages from Europe*. Lyme Regis, Dorset: Russell House Publishing. This book discusses some examples of different approaches to addressing child protection across Europe.

National Children's Bureau (2010) *Understanding Why: Understanding Attachment and How This Can Affect Education with Special Reference to Adopted Children and Young People and Those Looked After by Local Authorities*. London: National Children's Bureau. This booklet describes behaviours and feelings that are common among children and young people who have experienced a major loss or trauma early in their lives. It will help practitioners recognise attachment difficulties and consider how to help a child or young person achieve their full potential.

Plummer, D (2010) *Helping Children to Cope with Change Stress and Anxiety*. London: Jessica Kingsley. A photocopiable activities book suitable for use with children aged 7+.

Yorkshire and Humber Regional Leaving Care Forum (2010) *Good Practice Guide on Health and Wellbeing for Young People Leaving Care* **(www.leavingcare.org/data/tmp/6039-12734.pdf)**. This resource provides a range of good practice examples, looks at current research, and identifies issues for service development.

On the website Child Abuse: A History Website you can read about the case of Mary Ellen that led to the founding of the New York Society for the Prevention of Cruelty to Children, the first organization of its kind, in 1874. **www.library.index.com/pages/1361/ Child-Abuse-History-ABUSE-DURING-INDUSTRIAL-REVOLUTION.html**

5 PARTICIPATORY COMMUNICATION

Richard Kimberlee and Jonathan Coles

COMMON CORE OF SKILLS AND KNOWLEDGE FOR THE CHILDREN'S WORKFORCE: EFFECTIVE COMMUNICATION AND ENGAGEMENT WITH CHILDREN, YOUNG PEOPLE AND FAMILIES

Listening and building empathy

- Establish a rapport and build respectful, trusting, honest and supportive relationships with children, young people, their families and carers, which make them feel valued as partners.

- Use clear language to communicate with all children, young people, families and carers, including people who find communication difficult, or are at risk of exclusion or under-achievement.

- Be able to adapt styles of communication to the needs and abilities of children and young people who do not communicate verbally, or communicate in different ways.

- Build a rapport and develop relationships using the most appropriate forms of communication (for example, spoken language, visual communication, play, body and sign language, information and communication technologies) to meet the needs of the individual child or young person and their families and carers.

- Hold conversations at the appropriate time and place, understanding the value of regular, reliable contact and recognising that it takes time to build a relationship.

- Actively listen in a calm, open, non-judgemental, non-threatening way and use open questions. Acknowledge what has been said, and check you have heard correctly.

- Make sure that children, young people, parents and carers know they can communicate their needs and ask for help.

(CWDC, 2010a)

CHAPTER OBJECTIVES

By the end of this chapter you should have an understanding of:

- key participatory techniques for children, young people, and their families;

- policy and legislative context of participatory communication;

- theories or models that underpin the practice;

- different agencies, services and professionals offering support;

- tools and techniques for use in practice to support participatory communication;

- useful resources to improve knowledge and practice.

Introduction

Effective communication extends to involving children, young people, their parents and carers in the design and delivery of services and decisions that affect them.

(CWDC, 2010a, page 6)

Effective communication for children and young people is about participation. In the early seventies Pateman (1970, page 1) noted that the term *participation* was used to refer to a wide variety of situations by different people. This complexity continues today. A minimalist view of participation would suggest that simply encouraging children and young people's voice is a practical precondition for effective participation. A maximalist view would see young people having power to determine both the type of decisions and the actual decisions to which they are giving voice, and that this is seen as a complete expression of citizenship for children and young people to achieve (Hart, 1992). What are not in doubt are the potential benefits that occur from children and young people's participation in decision-making. In the UK these have been suggested to be:

- preservation of rights as citizens and service users;
- fulfilment of legal responsibilities related to international and national legislation;
- improvement and influence in services through better informed decision-making;
- enhancement of democratic processes;
- protection from abuse;
- enhancement of skills;
- empowerment;
- enhanced own self-esteem.

(Sinclair and Franklin, 2000)

Governments in recent times have come to believe that it is important to consult children and young people and hear their voice especially when they use and are affected by services delivered by local or national government. They also believe that it is important to consider children and young people's opinions and perspectives from the outset of their experience of a service. With effective communication comes the development of trust between the workforce and children, young people, parents and carers, as well as within different sectors of the workforce itself (CWDC, 2010a). However this stated aim has not always been recognised or granted to children and young people. In fact it is the outcome of several policy initiatives that have sought to engage them and enshrine their right to a voice in practice.

This chapter includes three discrete sections. The first explores the policies and legislation that support the engagement and participation of children and young people. The second section discusses some of the practitioner values and skills that enable and support the participatory communication of children, young people and their families. The third section pulls these together in describing a project that used some of the policies, values and skills identified previously to engage children and young people in an aspect of community safety. It is our belief that effective practice requires knowledge and understanding of social policies that support participation as well as positive values and communication skills in working with children, young people and their families.

Policy and legislation

The first post-Second World War Labour government in 1945 established the importance of state intervention as a policy choice to address urgent national needs after a long war. They developed social democratic policies to ensure they could intervene and manage the economy. They also expanded on and developed the welfare state to ensure it delivered universal services to people in need. Benefits such as child benefit (formerly family allowance) were available to all. Some commentators saw these new arrangements as being paternalistic. They felt that civil society was being ignored and criticised the lack of public participation in the development of the welfare state (Hughes, 1998). In other words they felt that these services were being planned by the state without consultation with the people who were likely to use their services. Instead the power and knowledge of professionals informed both policy-making processes and the delivery of services (Clarke and Newman, 1997).

Concern about youth voice and participation as a policy issue evolved in the 1960s when the *baby boomers* reached their teenage years. In this decade the growth of participation in civil society was symbolised by emerging new social movements, including feminism, the peace movement, environmentalism and the civil rights movement on both sides of the Atlantic. Universities became radicalised and new theorists and ideas emerged and became popular. This includes thinkers such as Carl Rogers (see below) who talked about the importance of a humanistic and person-centred approach to understanding relationships and decision-making. Young people and other marginalised groups were asking for a voice. By the 1970s the state intervention approach that had underpinned the post-war state came under further pressure from service users as it was increasingly seen to have failed to address the diversifying needs and the wishes of a more informed public. The state was seen as corporatist rather than paternalistic. When the long economic post-war boom ended the recession led both Labour and Conservative governments to consider more free market approaches to meet service needs. Privatisation of state services was seen as potentially more effective to meet the increasing demands for improved rights, choice and cost-effective services for service users.

Involving children and young people in decision-making as a policy principle had been largely ignored by successive governments. However external, international pressure led to change. In the UK the United Nations Convention on the Rights of the Child (1989) (UNCRC) served as a catalyst for a broad political consensus that children's opinions and observations must be taken more seriously. Article 12 stated that children and young people should have their opinions taken into account in all major decisions affecting their lives. They should have a voice. The treaty was ratified by the UK government in 1991 and this was subsequently endorsed by many local authorities. From this time the debate about children's involvement moved rapidly from the earlier philosophical debates as to *whether* they should be engaged to *how* and for *what purpose* they should be engaged, mirroring the debates on participation within the development discipline (Gaventa, 2006).

Have you heard of the UN Convention on the Rights of the Child (1989)?

The United Nations International Children's Emergency Fund (UNICEF) website outlines the principles of the convention. Have a look at this now and consider their implications for your own practice. See http://www.unicef.org.uk/UNICEFs-Work/Our-mission/UN-Convention/.The Department for Education website includes a link to a useful two-page leaflet that explains how the principles of the convention map against the five *Every Chld Matters* outcomes. See www.education.gov.uk/publications/standard/publicationDetail/Page1/32016

Following the establishment of the convention children and young people's right to be heard began to be incorporated into legislation. The Children Act 1989 gave children and young people involved in child protection proceedings the right to have *their wishes and feelings taken into account*. This heralded a new era. This was extended by the 2004 Children Act to all children and young people in need, which also replaced parental rights with the concept of *parental responsibility*. Since then the participation of children and young people has been included in seven separate pieces of legislation in the United Kingdom, including the Crime and Disorder Act 1998. The involvement of young people in the government's work received another boost with the European Community Youth White Paper (2001) that declared a stated European Common Objective on more youth participation. This led to increasing guidance and advice to service providers in local government to listen to young people's voice and engage young people in decision-making. For example the UK government's commitment to youth voice and participation was declared in the guidance on pupil participation *Working Together: Giving Children and Young People a Say for Schools and Local Education Authorities* (DfES, 2004c).

ACTIVITY 5.1

Identify any policy and/or procedures, in your setting, that are aimed at giving children or young people a voice in decision-making. Think of a time when you involved a group of children or young people in decision-making about a service they received?

Make a list of the costs and benefits of their involvement.

The need to build children and young people's capacity to engage as active citizens has long been acknowledged. The victory of New Labour in 1997 occurred at a time when concern about youth apathy and disengagement from politics and civil society was at its height (Kimberlee, 1998). Participatory structures for youth voice were subsequently slowly developed both across local authorities and within individual services (Willow, 1997). A United Kingdom Youth Parliament (UKYP) was formed in 2001 and following the Crick Report (Crick, 1998) citizenship was introduced into the secondary school curriculum in 2002. The importance of this educational reform was not simply about improving young people's political literacy (i.e. learning about politics) but it offered a clear approach that sought to promote *active citizenship* amongst young people. It envisaged that young people should be taught to realise their voice, work together and take practical action, using their knowledge and understanding of citizenship to contribute to a better society. Within the education sector the importance of children and young people's engagement was acknowledged when a new duty was placed on all maintained schools in England and Wales to consider their views with the passing of the Education and Skills Act (2008). This significant reform substantially strengthened the legal rights of children to participate in school decision-making and today it is not unusual to see young people involved in consultations around new appointees, funding bids and decision-making such as food provision in schools.

While education services received a boost from policy-makers to listen and positively encourage young people's voice and participation all services working with young people were forced into an assessment of their service delivery following the publication of the *Every Child Matters* (DfES, 2003) green paper. This was published alongside the formal response to the report into the death of Victoria Climbié, the young girl abused, tortured and killed by her great aunt and the man with whom they lived. With the Children Act (2004) the government provided a legislative spine for developing more effective and accessible services focused around the needs of children, young people and families. Consultation with and participation by young people was seen as an essential element if future services were going to be more effective in meeting needs.

As economies in Europe began to falter in the early 1990s, support for state intervention as a solution declined and policies that led to an increased voice for children and young people were re-evaluated. While these legislative initiatives appeared to have enshrined young people's rights the effectiveness of this approach has been challenged. Policy analysts who have tracked the increase in the privatisation of state services argue that the increasing commercialisation of private life and the breaking up of the corporatist social democratic welfare state has led to a withdrawal of state support for vulnerable people. In fact it is argued that it is now increasingly difficult to sustain the idea of public interest and a public space, defined in ways that are separate from market relationships (Gamble, 1996, page 127). Professionals (such as youth workers) delivering services have been encouraged to become target driven and to deliver cost-effective services as the withdrawal of the state and increasing commercialisation has contributed towards a more diverse service and policy (Rhodes, 1997).

The extent to which the state has lost influence and power in the policy-making process is contested but what commentators agree on is that public service workers and professionals working on the front line are now facing increasingly diverse and frequently contradictory pressures (Richards and Smith, 2002). Although participation and voice is encouraged it often leads to diverse voices and pressures. For some commentators *participation* has become one of the mechanisms through which the government attempts to govern (Newman et al., 2004). The *hollowing out of the state* shown in the decline of corporatism and the universal provision of welfare has led governments to adopt different governing strategies such as youth participation, which helps the state to reconstruct their relationships with individuals (Kooiman, 2003). This means that rights especially in relation to the welfare state and service provision have been rethought in response to external pressures from the United Nations and European Union, and internal pressures from target setting and new public management reforms under Conservative governments and the modernisation agenda of New Labour.

ACTIVITY 5.2

There are some important words used so far with which you may not be familiar. Use a dictionary of sociology or politics (see 'Further reading') to define their meaning more precisely then re-read the previous section:

Paternalistic	Professional	New social movements
Corporatist	Privatisation	Free market approach
Civil society	Welfare state	Social democratic

It is only relatively recently that children and young people have been given a voice. They have entered into policy discourses. Makrinioti (1994, page 274) has argued that in the immediate post-Second World War period children and young people had *their needs articulated and satisfied only implicitly and indirectly* in social policy. Policies affecting children and young people were made without their voice. Lacking access to participatory processes, which are integral to the exercise of democratic rights, children and young peoples' experiences had always remained largely hidden from view. They were denied effective recognition as citizens (Lansdown, 2000, page 7). New Labour policy initiatives encouraged the establishment of processes to engage children and young people and give them voice, but these may be seen as less significant than professionals striving to achieve policy outcomes. Social policies have often been output-driven, prioritising policy delivery. Targets such as reductions in child poverty and those concerning school performance have been more central to governing strategies. This might suggest that there has been less concern with enhancing young people's rights to have a voice, however other policy discourses have frequently called for *democratic renewal* and the need to build *social capital* in communities (Halpern, 2005), for example by expanding local government or through local regeneration schemes to improve local communities.

As the coalition government seeks to promote the notion of Big Society it is perhaps in the voluntary and community sector organisations where the rights of children and young people to a voice and participation will be sustained. The British Youth Council, a charitable organisation run by and for young people with an original aim of uniting young people against the forces of communism amid tense international relations just after the Second World War, continues to give young people opportunities to scrutinise the work of government and service delivery. With a consortium made up of five other agencies (Children's Rights Alliance for England, National Council for Voluntary Youth Services, National Youth Agency, National Children's Bureau and Save the Children UK) they have established the Participation Works network that enables professionals and organisations to involve children and young people effectively in the development, delivery and evaluation of services that affect their lives. The Children's Rights Alliance for England seek to protect these recently won human rights for children and young people by lobbying government and others who hold power and by bringing or supporting test cases using regional and international human rights mechanisms.

Discussion for the future might focus on how organisations balance the shift to marketisation and performance indicators in service delivery with the need to develop a culture of genuine participation. John (2003, page 196) highlights that there is an imbalance between children and those in power and argues: *In the case of children, their language, whatever its forms, about their worlds is rarely recognised by the powerful.* Tool kits have been devised and used to support professionals in their work to genuinely engage young people. It is important to avoid adopting a dogmatic approach that thinks any one tool kit or approach will work for all children and young people. Participation should be informed by the belief that all children and young people are of equal worth irrespective of ability, ethnicity, gender, health, religion, sexual orientation or social class. We have to be mindful that in the *current crisis in children's participation when the call for children's voices to be heard results in small, usually unrepresentative, groups of children being given limited access to adult forums* (van Beers et al., 2006, page 19) then the comprehensiveness and coherence of that voice must be considered and balanced against the democratic gains achieved.

ACTIVITY 5.3

If you are working with children and young people and want support to empower them to give them voice and involve them in decision-making you can find help and support from the Participation Works Partnership website. Here you will find tool kits for different scenarios, training opportunities and an opportunity to network with other professionals: www.participationworks.org.uk/.

Techniques and tools

Policy creates spaces and defines the scope and range of activity in which practitioners can engage with service users. This section considers both practitioner values and skills which support participation. It draws on the work of developmental psychologists and advocates of 'social pedagogy' and how this can translate into practical communication skills.

Practitioners often become involved with children, young people and their families when things are going wrong. The identification of a learning difficulty, problems with behaviour, criminal or anti-social activity, difficulties within the family, impairment, illness, loss and/or exclusion typically bring practitioners into the lives of children, young people and their families. In this section we look at the ways in which professionals engage with children and young people to hear their voice and enable them to participate and affect decisions. Reference will also be made to communication tools for engaging adult family members.

Communication roadblocks

Thomas Gordon (1974) observed that when children and young people show unhappiness or indicate that they have a problem most professionals respond with what he termed a 'communication roadblock'. This can involve the following:

Ordering/commanding	Warning/threatening
Moralising/preaching	Advising/giving solutions
Persuading with logic	Judging/blaming
Praising/agreeing	Name-calling/ridiculing
Analysing/diagnosing	Reassuring/sympathising
Probing/questioning	Diverting/sarcasm

He argues that all of these types of response claim some form of authority or power on the part of the professional and consequently disempower the child or young person. While such responses may serve a purpose (often compliance), they are unlikely to encourage participation.

ACTIVITY 5.4

A 12-year-old boy, Wayne, arrives in school extremely worried about his 14-year-old sister, who left the family home the previous evening after a fierce argument with their father and has not returned. During registration the teacher notices his distress and asks him to wait behind as the other students leave the room. The following interaction takes place between the teacher (T) and the student (S):

    T: You look a bit down in the dumps, Wayne. What's up?
    S: I'm OK sir.
    T: Is there something going on at home?
    S: No sir – I'm OK.
    T: Look, I know there's something wrong. Why don't you just tell me?
    S: [Silent].
    T: Well you either need to tell me so I can help you or else you need to cheer up and get on with the day.
    S: I'm OK sir.

It is quite clear that this teacher wants to help and yet the interaction is not working. Why might the student be reluctant to disclose what is really happening?

Values and attitudes

In considering how practitioners can encourage the participation of children, young people and families, both in one to one situations and when working with groups, this section builds on the idea that paying attention to how the practitioner constructs the relationship(s) is key. This inevitably involves consideration of the exchange of both overt and hidden messages – words and also non-verbal communication.

Gordon (1974) draws on the work of Carl Rogers in identifying a set of attitudes, values and skills that encourages genuine engagement between adults, children and young people. Rogers (1957) had identified six conditions of therapist attitude and behaviour in effective therapeutic relationships. Clearly practitioners are not usually therapists, however when children and young people are experiencing difficulties in their lives it seems logical for professionals to draw on the knowledge and skills developed within counselling and/or therapy, which invite engagement and participation. This section will briefly explore two of Rogers' key conditions: *unconditional positive regard* and *empathic understanding*, and consider their application.

Within mental health services and practice, the concept of *unconditional positive regard* is broadly accepted. When people are experiencing difficulties in life they risk harm to their self-worth – their self-esteem. There is a consequent risk that damage to their self-esteem can become a vicious circle. Repeated negative experiences such as being in trouble, rejection or failure provide a feedback loop that can negatively inform their self-image. The value position of *unconditional positive regard* should lead a skilled practitioner to the communication of acceptance of the other person – regardless of the current difficulties:

> When a person is able to feel and communicate genuine acceptance of another, he possesses a capacity for being an effective helping agent. Acceptance of the other, just as he is, is an important factor in fostering a relationship in which the other person can grow, develop, make constructive changes, learn to solve problems, move in the direction of psychological health, become more productive and creative and actualise his fullest potential.
>
> (Gordon, 1974, page 56)

Kwaitek et al. (2005) claim that many people with learning difficulties do not experience unconditional acceptance from practitioners, or from the general public. More usually they experience unequal 'doing to' instead of 'being with' relationships. Positive regard becomes conditional – experienced when they behave in ways which meet the approval of staff and/or parents. Perhaps this experience of conditional regard is true for many children and young people in their relationships with significant adults. *Unconditional positive regard* supports risk taking, growth and participation as positive regard is not withheld when mistakes are made.

Many of the individual children and young people with whom practitioners work may already have had negative experience of adults. Adult family members can also distrust service providers and professionals. When working with groups and seeking to encourage engagement and participation, practitioners need to communicate their belief that

- this engagement is worthwhile and valuable;
- the other person/people are 'up to' the task;
- there is little risk of failure.

ACTIVITY 5.5

Think about a situation in which you want to engage a particular child or young person into some sort of participation. How might you try to

- convince them that their engagement is worthwhile;
- communicate your belief that they will succeed and/or gain something;
- remove or lessen the fear of failure.

Now think about a situation in which you want to engage a particular adult family member into some sort of participation. How might you try to

- convince them that their engagement is worthwhile;
- communicate your belief that they will succeed and/or gain something;
- remove or lessen the fear of failure.

Rogers (1957, page 96) refers to *empathic understanding* as being: *To sense the client's private world as if it were your own, without losing the 'as if' quality.* Empathy can be described as a way of imaginatively experiencing another person's world. When practitioners achieve *empathic understanding*, they not only develop their understanding of how the other person experiences the world, they also attempt to communicate this back, with the intention of demonstrating their endeavours and perhaps encouraging the other person to further explain. At its best this can give rise to a sense of being understood, and the development of trust. The application of *empathic understanding* when working with groups will require the practitioner to imagine the thoughts or feelings of the group and communicate this attempt to understand, for example:

> *I would guess that you are already very busy.*
> *I expect some of you are worried about your exams next week.*
> *I'm sure that many of you would like to have more of a say in what food is available in the canteen.*

Both *unconditional positive regard* and *empathic understanding* are supported and advanced in the act of listening to children and young people. A precondition for effective listening is the ability to give one's full attention to another.

Attending

Egan (1998) discusses *attending* as a micro-skill of communication where *attending* means being with people in both a physical and psychological sense. Attending to others indicates that they are important to you and involves noticing and responding to both verbal and non-verbal cues. This is especially important when interacting with very young children and children or young people with learning difficulties, for whom spoken language may be problematic and non-verbal signals may be the main means of expression. Signalling attention indicates value and invites trust. Egan recommends a set of physical skills including posture and eye contacts which indicate attentiveness. However individual practitioners can develop their own ways to communicate this. These are likely to involve smiles, eye contact, nods and quiet verbal encouragements (*oh, I see, hmm*):

> *Attending to someone means giving them your total, complete, undivided interest. It means using your body, your face, your eyes, yes, especially your eyes, to say: 'Nothing exists right now for me except you.'*
>
> (Kottler and Kottler, 1993, page 40)

ACTIVITY 5.6

Try to identify some of the physical skills that you employ when you want to signal your attentiveness to another person. How do these skills differ when interacting with either adults or children or young people?

Avoiding distraction and focusing on the child or young person are paramount here. Bryant (2009) emphasises the importance of creating an environment for listening. For many practitioners this can prove difficult. Schools in particular are busy places and it can be hard for staff to find quiet spaces in which to give full attention without the risk of interruption. However even in busy spaces a skilled practitioner will use their skills to signal the importance of the other person and their best attempts to attend.

Active listening

Skilled listeners show that they are giving full attention, do not judge and work hard to try to understand the other person. They keep the *agenda* belonging to the other person, without introducing their own views or indeed, advice.

The particular skill of *active listening* starts with this emphasis on giving full attention to the message sender. It also involves practitioners in trying to show understanding by paraphrasing and feeding back or checking what they think has been communicated by the other person – both through words and also through non-verbal communication. A sensitive practitioner will often pick up on the mood of another person without words being exchanged and this can be fed back; for example, *You look a bit fed up today* or *Something's worrying you.*

This involves interpretation and as such there is no guarantee that the practitioner's perception will be accurate. However, at the very least this indicates concern, attentiveness and a willingness to listen. At best it may lead to a constructive interaction. Children, young people and adults are more likely to want to engage with practitioners who appear open and give the impression that they are trying to understand.

Indeed, language-based interactions also involve a good deal of interpretation. If someone tells you that they are feeling fine, but the way they say this – tone, body position, facial expression, eye-contact avoidance (remember Wayne?) – indicates something different then which do you believe? Non-verbal communication often provides a clearer indication of people's emotional states than words. McNaughton et al. (2007) describe active listening as a multi-step process, involving the use of empathic comments, asking appropriate questions and the use of paraphrasing and summarising. These skills indicate that the listener is trying to understand.

CASE STUDY 5.1   EXAMPLE OF ACTIVE LISTENING IN PRACTICE

You are a secondary school learning support assistant. You are in the drama studio getting the room ready for a class when Amanda (a 15-year-old student) arrives a few minutes early. She has her hood pulled low over her face, avoids eye contact with you and slumps heavily into a chair. The following conversation takes place.

Amanda: *I really hate drama.*
You: *You're not enjoying drama at all?*
Amanda: *[Pause] I suppose I enjoy some of it, but I can't concentrate.*
You: *Concentration's hard.*
Amanda: *Well I definitely can't concentrate when people are bossy.*
You: *You don't like being bossed about on the course?*
Amanda: *I don't like being bossed about by Tony [another student on the course]. For God's sake don't let Mrs Shah [teacher] put me in a group with him again.*

In a very short space of time a problem has been identified, however the conversation started in a different place. Consider the following:

- *What skills/tools did you use in this interaction?*
- *What did you avoid?*
- *Why?*

I-messages

Practitioners working with children or young people may occasionally need to confront, criticise or offer negative feedback when attempting to help them to change destructive behaviours. In these situations there is always a danger that the relationship between the practitioner and the child or young person will be damaged, often resulting in a loss of sometimes hard-earned trust.

ACTIVITY 5.7

Think of a child or young person with whom you work who sometimes behaves in ways that are harmful or hurtful to him/herself or others. Imagine this behaviour happening. How would you confront him or her? What would you actually say?

What response might the child or young person have to this message from you?

In situations like these Gordon (2000) recommends the use of what he terms confrontive I-messages. These are broken down into three parts:

- a non-blameful description of the actual behaviour;
- the effect that the behaviour is having;
- the speaker's feelings about that effect.

This can be given a more simple structure that practitioners can adapt and use in these situations:

When you . . . I feel ... because . . .

Some people respond very poorly to being given an order. Notice how this method of confronting describes a problem, but does not either criticise or order the child or young person to do something. As such, it is unlikely to seriously damage a relationship or undermine trust.

ACTIVITY 5.8

Think back to the child or young person from the previous activity. Try to construct a confrontive I-message in three parts using the structure *when you ... I feel ... because....*

What response might the child or young person have to this message from you?

Gordon also recommends the use of positive I-messages as a technique for praising or complimenting children or young people on their achievements. He recognises that some children find it difficult to accept praise, particularly if it sounds objective or authoritative:

Your story is very well written Jamil.
That's an excellent drawing Paula.

If Jamil does not think he is a good writer, perhaps because of previous adult criticism, and Paula is not confident about her drawing skills, they may not genuinely accept these well intentioned compliments. Indeed some children and young people will destroy their own work if they receive praise in this way. Gordon advocates that positive I-messages should include the speaker's feelings about what has been achieved. This makes a compliment more difficult to reject.

I loved reading your story Jamil.
I'd like to have your drawing on my office wall Paula.

Social pedagogy

In terms of the practice of working with children and young people, policy-makers have recently begun to advocate both the philosophy and skills associated with social pedagogy. The history or development of social pedagogy as an influence on education, social work and youth work is contested. What seems clear is that in the early nineteenth century the Swiss pedagogue and educational reformer Heinrich Pestalozzi (cited in Heafford, 1967) developed a method of holistic education that sought to engage the head, the heart and the hands of both the child and teacher in shared activity.

Petrie et al. (2005, page 22) identify the key features for those working with children to include:

- a focus on the child as a whole person, and support for the child's overall development;
- the practitioner seeing herself/himself as a person, in relationship with the child or young person;
- children and staff are seen as inhabiting the same life space, not as existing in separate hierarchical domains;
- the centrality of relationship and, allied to this, the importance of listening and communicating.

Further support for social pedagogy arrived from the Children's Workforce Development Council (CWDC, 2009b) in its discussion paper *Social Pedagogy and its Implications for Practice*.

When planning practice with either individual children and young people or with groups that seeks their participation then further considerations would be to appeal to them on these three levels – the head, the heart and the hands – and also to follow social pedagogy's emphasis of joining in shared activities.

In contexts that allow for this, expressive arts can create opportunities for collaboration between workers, children and young people and for the holistic, mutual engagement of head, heart and hands. Poetry, including hip hop/rap; music production and performance that employ both digital sequencing and analogue sound (instruments); drama, including role play; fine art such as painting and drawing (including graffiti, cartoons and comics); sculpture; graphics and the construction of graphic stories; film including animation; textiles and fashion; and photography all provide opportunities for expression, participation, engagement and collaboration, and all can involve the head, the heart and the hands.

Participation is, in part, about individuals and groups finding a voice, a way of saying things and of being heard, and thus being able to offer their opinions and make a mark on their own worlds. While the National Curriculum and formal education support this achievement to a greater or lesser extent for the majority of children and young people, they fail to do so for a significant minority. Some of those with learning difficulties and/or emotional and behavioural difficulties and children and young people with complex needs struggle to find a voice. Creative use of expressive arts allied with practitioner willingness to join children and young people and accept their perceptions, provides fertile ground for supporting and amplifying their voices.

CASE STUDY 5.2   STREETS AHEAD ON SAFETY

This case study looks at an example of engaging children and young people in decision-making to illustrate the social pedagogy approach – how heads, hearts and the hands of children were engaged in shared activity (Kimberlee, 2009).

Birmingham City Council's Streets Ahead on Safety *project aimed to improve road safety and quality of life in an area of multiple deprivation where 87,000 people from largely Asian backgrounds live. A third of residents were under 16 years old and 58 per cent self-defined their religion as Muslim. The project area had a poor traffic accident record leading to high levels of child KSI (killed or seriously injured). Between 2001–2005 there were on average 56 child pedestrian accidents per year in the project area, which gives an average of 2.18 child pedestrian accidents per 1000 of the child population. This was extraordinarily high compared to the Birmingham wide level of accidents (0.3 accidents/1,000 of the child population) and almost eleven times greater than the English average (0.2 accidents/1,000 of the child population). European child accidental injury is now seen as reaching 'epidemic' proportions (Vincenten, 2006) with both black and minority ethnic identity and social inequality having strong associations with road injury (Towner et al., 2002). Existing UK school-based road safety initiatives had rarely extended beyond the 'tokenistic'.*

This project endeavoured to encourage the Highways Authority, engineers and road safety officers to provide local young people with opportunities to participate in decision-making in the belief that the active engagement of young service users would lead to more effective and sustainable solutions to accident prevention. The project included 405 young people aged 9–11 years and involved environmental audits, interactive road safety awareness, citizenship training and engagement as decision-makers.

Involving the head in road safety

Young people can be disinterested in road safety (Audit Commission, 2007), so to stimulate their interest a new training technique was used based around interactive technology to explore safety issues and the Highway Code. In using Qwizdom *(LARSOA, 2006) road safety awareness was raised using a series of multiple choice questions where young people used individual, interactive keypads to learn road safety. Feedback to their responses was instantaneous and provided opportunities to discuss aspects of road safety such as crossing at road junctions, the prime cause of child KSI in the project area.*

Involving the hands in the environmental audit

Teacher-led exercises aimed at discussing 'moving around our community' provided an opportunity to understand routes taken by young people journeying to school. A familiar walking route was devised to undertake an environmental audit using cameras and question sheets. These were discussed on return to school.

Involving the heart in citizenship training

Young people were invited to reflect on what actions could be undertaken to improve their local environment to make it healthier and safer. This was based on techniques developed by the Children's Rights Alliance for England (2005) from their Ready, Steady, Go *participation packs. After considering responses given from the perspective of themselves, their family, City Council, police, local shopkeepers and school council, their ideas were collected and discussed in small groups. Groups were asked to select the best ideas for presentation to their class and the whole class voted on the best one for their school council.*

Engaging with decision-makers

To complete activities young people were invited to look at engineering plans as they affected roads, pavements and spaces outside their school. Question and answer sheets were devised to assist in exploration of key features and intended changes in road design. Young people were also shown a 3D graphic presentation of the options being considered.

Once the young people had participated in small discussion groups to explore the plans they were provided with an opportunity to ask questions and scrutinize the work of the project's engineers. All questions were answered in open forums, and where the engineers had insufficient information they were forced to research a response and come back. Young people voted on the options by secret ballot.

Outcomes of participation

Primarily, the purpose of this project was to engage young people in decision-making on the project. For the first time in this community young people were treated as stakeholders and engaged with engineering plans that sought to address the high level of child KSI. In terms of the local Highway Authority's commitment to participation they have become an 'emerging' authority on the National Youth Agency/Local Government Association standards in that it has started to make the active involvement of children and young people a central commitment of its organisation (Badham and Wade, 2005). This project has additionally created local spaces to empower young people to express their views to adults in their community. The eventual engineering development partially reflected young people's drive, commitment, contemplation and involvement in tackling this issue and achieved rung six out of eight (the 'Partnership' level) on Arnstein's Ladder of Participation *where* power is in fact redistributed through negotiation between citizens and power holders *(Arnstein, 1969, page 217).*

Engagement yielded many rich and unanticipated benefits to the project, the community and young people themselves. Insight into the beneficial outcomes of participation and engagement techniques were revealed through young people's completion of confidential evaluation sheets. Questionnaires were also sent to the teachers and members of the project team. Importantly one of the main outcomes was that participation was seen as fun, which is an important aid to learning and an appropriate response to those who believe that road safety is boring (Jones, 2002).

Green and Hert (1998) have suggested that road safety learning is not always transferable to different contexts; however, in their evaluations young people stressed that what they remembered most about their day of participatory activities was road safety: I learnt that road safety is very important. I also know how to look after the environment. I can now keep myself safe. *This was endorsed by their teachers:* It really improved their road safety awareness and their thinking skills and individual self confidence.

Improved self-confidence, enhanced personal and social development, and a greater sense of respon-sibility and understanding are all attributes that are often associated with young people's engagement in participative practices (Kirby and Bryson, 2002).

Active participatory approaches can also yield deeper insights into children's perspectives of the built environment and their local community, something demonstrated in the United Nations Educational, Scientific and Cultural Organization's (UNESCO) Growing Up in Cities project (Chawla and Malone, 2003).

In undertaking this participatory and head, hands and heart approach the project managed to understand and witness important features of the local community that provided material for future citizenship lessons and revealed issues and problems previously unknown to local service providers. Young people enthusiastically engaged with the engineering plans and engineers were able to listen to suggestions regarding young people's misuse of public space, traffic flow and the range of local languages spoken for improving signage.

The project included getting young people to consider ways in which their school council could develop issues raised from environmental audits. One school proposed that schools fine parents for parking over School Keep Clear areas to raise funds to support school trips.

Many young people were acutely aware of their parent's poor driving skills, a finding that is consistent with recent research on young people's safety awareness (Lupton and Bayley, 2006). References to accidents and road incidents revealed an understanding and recognition of a variety of problems including poor parking and speeding. This is important because one of the striking discoveries was that in every classroom someone could recall a recent road accident either involving themselves or a family member. Young people talk about road accidents and driving behaviour a lot and the Road Safe campaign (Wenham-Clarke, 2006) has made us acutely aware of the grief and trauma this creates. In the project area children and young people's awareness of death and injury is extraordinarily profound and revealed through participatory techniques.

Recent action research projects in Canada have put children and young people at the centre of processes of communal resolution by enabling them to develop local policy in partnership with service providers through processes of dialogue rather than consultation (Cairns, 2000). The Streets Ahead on Safety project sought to imitate this approach by adopting a child rights based method to addressing the problem of pedestrian injury that threatens children and young people's health and well being. Often the greatest obstacles to participation are the attitudes and working practices of adults and their adherence to processes and practices that are completely alienating for young people (Lyons, 2004). It is vital to build learning and accountability into the participatory process by continuing to foster a collaboration based on dialogue, learning and mutual reciprocity between young people and adults (Percy-Smith, 2005). This case study required an engagement with local and national policy, the demonstration of practitioner values, and use of creative practitioner skills to secure the full engagement and meaningful participation of children and young people.

CHAPTER SUMMARY

In this chapter we have provided you with some insight into:

- the key participatory techniques for children, young people, and their families;
- recent policy and legislative changes that form the context of participatory communication;
- some theories and models that underpin practice;
- how different agencies, services and professionals offer support by giving you a case study of good practice;
- potential tools and techniques for use in your own practice to support participatory communication.

USEFUL RESOURCES

www.youthaccess.org.uk/publications/upload/OpeningDoors_FINAL.pdf
Youth Access has published new guidelines for making advice services young person-friendly. The Opening Your Doors to Young People guidelines provide advice agencies with: basic information about barriers to access to services; a way of assessing how accessible, relevant and age-sensitive current services are; practical steps to take to improve services; examples of work undertaken by other advice agencies that have proved successful and could be replicated.

www.scie.org.uk/publications/elearning/cs/index.asp The Social Care Institute for Excellence (SCIE) website contains numerous resources and e-learning activities related to young people's communication and participation.

www.ukyouthparliament.org.uk This website is a rich source of information on youth issues and gives contact information on regional organisers and local projects. There are useful links on how to follow debates on Twitter and Facebook.

FURTHER READING

Koprowska, J (2010) *Communication and Interpersonal Skills in Social Work* (3rd edition). Exeter: Learning Matters. Exploring the communication skills required for effective social work practice, this book contains a useful chapter 'Communicating with children'.

McClean, I and McMillan, A (2009) *The Concise Oxford Dictionary of Politics*. Oxford: Oxford University Press. A useful resource for checking and learning about important political concepts discussed here and on other policy courses you may pursue.

Nind, M and Hewett, D (2006) *Access to Communication* (2nd edition). London: David Fulton. This details the communication technique 'intensive interaction', used to develop communicative relationships with children with profound and complex learning difficulties.

6 SUPPORTING TRANSITIONS

Bob Pitt and Billie Oliver

COMMON CORE OF SKILLS AND KNOWLEDGE FOR THE CHILDREN'S WORKFORCE: SUPPORTING TRANSITIONS

Understand how children and young people respond to change

- Understand issues of identity, delayed effects of change and be aware of possible signs that someone is going through a particular transition.

- Know about the likely impact of key transitions, both between services and life changes.

- Understand how transitions may affect those most at risk of exclusion or under-achievement and that it may be necessary to adapt or intensify support for these children or young people.

- Understand patterns of transition from childhood to adulthood.

- Understand that children and young people with disabilities or special educational needs (SEN) or at risk of not fulfilling their potential, and their parents or carers, may need additional support to manage transitions. Know when to seek specialist advice.

Know when and how to intervene

- Know about organisational procedures and legal frameworks, as well as appropriate referral routes within your own organisation and to other agencies.

- Know that in some family situations you may need to be more proactive about involving services.

- Know how to support young people to develop confidence in their own decision-making.

- Understand the importance of ensuring that information transfers ahead of the child or young person to support transitions.

(CWDC, 2010a)

CHAPTER OBJECTIVES

By the end of this chapter you should have an understanding of:

- key transitions in the lives of children, young people, and their families;
- policy and legislative context of transition;
- theories or models that underpin the practice;
- different agencies, services and professionals offering support;
- tools and techniques for use in practice to support those experiencing transition;
- useful resources to improve knowledge and practice.

Introduction

The term 'transitions' is used to refer to changes between services, such as moving from primary to secondary school, or transitions at 16 to school, college, an apprenticeship or part time training alongside full time employment or volunteering.

(CWDC, 2010a)

The Common Core of Skills and Knowledge for the Children's Workforce (CWDC, 2010a) also recognises a wider use of the term as referring to life changes of particular and personal transitions that may not be shared by others, for example experiences of bereavement, family splits, leaving care, disabilities, parental mental health, and crime. Children or young people with learning disabilities, those who are leaving care and young offenders may require specialist support and guidance to smooth their transitions to adulthood or to other services.

Skills required of the emerging professional workforce include being able to identify transitions by listening to children and young people's concerns in order to recognise signs of change in attitude or behaviour, and providing support by finding opportunities to discuss the effects of transition. Practitioners need to know and understand how children and young people respond to change, for example knowing the likely impact of key transitions. They also need to know when and how to intervene by having knowledge of organisational procedures, legal powers or duties, and referral routes. It is also important to acknowledge the role of parents and carers and to work in partnership with them to support children and young people at points of transition, and to understand their need for reassurance, advice and support. Practitioners need knowledge and understanding of the range of effective and appropriate resources that they can draw on, from other professionals and agencies, to help them support children and young people through these key transitions.

This chapter aims to set the context for reflecting on a range of transitions that children or young people might encounter. Different sections of the chapter will encourage you to reflect on some of the challenges and on some good practice approaches to supporting change and transition with children, young people and their families. You are encouraged to engage with the case examples and activities and to reflect on your own experience to develop critical thinking and learning.

Transition types

Children and young people experience complex transitions throughout their lives. Starting in early years they move away from the home and family into the wider community through pre-school activities. Education transitions take them from primary to secondary school, and some on to college or university. Young people move into adulthood accompanied by both greater independence through employment and housing, and more responsibility for their own health and well being, or by starting a family.

The nature of transitions is that they lead to changes or adjustments that may be transitory, persistent or permanent. This chapter acknowledges different types of transition and aims to represent these with case studies. The 'life stage' transition refers to transitions associated with a change of services provided to the child or young person. These transitions are expected and can be planned for, such as the move from primary to secondary school or leaving care. 'Life change' transitions are unexpected, resulting from 'critical events' (Plummer, 2001) such as bereavement or family breakdown and may need to be supported by multi-agency and specialist services.

Both 'life stage' and 'life change' transitions may lead to internal, emotional outcomes and challenges to the emerging identify of the child or young person. The way that a child copes with or manages a transition will depend on their previous experiences and the support they receive from their family and practitioners with whom they are involved.

ACTIVITY 6.1

Reflect on one of the changes that have taken place in your own life (such as changing jobs, moving school, moving home, giving up smoking, becoming a parent):

- Was the change planned or unforeseen?
- What emotions did you feel?
- What factors helped you engage positively with that change?

Policy and legislation

Wetz (2010) noted that *it is not easy to get a child through adolescence to adulthood, let alone with confidence and ambition*. He argues that schools should not undervalue the importance of developing children's social and emotional competencies. A report from Action for Children (2009) argued that ages 6 to 13 are a turning point and fundamental to the emotional and physical development of a child. While they are becoming more independent, spending less time with parents, experiencing physical changes and new relationships, they are also facing problems that, if ignored, may result in risk of crime, substance dependence, mental health issues or behavioural problems lasting into adulthood.

In response to reports such as these, and building on *Every Child Matters* (DfES, 2003), the development of Extended Services (DCSF, 2007a) means that primary and secondary schools are now expected to provide a 'varied menu' (Broadhead and Martin, 2009, page 48) of on-site support activities for all children between the hours of 8 am and 6 pm, all year round. Furthermore, schools are expected to provide support and information to parents at key transition points and to identify children with particular needs to ensure effective referral to relevant specialist support services. Models of delivery are emerging whereby schools within local communities work in partnership clusters to ensure this range of provision is met. Where they are well developed, these partnerships include voluntary groups and youth groups as well as the schools.

New roles have emerged within schools in response to this agenda. Teaching assistants are now widespread and many schools have learning mentors and staff responsible for family support links. Very often these practitioners have a greater understanding of children's lives outside school and the impact this can have on their learning (Broadhead and Martin, 2009). Together, the new range of roles within the wider school can reflect on and respond to the holistic needs of the child, rather than just focusing solely on their learning and knowledge acquisition.

Williamson (2009) noted a shift in policy responses to young people initiated under the New Labour government from 1997. Where once policy focused on education, training, youth services, special needs and youth offending, New Labour accepted the notion of the changing complexity of youth transition that *produced a corresponding risk and vulnerability for a significant minority of young people* (Williamson, 2009, page 135). For New Labour that risk was shown in young people's 'disengagement' or 'social exclusion' and their construction or labelling as NEETs (not in education, employment or training). The setting up of the Social Exclusion Unit in 1997 led to a wider focus on youth issues such as truancy and school exclusion, juvenile crime and youth justice, substance misuse, teenage pregnancy, homelessness and leaving care.

Williamson also recognised different policy directions within the UK as a result of devolving powers to the Assemblies of Wales and Northern Ireland, and Scottish Parliament. Initiatives such as the *Connexions Service* (DfEE, 2000) were established in England but rejected in Wales where young people were supported through *Extending Entitlements* (National Assembly for Wales, 2000). Other initiatives have tended to disappear before becoming established such as the Children and Young People's Unit in England and Child Trust Funds. In 2010, following a general election from which no one party emerged with an overall majority, a Conservative–Liberal coalition government was established. The new government introduced a rapid and radical re-thinking of most of the policy initiatives that had been introduced previously. In Chapter 9 we summarise some of these policy reviews and changes since May 2010 and suggest resources that you can access to follow the progress of this area of policy.

ACTIVITY 6.2

Identify any policy and/or procedures, in your setting, that are aimed at supporting social, emotional or personal transitions.

Theories or models of transition

Extended transitions

For the past 30 years or so, the dominant discourse for interpreting the experiences of young people has been what has become known as the 'transitions discourse'. It is widely accepted that young people's lives change rapidly and often dramatically between the ages of 13 and 25 as they move towards independence (Coleman et al., 2004). However, increasingly commentators refer to 'extended transitions' and 'precarious transitions'. It is recognised that a number of transitions occur at different times during adolescence, and that how these are experienced will vary according to social background, ethnic origin, gender and living circumstances: *It is important to recognise that the overall transition from child to adult is accomplished through multiple smaller transitions all of which may potentially be stressful or difficult in themselves* (Coleman et al., 2004, page 227).

In recent years, much has been written about the 'extended' nature of 'youth transitions' (Furlong and Cartmel, 1997; Miles, 2000; Coles, 2004; Bradley and Hickman, 2004; Thomson et al., 2004, Roche et al., 2004). It is a widely held view that for young people the transition to adulthood or independence has become much more protracted, unpredictable and increasingly 'fragmented' in that the different markers of adulthood are *increasingly uncoupled from each other* (Thomson et al., 2004, page xiv). This has led to a growing recognition that *the goal of independence as a model of adulthood has to be questioned*. Increasingly commentators are referring to *uneven transitions* or *fragmented transitions* (Roche et al., 2004, page xiii) where different groups of young people have very different and complex experiences of the transition to adulthood. The implications of all this are that, for young people, the beginnings and endings of particular transitions are 'ill-defined' and are 'taking longer and longer' (Coleman et al., 2004) with a resulting increase in uncertainty and anxiety.

Early transitions

Coles (2004, page 91) refers to the emergence of the conceptualisation of 'early transitions' as being associated with a sense of 'failed' transitions, when, for example, teenaged parents 'leave home prematurely' or when young people leave the support of family or carer without other forms of support or housing. According to Coles (2004, page 92), much of the policy agenda in the late 1990s was focused on how vulnerable young people experienced *failed transitions* leading to various forms of social exclusion.

Policy and legislation is often both a response to, and has an impact on, transitions. For example, the introduction of initiatives such as New Deal for Young People in 1998 and the Connexions Service, following the Learning and Skills Act 2000, were responses to New Labour government (1997–2010) concerns about young people labelled as NEET or at risk of social exclusion. Some commentators see policy-makers keeping young people in prolonged dependencies on schools, families and training schemes, thereby excluding them from full participation as citizens (Mizen, 2004). For example, the Schools White Paper, published in November 2010 confirmed the coalition government's intention to *raise to 17 by 2013 and then 18 by 2015 the age to which all young people will be expected to participate in education or training* (DfE, 2010b).

Class-based transitions

Bynner (2001) has argued that government sees youth transitions in principally economic terms with the shift from immature unemployable child to independent employable adult suggesting a uniform view of all youth in transition. However class differences indicate a lack of homogeneity in youth transitions. For the middle classes there tends to be a traditional expectation of a prolonged period of education and training before moving into employment. The working classes are more likely to leave school at the minimum statutory age to get a job and thereafter get training 'on the job'. However, during economic recession and lack of employment opportunities then gender may become allied to class differences with young men postponing commitments to getting a job thereby prolonging their adolescence and lifestyle based on alcohol, drugs and crime or resulting in young women starting their own family and being drawn into domestic routine (Bynner, 2001).

Personalised transitions

Personalised transition (Cowen, 2010) is a system for enabling young people with complex needs to leave school and to achieve citizenship within their community. According to Cowen in the past many professionals have not seen this as a priority and as a result many young people with complex needs have gone on *to lead institutionalized, unfulfilled lives* (2010, page 24). The personalised transitions model draws on the experience of using person-centred planning, an approach that designs and delivers services based on what is important to a person. Used particularly within mental health and learning disability services the approach draws on the person's own perspective of their situation and aims to contribute to their full inclusion in society (DH, 2001). These approaches aim to give more control to young people and their families. Personalised transition advocates using self-directed support to bridge the gaps between children and adult services and the pooling of resources from education, health and social care to equip young people for adult life and for being active citizens.

ACTIVITY 6.3

Identify recent government policies or proposals (such as the proposal to raise the school leaving age to 18) that may have an impact on transitions. Are they likely to extend or shorten the period of transition? How may the policies affect children or young people and their families differently?

Life stage transitions

Life stage transitions are those transitions associated with a change of services provided to the child or young person. These transitions are largely to be expected and can be planned for, such as educational transitions as children start school, move between primary to secondary school or transitions such as leaving care that occur at particular ages. Being expected, however, does not necessarily mean that the transition will be smooth or unproblematic for the child. These transitions require children to acclimatise to new surroundings, to adapt to new ways of working, to make sense of new rules and routines and to interact with unfamiliar adults and peers. Ability to respond to these challenges may influence the ways in which the child progresses and develops (Sanders et al., 2005).

In every case, transition should be seen as a process, not an event, and should be planned for and discussed with those involved. A number of agencies have developed tiered models for thinking about how best to approach supporting transitions. Typically, these models define three different levels of provision, as guidance for practitioners, when managing transition: universal, targeted and specialist.

- *Universal* – all children and their families require a planned approach to support this transfer process, with effective communication between settings.
- *Targeted* – some of the children will have additional needs that require specific strategies being in place to support their needs. Children's additional needs and strategies for support need to be shared between settings in partnership with parents.
- *Specialist* – a few children will have substantial needs. For children with substantial needs, a specific, structured process that includes a clear action plan with roles and responsibilities must be followed to ensure a smooth and positive transfer.

(BANES, 2008)

Now read the following case study from a Children's Centre. Reflect on how practitioners in this setting apply some of the theories or models discussed above.

CASE STUDY 6.1 SUPPORTING TRANSITION FROM NURSERY TO SPECIALIST PROVISION: THE LIMES CHILDREN'S CENTRE

The Inner City Children's Centre supports families from a wide range of social, economic and cultural backgrounds. Staff work in partnership with a number of primary schools and special schools, to whom the children transfer, in a child-centred, multi-professional team approach: We all work together to make it right for the child.

Working in partnership

Staff begin working with the child and the family in March/April to prepare them prior to transition in September. The teams of staff work to gradually build up confidence and trust. Often, when a child is transferring from the Children's Centre to a Special School, as much work needs to be done supporting and preparing the parent as it does for the child so the staff work with the whole family to ensure everyone feels comfortable with the transition.

In the summer term, staff from the receiving specialist school come to the nursery to meet the child in their familiar environment. Staff hold a 'round table' multi-professional meeting to explore the particular physical or emotional needs of the child.

Introduction to the new school is staggered: firstly, in the summer term, the child makes a visit to the new school with their parent/carer. Next the child visits the new school without their parent/carer. At the beginning of the new term the child is gradually integrated into the new class/school with a 'staggered' start beginning with mornings only. The school and the Children's Centre continue to work in partnership after the transfer to ensure a smooth transition.

The child's learning diary, which includes reflections on their daily activity, learning and development, is given to the parent when the child leaves the nursery, for the parent to pass on to the new teacher – encouraging the building of a new partnership around the child.

Preparing the child for transition

The teacher compiles a **photomontage** *of the child 'at work and play' to illustrate their capabilities and preferences. As well as passing this on as an accessible record to the new school, staff use it as an 'ending' tool to help the child review some of activities and milestones achieved at nursery. The teacher increasingly prepares the child for transition by talking about the transfer in* **Circle Time** *(or Group Time), encouraging the child to talk about the school they will be transferring to and the visit they have made. In schools, Circle Time is a special time in the day for sharing experiences, rhymes, songs and stories. It provides a time for listening, developing attention span, promoting communication and learning new concepts and skills.*

The teacher makes a **personal book** *with each child, illustrated with photos of the child at the nursery. The book acts as a record of 'things I like to do', 'things I am good at', 'things that made me laugh'. The book is passed on – one copy for the parent and one for the receiving school. This is a tool that is used to engage the child in a conversation about what they enjoy doing by the new teacher. At the end of term the teacher has an individual conversation with each child, often using the child's book as a focus for reviewing their experiences at nursery and preparing the child emotionally for the closure of that relationship.*

Consider the 'good practice tips' that practitioners in the Children's Centre have suggested in Table 6.1. Do you have any further suggestions of your own to add?

SENDING	CLOSING	RECEIVING
• Multi-agency meetings to discuss children's needs with parents and range of professionals • Calendars for children to count down the days • Circle Time to prepare children • Photos of 'new' schools on display – who is going where	• Pack to take away • Graduating party – photos taken, books/certificates handed over • Diary of special events • Leaving cake	• Clear key worker roles • Photo book exchanges • Favourite activities set out for planning time • Staggered entry • Welcome celebrations • Buddy system (for parents and children)

Table 6.1 **Good practice tips: ensuring a smooth early years transfer**

Figure 6.1 is an example of a set of principles used in one particular setting – the Connexions Service. Consider these principles in relation to the Children's Centre example above. Can you identify how these principles might also be applied to that setting?

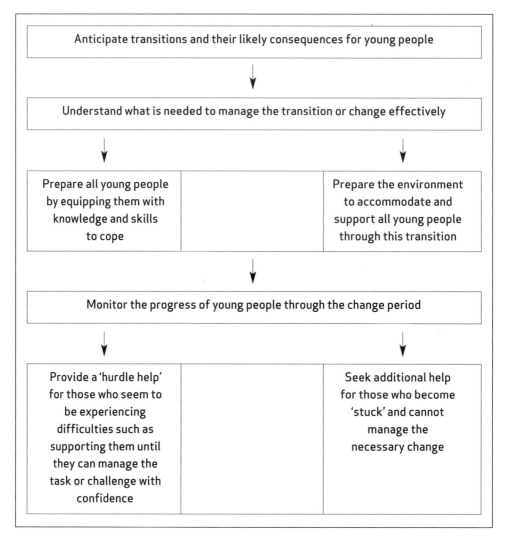

Figure 6.1 **Principles for managing transitions**

Source: Adapted from Diploma for Connexions Personal Advisers Module 3, page 84.

Now read the following case study of supporting the transition from primary to secondary school. To what extent can you identify the application of the principles outlined in Figure 6.1? Can you identify any further principles that the practitioners in this example consider important?

CASE STUDY 6.2   SUPPORTING TRANSITION FROM PRIMARY TO SECONDARY SCHOOL:
THE PYRAMID CLUB

Pyramid clubs are an early intervention preventative programme used to support pupils of primary school age to build resilience, raise self-esteem and improve learning behaviours. The transition between primary and secondary school can be a difficult time for young people. Some might begin to have behavioural issues, others might become withdrawn and depressed. Pyramid clubs, usually run by a teaching assistant or learning mentor supported by volunteers, offer a safe place for children where they can relax, have fun, have their voice heard, learn new skills and develop positive relationships with their peers. They are an effective way to support shy, quiet and withdrawn children who are often easily overlooked in a busy classroom.

Typically, clubs run for ten weeks, usually straight after school. The clubs are aimed at quieter, withdrawn pupils who may be lacking in self-esteem and are considered vulnerable at the point of transfer to secondary school. The emphasis throughout is on praise, encouragement and security.

Clubs have a clear structure, including Circle Time at the beginning and end of each session, sharing healthy food, games, art/craft/food preparation and other activities depending on the interests of the children and the leaders. A review meeting is held with the young people at the end of the process to assess their progress and the impact of the intervention.

Typical comments from Year 6 pupils:

> *I liked the circle time games because it made me realize that I wasn't the only one who felt like that.*
> *I learned I can do things, even if they are scary at first.*
> *Before pyramid club I used to feel left out but now I feel more confident in group work.*

The list that follows is a selection of 'good practice tips' from practitioners working to support the transition to secondary school. Do you have any further ideas to add here?

- Focus on specific personal targets selected by the young person.
- Work with the young person on a structured planner or diary of activities.
- Use Circle Time to provide a focus for the session and allow the young people an opportunity to 'switch off' from school mode.
- Use Circle Time to play 'social games'.
- Come together as a group for a 'compliments circle' where all children get a sticker for their achievements in the session.
- Share information between agencies to give the child the greatest opportunity to succeed.
- Compile a photo 'comic' with each child that records their activities and progress, using their own words in 'bubbles'.
- Provide 'pen pictures' of the young people and the activities they have been involved in.
- Use the summer break to run activities, such as treasure hunts, based in the receiving secondary schools.
- Hold a 'transfer celebration' event and/or a reunion.

ACTIVITY 6.4

Reflect upon a child or young person that you know. What activities, tools or techniques would you adapt from the case studies to help them make their next transition? What strategies would you put in place to help them feel secure, happy and confident to progress and learn?

Life change transitions

Life change transitions are often unexpected and may result from *critical events* (Plummer, 2001) such as bereavement, family breakdown or sudden homelessness. The impact of such transitions may need to be supported by multi-agency interventions and specialist services. Preparatory work can reduce the disruption and trauma that transitions may cause for young people. However, even with high-quality preparation there are some young people who still find transitions very challenging.

Identity and resilience

Markus and Nurius developed the idea of *possible selves*. They defined *possible selves* as representations of individuals' ideas *about what they might become, what they would like to become, and what they are afraid of becoming* (1986, page 954). In this framework, *possible selves* are seen as the essential link between self-concept and motivation. Gilligan (2000, page 38) drew on this notion of '*possible selves*' arguing that, for young people, developing a sense of '*worthiness*' and competence usually involves some comparison by the individual between how they would like to be and how they think they actually measure up. Recent research into the '*possible selves*' construct has tended to suggest that possible selves emerge during *affectively significant relationships* (Kerpelman and Pittman, 2001; Rossiter, 2003) such as that with a youth worker, mentor or peers.

Theorists have drawn on this notion of '*significant relationships*' and incorporated it into the concept of 'resources' (things that sustain people) in the process of identity formation and transition (Stets and Burke, 2000, page 225). This idea has also been applied to thinking about the nature of resilience. Resilience has been described as *the ability to bounce back having endured adversity* (Gilligan, 2000, page 37); as *the ability to thrive, mature, and increase competence in the face of adverse circumstances or obstacles* (Gordon-Rouse, 2001, page 461); and as *the degree to which the system is capable of learning and adaptation* (Cumming et al., 2005, page 975).

In recent years, there has been a growing interest in uncovering the factors that contribute to some people developing resilience and one of these is thought to include having a social network or secure '*base-camp*' that encourages both exploration of possible selves and attachment-type relationships (Gilligan, 2000, page 39) (see Chapter 3 for a discussion of what is meant by 'attachment'). Gilligan argued that strengthening social networks is an important factor in promoting a sense of belonging and a sense of mattering. Coleman and Hagell (2007) have also argued that we can achieve *far more for young people who experience adversity if we emphasise their strengths and capabilities* rather than their weaknesses. Through the experience of being homeless, excluded from school or being in care, for example, a young person may have developed many coping skills that indicate personal resources and strengths that can be applied in other settings.

Houston (2010, page 358) supports this point of view, arguing that *building up self-esteem and self-efficacy, through supportive school environments, cultural activities and sporting pursuits, appears to accentuate a child's resistance to adverse events, thereby creating the conditions for optimal mental health and activating positive chain reactions in life trajectories.*

CASE STUDY 6.3   BEN

Eighteen-year-old Ben has called at the youth housing project where you work as a support worker. Following family conflict over his use of drugs he has been thrown out of the house due to parental concern about his behaviour impacting on two younger siblings. Ben presents himself in an exhausted,

---

shocked and disoriented state. He wandered the streets last night and has not eaten. He tells you he's in full-time education at the local college.

What would you do?
Consider the aims of your intervention:

- *What values or principles will underpin your work with Ben?*
- *How will you make an assessment of what he needs?*
- *What information, advice or guidance will you offer?*
- *What other agencies or professionals will you involve?*

You might want to look up the Homelessness Act (2002) Part VII. You could refer to the Southwark Judgment (see 'Useful resources' at the end of the chapter) and the duty to see a homeless young person as a 'child in need' under Section 20 of the Children Act (1989).

Techniques and tools: approaches to supporting life change transition with young people

The scope of this book does not allow for an in-depth discussion or explanation of the range of different approaches to supporting young people through transitions. A sample of techniques is introduced here for illustrative purposes and to indicate areas for further study.

Informal education

Informal education is an approach used by youth workers. It entails working with young people often in unplanned and unpredictable ways. For Smith (2009) the skill of informal education is to *catch the moment* in conversations with young people in order to *deepen their thinking or to put themselves in touch with their feelings* with the aim of *exploring or enlarging* their experience. Informal educators engage in a range of activities with young people. Sometimes these activities might allow for *sitting down having long conversations* (Crosby, 2005). At other times contact may be short and fragmented. In whatever situation or environment informal educators work, they seek to build a relationship of trust, to understand and respect the context of the young person's experience, and to engage that young person in a conversation that helps them to both deepen their understandings and to act on them.

Advocacy

Advocacy is an approach to use where the child, young person or their family is in the middle of a structure or process where they are relatively powerless and in which they need support to develop the confidence to express their own needs or opinions. There are different forms of advocacy.

Citizen advocacy developed as a way to support people who were unable to advocate for themselves or who required support to do so. A citizen advocate has been described as someone who *may become a friend, helping their advocacy partner develop the skills needed to get the most out of life* (Kennet and North Wilts Advocacy Project, 2002). *Professional advocacy* is a response to the difficulties some young people and adults experience when communicating with powerful professionals and because of *the diminishing advocacy role undertaken by professionals* (Boylan and Dalrymple, 2009, page 105). A form of professional advocacy has been proposed for young people making a complaint under the Children Act 1989 and Independent Complaints Advocacy Services (ICAS) within the National Health Service. *Peer advocacy* involves the advocate working in partnership with the young person around their shared experiences or similar circumstances to build a supportive relationship. For some young people, peer advocates may be more acceptable than other people because of this common understanding (Atkinson, 1999). While peer advocacy has similarities to other forms of peer support, such as peer mentoring, the difference is that peer advocacy is concerned with *representing young people's views with the intention of influencing change* (Harnett, 2004, page 1).

Boylan and Dalrymple point out that a recurring theme across all these forms of advocacy is the importance of advocates *being able to listen and speak up for young people* (2009, page 79).

Mentoring

The role of mentor has been defined as *an older experienced guide who is acceptable to the young person and who can help ease the transition to adulthood by a mix of support and challenge* (Philip, 2000). In this sense it is a developmental relationship in which the young person *is inducted into the world of adulthood*. The relationship is based on the sharing of information and advice from the mentor to the mentee.

Peer mentoring projects match young people with someone their own age or older, in a one-to-one relationship to provide positive role models and an effective relationship. In this way, young people receive support from those they believe to have relevant and accessible knowledge and so can be more empowering in enabling them to reflect on their own ideas and experiences. A key element in peer mentoring is that the relationship is seen as one that benefits both sides with the mentor also benefiting from the processes (Philip and Hendry, 1996).

This idea of mentoring currently holds great appeal to politicians (Lepper, 2010). As Philip (2000) has observed it *conjures up a positive way of bridging boundaries between generations and harks back to notions of large extended families and friendly neighbourhoods within which young people and elders could establish common ground*. Studies have suggested that mentoring relationships can help promote resilience in young people. Philip (2000) found that mentoring relationships contribute to young people developing a form of *cultural capital or a set of recipes* to deal with the challenges they face in their daily lives.

Motivational interviewing

Motivational interviewing (Miller and Rollnick, 2002) is a non-confrontational technique designed to help someone make changes in their behaviour. Developed in the 1980s it emphasises the importance of commitment and motivation in making change. It uses a counselling approach that is designed to help build commitment to change. It recognises that if the idea of change is entirely positive then it is easy to carry out.

Important aspects of the approach include a *de-emphasis on labelling in negative terms* (Goodman, 2009) and instead emphasising personal responsibility for deciding future behaviour. It aims to help build self-awareness of the discrepancy between current behaviour and one's goals. For example, a young substance misuser, keen to overcome their addiction, may be encouraged to reflect on the structure of their day and the people they socialise with to explore whether these might be related to difficulties in achieving their goal. Resistance is seen as an inter-personal dynamic that is interesting and worthy of exploration. Goals and change strategies are negotiated with the young person and their involvement and acceptance of the goals are seen as vital.

Cognitive Behavioural Therapy

Cognitive Behavioural Therapy (CBT) is based on the idea that behaviour is learned and that feelings and emotions are based on thoughts rather than having an independent existence. The focus is on the young person's thinking processes and it aims to teach young people to manage themselves by changing the way they think about situations. The approach involves helping a young person to develop new approaches to thinking about and responding to situations.

The perspective on CBT developed by Beck (1976) is the approach that is most frequently practiced in the UK. Beckian CBT assumes that people are 'active agents' who interact with their own individual world through interpretation and evaluation of their environment. This results in 'cognitive processes' that are thought to be accessible to consciousness and therefore there is the potential to change them (Grant, 2010). For example, following bereavement, a young person may feel prolonged and extreme sadness because they believe they have lost 'the only person' with whom they can feel happy in life. CBT approaches aim to challenge this assumption and to look for behaviours, such as avoiding engaging in activities that they had previously experienced as enjoyable, that might be reinforcing the belief.

ACTIVITY 6.5
Understand and use your own experiences of transition to move from biography to practice (Henderson et al., 2007):

- Map your personal experiences of transition from secondary education to adulthood.
- Individually identify dates and 'critical events' under headings such as family, education, health, work, neighbourhood or community. What happened? What impact did the transition have on you? How were you supported?
- Reflect to consider if you were a professional helping someone like you through that transition today then what would you do to ensure a successful or improved transition? How are you judging 'success'?

Discussion point: In a group discuss with others how your experience compares with theirs. What do you notice about differences and complexities in transitions?

CHAPTER SUMMARY

Children and young people today experience multiple transitions and have to cope with many discontinuities in their lives. Although discontinuity can be very challenging, it can also encourage children to develop new patterns of behaviour and new skills that can offer opportunities for development.

This chapter has set out a range of transitions that children might face. It has classified these as 'life stage' transitions that are expected and planned for, and 'life change' transitions that might be unexpected or complex. The chapter has discussed theoretical perspectives surrounding the concept of 'transition' and has encouraged the reader to reflect on practice and personal examples to help make sense of this theory. The chapter presented an overview of some practical techniques. It concludes with useful resources to support practice.

USEFUL RESOURCES

www.actionforchildren.org.uk/uploads/media/37/9740.pdf Link to the report 'Stuck in the middle' published by Action for Children.

www.centreforwelfarereform.org The Centre is an independent research and development network that works to reform the current welfare state. It aims to enable and promote active *citizenship* for all; encourage and strengthen *family* life; build stronger forms of *community* and a more vibrant civil society.

www.c4eo.org.uk/themes/general/resources.aspx?tab=tools&dm_i=7SL,4XOA, 12Q33V,FC8F,1 Centre for Excellence and Outcomes in Children and Young People's Services (C4EO) has a wealth of resources.

www.leavingcare.org Link to the National Care Advisory Service (NCAS). This national advice and support service focuses on young people's transition from care. NCAS supports young people in and from care aged 13–25, their corporate parents and those who work with them.

www.leavingcare.org/admin/uploads/87fe6ee0fa282a244ec64e4fab764aca.pdf Briefing paper produced by NCAS on the Southwark Judgment entitled *Law Lords Judgment: G vs. Southwark.*

www.teachernet.gov.uk/_doc/10867/PromotingChildrensMentalHealth2001. pdf A guide to promoting children's mental health in early years and school settings.

www.teachers.tv/videos/transition-from-primary This programme provides an insight into how a large secondary school works to ease the transition from primary to secondary school for their new set of Year 7s.

www.transitioninfonetwork.org.uk The Transition Information Network (TIN) is an alliance of organisations and individuals who work together with a common aim: to improve the experience of disabled young people's transition to adulthood. This web resource is a source of information and good practice standards for disabled young people, families and professionals.

www.transitionpathway.co.uk The Transition Pathway is a resource pack that can be used by anybody who is involved in supporting a young person in transition to adult life. It gives information and guidance about transition and provides tools, using person-centred approaches, to help young people think about, plan and lead the lives they want.

www.youngminds.org.uk Website of YoungMinds, 'the voice for young people's mental health and wellbeing'.

Further reading

DCSF (2006) *Seamless Transitions: Supporting Continuity in Young Children's Learning*. Nottingham: DCSF Publications. This publication aims to disseminate examples of effective practice that will stimulate professional dialogue, encourage reflection and support further training to develop seamless transitions throughout and beyond the Foundation Stage.

Hannon, C, Wood, C and Bazalgette, L (2010) *In Loco Parentis*. London: DEMOS. This report considers transitions within the care system and the abrupt transitions that many young people still experience when leaving care. The authors put forward suggestions for working towards 'smoother exits' and supported transitions for young people entering and leaving care.

Morris, J (1999) *Hurtling into the Void: Transition to Adulthood for Young Disabled People with Complex Health and Support Needs*. Brighton: Pavilion Publishing. This skills resource is divided into two parts. The first discusses what is meant by 'complex health and support needs' and 'transition to adulthood'. The second section summarises existing research and includes information from six case study sites.

Plummer, D (2010) *Helping Children to Cope with Change, Stress and Anxiety*. London: Jessica Kingsley. A photocopiable activities book suitable for use with children aged 7+.

Sanders, D, White, G, Burge, B, Sharp, C, Eames, A, McEune, R and Grayson, H (2005) *A Study of the Transition from Foundation Stage to Key Stage 1*. London: DfES. This report sets out to provide an evidence base concerning the effectiveness of transition from the Foundation Stage (which applies to children aged three to five years) to Year 1 (for children aged five to six years). It includes recommendations on activities that can support early transitions.

7 MULTI-AGENCY WORKING

Jane Tarr and Adele Gardner

COMMON CORE OF SKILLS AND KNOWLEDGE FOR THE CHILDREN'S WORKFORCE: MULTI-AGENCY WORKING

Knowledge of your role and remit

- Understand that different factors may combine to cause particular risks for children and young people, and that it may be appropriate to seek support from colleagues in other agencies, before problems have developed.

- Have a general knowledge and understanding of the range of organisations and individuals working with children, young people, their families and carers.

- Be aware of the roles and responsibilities of other professionals.

Knowledge of procedures and working methods

- Know what to do in given cases involving appropriate services or raising concerns when a child or young person is at risk of harm or of not achieving their potential.

- Know how to work within your own and other organisational values, beliefs and cultures.

- Know about tools, processes and procedures for multi-agency and integrated working, including those for assessment, consent and information sharing.

Knowledge of the importance of information sharing

- Know the importance of ensuring that information sharing is necessary, proportionate, relevant, accurate, timely and secure.

- Know what to record, how long to keep it, how to dispose of records correctly and when to feed back or follow up.

- Be aware that different types of information exist, for example personal information, confidential personal information and sensitive personal information. Understand the implications of these differences.

(CWDC, 2010a)

CHAPTER OBJECTIVES

By the end of this chapter you should have an understanding of:

- why working together with other professionals across children's services is important;
- policy and legislation that has encouraged and supports such practice;
- theories that underpin the process of multi-agency working;
- multi-agency practice through a range of different case studies;
- multi-agency assessment tools and strategies for sharing information;
- useful resources to support your knowledge and understanding of other professionals.

Introduction

This chapter aims to introduce the reader to the concept of multi-agency working. Multi-agency and integrated working are practices that all those involved in children's services are required to understand and engage with. This approach to practice arises from the recognition that the healthy development, care and education of children and young people are the responsibility of all parents supported by a wide range of different agencies, professionals and voluntary organisations. *Every Child Matters* (DfES, 2003) introduced the concept of *five outcomes for children and young people*. These are that children and young people will be healthy, stay safe, enjoy and achieve, make a positive contribution and achieve economic well being. If these outcomes are to be achieved then all agencies working with children, young people and their families will need to be co-ordinated and working together.

This chapter explores the challenges that are faced in developing such practice and the importance and value of that practice will be clarified through the use of case studies. A range of strategies, tools and approaches has been introduced and developed to support collaborative working. These include creation of a new role – the lead professional – and the *Common Assessment Framework* (CAF) (CWDC, 2009a). Both these strategies aim to bring colleagues together in meaningful dialogue to ensure that the best possible provision is accessible to families and their children.

This chapter aims to encourage reflection on a range of contexts where multi-agency working takes place. Different sections of the chapter will encourage you to reflect on both the challenges and on the good practice in working in an integrated way with other practitioners to support children and families. You are invited to engage with the case studies and activities, to reflect on your own experience to develop critical thinking and learning.

The concept and terminology of multi-agency working

There are many terms used to describe the process of different professionals working together for the benefit of children, young people and their families. These range from 'multi-disciplinary', 'multi-professional' and 'multi-agency' to 'inter-disciplinary', 'inter-professional' and 'inter-agency'. Pollard et al. (2005, page 10) have suggested that *a broad rule of thumb* that can be used to understand these differences is that *the prefix 'multi' tends to indicate the involvement of personnel from different professions, disciplines or agencies, but does not necessarily imply collaboration. The prefix 'inter' tends to imply collaboration, particularly in areas such as decision making.*

Further terminology that you might come across may refer to 'joined-up working' and 'joined-up practice' emphasising the process of linking together. There may be nouns or adjectives used to describe the process, for example 'partnership working' or 'networking', and 'cooperative practice' or 'collaborative practice'. This wide vocabulary reveals the breadth, complexity and contested nature of our conceptual understanding about the process. What can be agreed is that working together is challenging and the purposes and processes need to be clarified before the practice can be effective.

ACTIVITY 7.1

Read the 'Multi-agency working' and 'Information sharing' sections of the Common Core Skills and Knowledge for the Children's Workforce (CWDC, 2010a).

Reflect on the ways that the skills and knowledge listed are embraced within your practice setting.

Talk to other people in your practice setting. What are their views on the value of multi-agency working?

Policy and legislation

Public and social policy over the past 20 years has increasingly recognised the need for collaborative practice to improve the quality of service delivery. Numerous reports during that time have concluded that inter-professional relationships across health, social services, education and the voluntary and community sector have not been sufficiently co-ordinated. Pollard et al. (2005, page 12) have observed a *long term consensus* despite changes in government during that period.

As early as 1978, *The Warnock Report* considered the needs of children with disabilities and recommended that health, social and educational professionals should work together with parents to ensure the best provision for the child. The Children Act (1989) recognised the need for professionals to work together to protect vulnerable children. In the early 1990s the concepts of 'inter-professional collaboration' and 'partnership' were increasingly referred to. However, Le Riche and Taylor (2008, page 11) have observed that *although an understanding of partnership is taken for granted there is little theoretical clarity about the concept [and] the danger is that this lack of clarity will lead to an uncritical approach to partnership learning . . . and in practice.*

In 1997, the Social Exclusion Unit (SEU) noted that existing services were *separated, independent and often did not exercise the possibility of maintaining open lines of communication among professionals* (Artaraz, 2005). The parents of children with particular challenges such as disability, for example, have often expressed the need for professionals to communicate with each other as they are frequently asked to relate the story of their child's development to each different professional they meet (Case, 2000).

It was increasingly suggested that while professionals and agencies continued to work in traditional uni-professional ways there was an increased likelihood that children, young people and families would *slip through the net* of service provision and experience greater social and educational disadvantage. The core of this analysis was the belief that a key cause of the ineffectiveness of provision was the proliferation of specialist agencies, each dealing with a disconnected part of a person's life (Oliver, 2006). Taylor (2004) argued that the continuing presence of complex and seemingly insurmountable social problems had led to an acknowledgement that no agency or profession could be expected to address these issues single-handedly.

Such concerns generated a number of calls for the development of a culture of collaboration and partnership between and within organisations and professions. The purpose behind this strand of policy has been to encourage inter-professional collaboration, and to identify and disseminate 'best practice'. Increasingly, also, there has been a growing policy focus on encouraging – or requiring – agencies and professionals to build partnerships with service users and to involve them in service planning, delivery and review. Such partnerships are expected to produce a deeper understanding of the problem and its context, and consequently more creative and mutually owned responses. *They are a means to generate information sharing, improve communication, enable a better understanding, avoid duplication, reduce inefficiencies and identify opportunities for the effective sharing of resources* (Miller, 2004, page 142).

However, as Oliver (2008) has pointed out, *despite this espousal of the principles and values of user involvement and flexible integration of services, this area of policy continues to be a contested territory.* In particular, the concept and definition of terms such as 'participation' and 'involvement' are notoriously difficult to unpick and one of the main difficulties with any such exploration is that the language is complex and that *the same term means different things to different people* (Braye, 2000, page 18). Too often the words are used with an assumption that there is agreement over their meaning, whereas, when examined more closely, one begins to uncover a confusion that suggests more support for the rhetorical principles than for examining the reality of how to make it work in practice (Oliver, 2008). Furthermore, as Miller has argued, a number of obstacles have been experienced in trying to make joint working across professional boundaries a reality because calls for collaboration came *at the same time as specific professions feel threatened by a loss of identity and autonomy and are struggling to maintain a professional role* (2004, page 152).

Over the years, there have been a number of high-profile cases where children have been abused by their carers. Inquiries into the factors leading to such tragedy have invariably drawn attention to the need for public services to work more closely together and to share information. In 2003, the inquiry set up to investigate the death of Victoria Climbié made a series of recommendations that led to the publication of *Every Child Matters* (DfES, 2003). Laming (2003) concluded that children's needs were being neglected or overlooked through a lack of 'joined-up' working, poor systems for information sharing and too great a reliance on professional and agency boundaries. *Every Child Matters* became the launch pad for the creation of new working practices that emphasise the integration of services through multi-agency working and partnerships between the voluntary, community and statutory sectors including common assessments, information sharing and joint training. As noted above, these integrated practices can be complex and challenging to services and individuals engaged in supporting children, young people and their families due to the different meanings inherent in the language that each agency uses. *Every Child Matters* sought to create a common language and a common core of skills and knowledge that would be required of anyone working with children and young people.

The Children Act (2004) led to the introduction of new local authority-based integrated services that merged education and social services into Children's Trusts and to the identification and allocation of what it called a *lead professional*, described as *one practitioner who takes a lead role to ensure that front-line services are co-ordinated, coherent and achieving intended outcomes* (DfES, 2006b).

Support for families during the early years of childhood and the co-ordination of different agencies that might work with families has been seen as an important strategy since the mid-1990s. It was recognised that families with young children may need to travel between care facilities, health clinics, playgroups or benefits offices. Awareness of this complexity of need resulted in the Sure Start (1999) initiative aiming to bring all such services together under one roof so that families could access services *within pram-pushing distance* from their home. In the earliest years, Sure Start Centres were set up in disadvantaged communities where families experienced greater levels of poverty and faced challenges in accessing support. From 2004 Sure Start Centres evolved to become Children's Centres in many locations, where education, care and sometimes health facilities are provided for all local families. These centres have become hubs of the community and enable families to share experiences and meet up with the different agencies as and when they require them. It has proved more challenging to provide the same level of co-ordinated support during the later years of a child's life, but the Extended School initiative (DfES, 2005b) aims to support access to a range of community support. All schools are encouraged to build stronger partnerships with the local community they serve and to recognise the contribution that community members can make to the education and care of children, young people and their families.

Challenges in multi-agency working

One of the key strategic aims in all of these initiatives was to stress that those working with children and young people should be enabled to work across professional boundaries and to understand how their role fits in with the work of others. The radical restructuring that these changes introduced has proved to be very challenging for the practitioners and agencies involved. There is ongoing debate as to whether such integration has resulted in greater levels of collaborative practice or whether the new structures have proved to be detrimental to the provision of services to children and their families.

In 2001, *Raising the Achievement of Children in Public Care* (Ofsted, 2001 page 7) observed that *there is still a lack of understanding between Education and Social Services of their distinctive roles in working together to support the children in public care. Quality Protects* (DfES, 1998) and *Care Matters* (DCSF, 2008c) have both informed the thinking of professionals who, in a multi-professional context, work with children in public care, who are sometimes also referred to as 'looked-after' children. These documents have established, as good practice, that we must have high aspirations for children in public care and that 'corporate parenting' (the official term used for those employed by, or otherwise engaged with, children in care on behalf of their local authority) achieves better outcomes for children and young people through effective multi-agency collaboration. Ofsted recognised how vital the partnership between social care and education is with regard to achieving better outcomes for children in care and issued the following statement to clearly illustrate what this would mean in practice:

> *To ensure a common understanding of the needs of children and young people in public care, training is required for key teachers, governors, social workers, local authority personnel and elected members with an expectation that they will disseminate this training to their colleagues. The training could focus initially on shared knowledge of the requirements of the education and care services.*

(Ofsted, 2001, page 7)

However, one of the biggest challenges faced by those trying to create an integrated and collaborative workforce has been supporting all those who work with children in understanding what other people do, why they do it and why it is important to overcome resistance to multi-professional working practices that may exist.

The challenges faced by practitioners and by agencies in working collaboratively to ensure a co-ordinated approach to supporting children and young people is evidenced by the knowledge that there have been further tragic, high-profile child deaths since 2003. The inquiry into the death of Peter Connelly (Laming, 2009) concluded that better outcomes for children could be achieved if professionals pooled their expertise and co-ordinated their services in proactive and meaningful ways. It is recognised that no one person can be expected to have all the knowledge, skills, time or professional understanding to successfully support children and families whose needs may be complex. By working together, it is argued, multi-professional teams can strengthen the support that children, young people and families receive.

ACTIVITY 7.2

Make a record of your own experiences of multi-agency working practice. Which agencies do you feel that you know well and feel comfortable with? About which agencies do you need to find out more?

Strategies and approaches to support multi-agency working

To ensure the highest quality provision we need to work towards deeper levels of collaborative practice across the different agencies working together with children, young people and their families. Barrett and Keeping (2005, page 18) have pointed out that despite the continuing imperative within health and social care policy for inter-professional and interagency working, *policy directives alone appear insufficient to ensure the desired outcome.* They go on to explore a range of factors *that are likely to enable and encourage different professions to work collaboratively.* These include:

- knowledge of other professional roles;
- a high level of motivation and willing participation;
- confidence in one's own role and responsibilities;
- open communication;
- trust and mutual respect;
- equality in terms of power;
- reflection and supervision.

Working together with someone from a different disciplinary and professional background calls for a high level of self-awareness and self-confidence. The language and culture of interaction can be very different. Individual practitioners need to be flexible and tolerant in their interactions to enable effective communication to take place. The capacity to engage in basic interaction with warmth and acceptance provides a useful starting point when meeting another professional for the first time. Acknowledgement that everyone has the best interests of the child, young person and family in mind is a beneficial starting principle and tolerance of individual's different ways of enacting such a principle is very important.

Kimberlee and Coles have discussed the significance of inclusive communication with children and families in Chapter 5. Most practitioners working in children's services will be aware of their responsibilities to listen to their clients. It is just as important to use these effective communication skills in one's interactions with other practitioners and agencies. The ability to listen to the contribution and experience of another practitioner, as well as a family, and to be able to clearly express your own experience and knowledge is a valuable skill. The avoidance of jargon and successful sharing of knowledge can result in innovative approaches and joint problem solving, together with the challenging of assumptions and old ideologies (Tarr, 2005, page 45).

Building effective partnerships with families and other practitioners requires everyone involved understanding and recognising that status and power impact upon individuals in different ways. More confident individuals can be more resilient and less affected by power struggles, whereas less confident or more vulnerable colleagues and families may feel very powerless and unable to be proactive in engaging in collaborative working processes. All practitioners, whatever their level of experience, need to be able to respect differences and to develop levels of empathy for each other, to build upon commonalities rather than identify the differences.

A further factor, identified by Milbourne et al. (2003), is the time required to build inter-professional relationships and attend multi-agency meetings. Many practitioners argue that this frequently takes them away from what they see as their 'core work' with children, young people and their families: *The time and effort required for agencies and individuals to establish positive working relationships in order to build up the team trust necessary for collaborative multi-agency work is often not recognized* (Milbourne et al., 2003, page 22).

ACTIVITY 7.3

Reflect on your own experience of multi-agency working or partnership working. What are some of the challenges that you have experienced?

What are some of the strategies you have used, or support you have received, to help you overcome those challenges?

Knowledge of other professional roles

All children will meet a range of different professionals during their life. At birth health professionals, such as midwives, nurses, paediatricians, will be present to ensure entry into the world is safe and comfortable. In the early years of life, the health visitor may oversee the child's developmental milestones. If the family faces social or economic challenges, then sometimes a social worker or community support worker may be involved to support the family in their parenting processes. As the child grows, educational professionals become involved through nursery or playgroups. These may be nursery nurses, early years professionals or teachers. Into childhood other health practitioners such as dentists and opticians might be called upon. Those working in the community or voluntary sector will provide services for children and young people – for example babysitting, cubs and brownies, play schemes, church crèche, sports facilities and leisure centres. A range of teachers, teaching assistants, youth workers, careers advisers and mentors will support young people through their days of schooling and into adult life.

ACTIVITY 7.4

Talk with the parent/carer of a child you know and ask them to name the different professionals they have spoken with about their child. Record their responses under the following headings:

- overall profile of the child and family including the context and background;
- community support around the family, the social network;
- health provision and support;
- social care provision and support;
- educational provision.

It can be useful, when thinking about multi-agency working, to focus on a particular group of children and young people. In this chapter we have used this approach to enable us to understand the contribution of different professionals working together in a series of case study examples.

Children with additional educational needs

It has been estimated that around 20–25 per cent of children and families will, at some time in their lives, require the additional support of other professionals working within children's services. Such children or families might be vulnerable in terms of health, education, social or economic aspects and these might be judged to be impacting upon the child's development. Case Study 7.1 aims to illustrate the range of different professionals that might support Henry, a child who has been identified and diagnosed as falling within the autistic spectrum.

CASE STUDY 7.1   HENRY

Eight-year-old Henry is the middle child of three children born to African Caribbean parents. He received a recent diagnosis of Asperger's Syndrome and is a quiet child who enjoys playing the piano. He lives with his mother, father, brother and sister. His grandparents live far away. A range of professionals, including voluntary sector and community networks, provide additional support – e.g. National Autistic Society and the Jehovah Witness community.

*Social care provision received by the family comes in the form of the Disability Care Allowance, and they have involvement with a range of health care professionals, including: a **health visitor**, **community paediatrician**, the **family doctor**, an **occupational therapist**, plus a **speech and language therapist** who is attached to the communication disorder clinic.*

*Henry attends a mainstream school where he receives additional support from a **learning support assistant**. The school's **special educational needs co-ordinator (SENCO)**, an **educational psychologist** and **local authority administrators** are also involved as Henry currently has a statement of special educational need.*

In the early days of Henry's life the health visitor was a key person in supporting the family. If a child has challenges related to their physical development it is usually a medical professional who is called upon to support the child and the family. Depending upon the stage of development when such physical needs are identified the first health worker to be involved will vary. The health visitor makes visits to a family in the home when the child is a baby and can be the first person to which the family turn if they have concerns about their child's development. In the case study of Henry, the health visitor played a very important part in supporting the family particularly in the early stages. The family developed very strong relationships with the health visitor who took the role of lead professional for several years and supported the family in arguing for a clear diagnosis for their child.

*Henry was diagnosed at the age of 9 years with Asperger's Syndrome but throughout his early years there was engagement with health professionals such as the speech and language therapist who was particularly concerned about his communication and language skills. Henry was allocated a **paediatrician** at the hospital from an early age as the health visitor encouraged such communication for the family. Sometimes the speech and language therapist or **physiotherapist** might visit Henry at school but in many cases the family has to take him out of school to attend consultations. This can be disruptive to his education if the **teacher** and learning support assistants are not sensitised to this process.*

Henry also had support from an occupational therapist to enable him to interact with others. An occupational therapist helps people of all ages who have physical, mental health or social problems to adapt to any aspect of their life and gain more independence, confidence and control. The broad range of this role has led to their working across health and social services.

Throughout his life the church as a community also played a highly influential role in ensuring that the family felt supported as they gradually came to terms with the challenges facing Henry in his life. For the family to feel supported, this range of different practitioners needs to understand what each of

---

> *them can offer and how the child and family might be able to co-ordinate their different contributions. The family is central to this process and where so many people might be involved it may be necessary to appoint a* **lead professional** *to manage the team around the child and family.*

Children in care

Jackson and Sachdev (2001) remind us that it is through school that children earn passports to different kinds of futures. Therefore it is particularly important that education and social care workers operate collaboratively to ensure positive outcomes for children with additional social and emotional needs, such as children in care. While the majority of children in care are 'looked after' by *foster carers* who may be engaged in fostering through their local authority or an independent provider, the day by day parenting of children is often supported by a *social worker*. Both the social worker and the foster carer have the opportunity and responsibility to encourage and support the engagement of children and young people with education. Other practitioners who may be involved with the child include *teaching assistants*, *Connexions personal advisers*, *family support workers* and *school nurses*.

In Case Study 7.2 we can see how a range of practitioners may need to work collaboratively to support Alison and her foster carers in addressing concerns that her behaviour may be affecting her education, health and relationships with others.

CASE STUDY 7.2   ALISON

Alison is a 13-year-old who has lived with her **foster carers** *for the last three years. Recently her foster carers have raised concerns about her drinking and are worried that she may be engaging in sexual activity with her 17-year-old boyfriend. The foster carers have shared their concerns with Alison's school that they are worried her attendance has become less regular than it used to be.*

Alison is currently supported by a **Connexions personal advisor** *and is known to the* **designated teacher** *for Children in Care at her school. The local authority provides the support of an* **educational welfare officer (EWO)** *and the* **school nurse** *is also involved.*

As a Child in Care Alison has her own **social worker***, and she also has access to a* **youth worker***. Additional support can also be drawn from, for example, Counselling Services and the Alcohol Abuse Team within the Youth Service. So far, the Health Service has needed to provide no further support other than access to a* **general practitioner (GP)** *for Alison.*

Reflect upon the different agencies and range of practitioners working with Alison and her carers. What might each of them contribute to the education and care of Alison?

Imagine that you are Alison's social worker. Make a list of four priorities that stand out for you in response to the issues raised in the case study. Now imagine that you are in one of the other professional roles identified around Alison:

- *designated teacher;*
- *foster carer;*

- *family support worker;*
- *school nurse.*

In what ways do you think your professional role might influence the ways in which you think about and respond to the concerns that have been raised about Alison's drinking/her boyfriend/her truancy? Are there any concerns that you think other professionals would share with you?

Around what issues might practitioners seek the involvement of other agencies in order to achieve better support for Alison and her foster carers? How do you think professionals might work together to achieve this?

Children in care can be vulnerable due to a history of abuse and neglect prior to entering care. They are more likely than the general population to have special educational needs, but may also be capable of a high level of academic achievement, which should be noted and nurtured so that opportunities for high attainment are not missed. Since 2001, there have been a number of initiatives both at local and national level to improve outcomes for children in care and to support those who wish to remain in care past the age of 18 so that they have a secure base from which to continue with education or training. The Children Act (2004) gave a clear message to all those who worked with children in care that the level of educational attainment among children in care was unacceptably low compared to other children, and that this could not continue. The Act instructed local authorities to *promote* the education of children in care *proactively* rather than *reactively*. However, government figures in 2008 indicated that only 14 per cent of children in care achieved five A* to C grades at GCSE, compared to 65.3 per cent for all children (DCSF, 2008c). This suggests that there is still much work to be done with regard to achieving better outcomes.

Disabled children

In Case Study 7.3 you can see the wide range of practitioners who are involved with the family. Use the 'Useful resources' section of this chapter to find out more about roles, such as that of the educational psychologist.

CASE STUDY 7.3   SOPHIE

*Sophie is a profoundly deaf six-year-old who was born with a bilateral centro-neuro hearing loss. Sophie lives with her mum and her stepfather and she attends a mainstream school that has specialist support for children with hearing difficulties, including **teachers** and **learning support assistants** who communicate using British Sign Language (BSL). Sophie's mum is involved with the school in the role of **parent governor** and is also employed by the school as a **school meals supervisor**. So that Sophie has access to the Deaf community for whom BSL is the main means of communication, Sophie attends a club for the Deaf and a Centre for the Deaf.*

*At school Sophie also receives additional support from a **peripatetic teacher of the Deaf** and an **educational psychologist**. These specialists consult with her teachers and learning support*

> *assistants to ensure that Sophie's language skills are developed and that her access to the National Curriculum is maintained.*
>
> *The Health Service co-ordinates a range of professional support for Sophie that includes: an **audiologist**, an **ear nose and throat consultant**, a **paediatrician** to support her general health and also access to a **nutritionist**. The family **GP** is also involved with Sophie's care.*
>
> *Sophie does not currently have a **social worker**, though her mother does receive disability living allowance for Sophie. However the family have received support from their local housing department.*

The voluntary and community sector

Public services provide the main aspects of education, care and support for children, young people and families. However, the voluntary and community sector increasingly complement and supplement this provision. Families with a wide network of friends, who are able to take time to talk together, entertain and care for the children or go out socially, may not require such a high level of support from public services. They will also be able to choose those people who they get on with and understand to support them which can be very valuable.

This sector includes the main children's charities such as Barnardo's, National Children's Society, National Children's Home and National Children's Bureau, all of whom receive government support to work collaboratively with public services – education, health and social services. The voluntary sector has had an impact on the way public services work with children and families, often encouraging a more participatory approach in decision-making. The voluntary sector has also led the development of additional provision before and after school and the creation of children's centres for families with children in the early years. The value of voluntary and community sector provision is its capacity to be responsive to the needs of children and families. However, the sector frequently faces limited financial stability and users may be asked to contribute to the running costs.

An example of such community activity is the supplementary school movement. Here parents and community members co-ordinate themselves to provide after-school and weekend education for their children in aspects of education they feel are important. Many of the communities are minority ethnic groups and the education covers, for example, additional support in learning English or mathematics through to understanding aspects of their religious faith and cultural insight. Mainstream schools can benefit from building partnerships with supplementary schools to enhance their understanding of the children, young people and community they serve.

Information sharing

One of the acknowledged difficulties in effective collaborative working is the barrier created by different agency protocols for the sharing of information about children, young people and their families. This process is frequently managed differently among professional groups and the professional judgements required when deciding whether to share information are often drawn from a range of differing perspectives. There are policy statements, legal requirements and recommendations (see under 'Useful resources') about when and how to share information about a child or young person, and all rely heavily upon the professional judgement of the individual. There is considerable debate about the sharing of information in the field of children's services, and practitioners need to have a clear understanding about what is required of them by law and what might be seen as good practice.

The Common Assessment Framework (CAF)

The CAF (see also Chapter 4) is a shared assessment and planning framework for use across all children's services in England. It aims to promote efficient multi-agency working by supporting practitioners to build a *team around the child*. The term a team around the child acknowledges the necessity of multi-professional teams whose role is to follow integrated working practices to support young people and those who care for them to achieve better outcomes.

The purpose of the CAF is to help the early identification of children's additional needs and promote a standardised approach to conducting an assessment and co-ordinated service provision to meet the child's needs. The CAF is generally used with children and young people up to the age of 18, but its use can be extended beyond 18 where appropriate, to enable the young person to have a smooth transition to adult services and up to the age of 24 where a young person has a learning difficulty or disability (CWDC, 2009a).

The CAF consists of a pre-assessment checklist to help decide who would benefit from a common assessment; a process to enable practitioners in the children and young people's workforce to undertake a common assessment and then act on the result; a standard form to record the assessment; and a delivery plan and review form. The assessment covers three domains: development of the child or young person; parents and carers; and family and environment. There are four main stages in completing a common assessment: identifying needs early, assessing those needs, delivering integrated services and reviewing progress.

The most recent guidance (CWDC, 2009a) advises that the CAF has replaced other assessment frameworks such as the *Connexions Framework for Assessment, Planning, Implementation and Review* (APIR). While other assessments, such as universal checks and specialist assessments for Children in Need, remain in place, the CAF may appropriately be used before, after, or in conjunction with these assessments to help understand and articulate the full range of a child or young person's needs. A common assessment will be carried out when a young person has unmet needs that cannot be met by one agency alone and where a multi-agency response is required.

A common assessment can be carried out at any time if a practitioner is worried about a child or young person's progress towards the five *Every Child Matters* priority outcomes. For example, a practitioner might be worried about a child's health, development, welfare, behaviour, progress in learning or any other aspect of their well being. Alternatively, a child or young person or their parent/carer might raise a concern themselves. It is important to remember that the CAF is entirely voluntary. A practitioner must discuss their concerns with the child or young person and/or their parent/carer before deciding on a common assessment. The child or young person is seen as the key to finding effective solutions and so it is crucial they are involved in the design.

The use of CAF was never intended to *become overly bureaucratic* (Barker, 2009) but it was designed to support multi-professional engagement and information sharing. Like all new initiatives the CAF experienced teething difficulties that have varied between local authorities. This is why CAF training has been given such a high priority as it impacts on the working practices of all those within the children's workforce, whether they are public or voluntary sector workers.

Throughout the common assessment process any information provided by the young person or their family will only be shared with their consent. There are, however, certain circumstances where professionals will need to share information outside of the consent boundaries, for example where a young person is at risk of harm.

Role of the lead professional

The person who co-ordinates the delivery of a CAF is called the lead professional and while this role is assigned to one person, there is no hard and fast rule about which professional this should be. The CAF is intended as a non-judgemental tool to support professionals in identifying what the needs or issues are for a child and their family, so that timely support can be put in place. The Children's Workforce Development Council describes CAF as: *a three step process – prepare, discuss, deliver* (CWDC, 2009a). The role of the lead professional has been designed to support this three-step staged approach and also to reduce the previously often overwhelming number of professionals with whom a child, young person and their parents or carers might need to have contact.

Some children with complex needs will not require a CAF because the need for support has already been clearly identified and a number of professionals are already involved. Children in this category may include: children who are subject to a child protection plan; children in care; young offenders; and children who have complex health or mental health needs. However it is always important to never presume what a child may have in place to support them, but clearly understand how to find out about the support they are receiving. Analysis of the situation will enable one to ascertain whether a CAF is a useful tool to co-ordinate services for a particular child or young person.

The role of the lead professional is:

- to provide a single point of contact for families and other professionals who support the family;
- to co-ordinate the assessment and ensure any actions agreed as part of the CAF are delivered;
- to reduce an overlap of services and to ensure that children, young people and families do not receive inconsistent responses to their needs or requests for support.

ACTIVITY 7.7

Think about the range of different professionals you work most closely with and who might be suited to the role of lead professional with a child, young person or family with whom you work.

Good practice suggests that families or young people should be able to indicate who they would prefer their lead professional to be. For example, in school multi-professional teams this may include learning mentors, teaching assistants, parent support advisors who are in school most of the time and also health professionals such as physiotherapists and speech therapists who may work in a more peripatetic way. Any of these people could potentially take on the role of the lead professional.

Important considerations might include their knowledge and understanding of the major issues, whether the child or their family is happy with the choice of lead professional, and the professional capacity of the individual to take on the role and carry it out effectively.

One of the major reasons for the introduction of the CAF was to prevent children, young people or those who care for them, from reaching crisis point because their needs had not been properly identified and met. We will now use a case study approach to think about whether undertaking a CAF is a suitable response to the increased levels of disruptive behaviour displayed by 10-year-old Andy (see Case Study 7.4).

CASE STUDY 7.4   ANDY

Andy is a 10-year-old who has co-ordination and learning difficulties. Andy's mother describes him as immature for his age and also says that his behaviour can be challenging at times because he often experiences frustration and finds it difficult to control his emotions.

Andy lives with his mother and father and has two brothers. His father works away from home a lot, but his grandparents live close by and are supportive of the family. Andy also has an aunt who looks after the boys occasionally. Andy's mum runs a support group for parents of children with additional needs.

Further support for the family is provided by Health and Social Services. Andy was referred to a co-ordination clinic by a **consultant paediatrician**. *He has support from his family* **GP** *and for his emotional difficulties via a* **psychiatrist** *and a* **psychologist**. *Andy's mum is in receipt of disability living allowance for Andy and he has received support from his* **social worker**. *The* **police** *have been involved in supporting the family and a project run by Barnardo's provides further support for him.*

Because of his learning difficulties Andy requires additional help at school. The school's **SEN co-ordinator** *and an* **educational psychologist** *support mainstream teachers in delivering Andy's Individual Education Plan and if he is not able to attend school additional support is provided by the Home Tuition Service and an* **education welfare officer**. *Because of Andy's level of disability he is transported to school via a taxi that is paid for by the local education authority.*

With his father away for much of the time, much of the parental responsibility with regard to behavioural boundary setting is left to Andy's mum. She mostly has sole responsibility for the three boys. She has recently explained to a **family link worker** *that she is worried about Andy's behaviour, which is becoming more of a problem now that he is growing physically stronger and is also showing a greater level of concern about his co-ordination and learning difficulties.*

Educationally this is a key time for Andy because the primary phase of his education will soon end and he will enter the Key Stage 3 stage of compulsory education. Regardless of whether Andy receives his education within a mainstream or special school, or through some alternative arrangement such as home tuition, if Andy's behaviour continues to deteriorate this may prevent him from engaging with education in a positive way.

Use the information above to think about whether a CAF would be a useful tool for supporting Andy in his transition from Key Stage 2 to Key Stage 3. Consider the following:

- *Andy's transition from Key Stage 2 to Key Stage 3 of his schooling.*
- *His poor behaviour and whether plans are already in place to manage this.*
- *Whether his co-ordination and learning difficulties have been clearly identified – for example, is Andy dyspraxic?*
- *Is there a link between Andy's poor behaviour and his learning needs?*
- *Consider which professionals are already involved with this family and how successful their intervention has been or continues to be.*
- *Give thought to how information is shared so that respect is shown and assumptions are not made. Think about how the classifications of personal, confidential and sensitive information might apply to Andy.*

- *If a CAF is required who is best suited to the role of lead professional? What challenges in co-ordinating roles and responsibilities might exist and how might the lead professional and other professionals overcome such challenges?*

Record keeping

An important aspect of multi-agency working and information sharing is the clear recording of decisions together with the reasons for the decision. If it has been agreed to share information with other practitioners or agencies you should record what is to be shared and with whom. All practitioners need to work within their own agency's arrangements for recording information and within any local information sharing procedures that might be in place. These arrangements and procedures must be in accordance with the Data Protection Act 1998 (see under 'Useful resources' for further information on the Act).

ACTIVITY 7.8
Find out what it says in your agency's Information Sharing Protocol (ISP) that can help you understand the circumstances in which you should share information about a child or young person with other practitioners. What sort of information should you share and not share?

One of the strategies devised to support record keeping and to enable education and social care services to work collaboratively to promote educational achievement is the personal education plan (PEP). The PEP is a form for children in care that is designed to record barriers to learning that need to be addressed, to celebrate what has been achieved and to indicate what support a child or young person may need if they are to continue to make progress. While the PEP is instigated by the child's social worker and is a record of their educational history, it is also part of the wider care plan. PEPs support and provide evidence of children and young people's engagement with education, and therefore demonstrate enjoyment and achievement in line with *Every Child Matters*. As with all forms of record keeping and information sharing tools, PEPs raise issues with regard to the legislation and ethics that surround confidentiality and security of information as outlined in the Common Core. Go to the 'Useful resources' section of this chapter and use the information section of the Common Core of Skills and Knowledge publication to support you in understanding the skills involved in *Information Handling and Engagement* as well as the *Knowledge* with regard to how information is collected and shared, plus the *Roles and Responsibilities* that govern individual cases and professional boundaries.

All professionals who work with children in a multi-professional way have to be aware of the impact of their service both as an individual service, and also as a collaborative attempt to better support children and those who care for them.

ACTIVITY 7.9

How might two professionals, one from social care, for example a support worker, and another from education, for example a learning mentor, jointly demonstrate that the impact of their joint intervention is positive for an eight-year-old child in care who is aggressive towards other children?

Finally, create your own case study and use this to demonstrate reflective practice by explaining how integrated working was useful in this case. Reflect on the potential difficulties that may arise from differing professional perspectives of what a successful outcome might be. Indicate how the Common Core can support you in working together and identify any tensions that working in this way might cause.

CHAPTER SUMMARY

This chapter has focussed attention on the range of professionals who work within a multi-professional context to support children and their families. The coming together of professionals from the fields of education, health and social care has required professionals to challenge working practices that have been resistant to change in order to create and facilitate better ways of responding flexibly to the requirements of children, young people and families. While changes in government may have led to changes in policy over the years, there has remained a consistent theme in support of a multi-agency approach to supporting children, young people and families.

In this chapter we have introduced an overview of a range of organisations and individual roles who work to support children, young people and their families. We have discussed some tools, processes and procedures that have been introduced to support multi-agency and integrated working and information sharing. At different points throughout the chapter we have encouraged you to reflect on your own experience and practice that you may be familiar with in order to support you to develop your own critical thinking and learning.

USEFUL RESOURCES

www.continyou.org.uk Use this link for further details into the nature of the activities that supplementary schools might support.

Useful website links to resources that will support you in engaging more fully with the CAF and the role of the lead professional are:

www.cwdcouncil.org.uk/caf
www.cwdcouncil.org.uk/lead-professional
www.cwdcouncil.org.uk/educational-psychology This link provides occupational and training information on the role of the educational psychologist.
www.cwdcouncil.org.uk/cwdc-share This link provides a range of good practice examples of multi-agency working.
www.cwdcouncil.org.uk/common-core Use this link to download the Common Core of Skill and Knowledge. Go to page 22 of the downloadable Common Core:

Information Sharing in the context of multi-agency and integrated working.
Find a range of useful case study examples of multi-agency working, together with explanations about the role of the practitioners involved on:

www.uwe.ac.uk/elearning/edu/maw/cs/Presentation_Files/index.html

The Department for Education has produced information sharing guidance for practitioners and other supporting advice:

www.education.gov.uk/childrenandyoungpeople/strategy/integrated working/a0068938/integrated-working
www.education.gov.uk/schools/leadership/governance/becoming agovernor/rolesandresponsibilities/a0056705/information-sharing-guidance-for-practitioners-and-managers
www.education.gov.uk/schools/careers/careeropportunities/ a0014613/educational-psychologists This link takes you to a range of resources that will tell you more about the professional role and training requirements of educational psychologists.
www.education.gov.uk/publications/standard/publicationdetail/ page1/DCSF-01046-2009 Use this link to find details on the role and responsibilities of the designated teacher for looked after children.

www.ico.gov.uk/for_organisations/data_protection/the_guide.aspx Use this link to the Information Commissioner's Office for further information on the Data Protection Act.

FURTHER READING

Anning, A, Cottrell, D, Frost, N, Green, J and Robinson, M (2010) *Developing Multi-Professional Teamwork for Integrated Children's Services*. Maidenhead: McGraw Hill. This book reflects on the numerous changes to policy and practice in the delivery of Children's Services.

Barker, R (ed) (2009) *Making Sense of Every Child Matters: Multi-Professional Practice Guidance*. Bristol: Policy Press. This book provides practitioners with a guide to integrated practice from a range of different agency perspectives.

Barrett, G, Sellman, D and Thomas, J (eds) (2005) *Interprofessional Working in Health and Social Care*. Basingstoke: Palgrave. This book contains a helpful overview of the range of roles and perspectives of delivering integrated health and social care practice.

Horner, N and Krawczyk, S (2006) *Social Work in Education and Children's Services*. Exeter: Learning Matters. This book has useful background on the role of social workers in supporting multi-agency practice with Children in Care.

Pollard, K, Thomas, J and Miers, M (eds) (2010) *Understanding Interprofessional Working in Health and Social Care*. Basingstoke: Palgrave. This book uses real-life interview extracts to draw together a range of views and standpoints on inter-professional working.

8 LIVING AND WORKING IN A DIVERSE WORLD

Shekar Bheenuck and Tillie Curran

COMMON CORE OF SKILLS AND KNOWLEDGE FOR THE CHILDREN'S WORKFORCE: EQUALITY AND DIVERSITY

- Be self-aware. Know how to demonstrate a commitment to treating all people fairly. Be respectful by actively listening and avoiding assumptions. Make sure your actions support the equality, diversity, rights and responsibilities of children, young people, their parents and carers.

- Encourage children or young people to value their personal experiences and knowledge.

- Know and recognise the child or young person's position in their family or caring network, as well as a wider social context. Appreciate the diversity of these networks.

- Build a rapport and develop relationships using the most appropriate forms of communication to meet the needs of the individual child or young person and their families and carers.

- Understand the effects of non-verbal communication such as body language, and that different cultures use and interpret body language in different ways.

(CWDC, 2010a)

CHAPTER OBJECTIVES

By the end of this chapter you should have an understanding of:

- concepts of diversity and equality as they apply to services for children, young people and their families;

- inequality, discrimination and oppression and how these manifest themselves in the provision of services;

- how to reflect on your own experiences of living and working in a diverse world;

- creative approaches to developing and implementing inclusive practices.

Introduction

We live and work in a world that is increasingly diverse. Those working with children and young people need to recognise the richness, possibilities and challenges this brings to their practice. The main reasons for learning about diversity and equality when working with children, young people and families are that as practitioners:

- our practice and workplace reflect the principles of equity, fairness and inclusivity;
- we recognise and harness the benefits that diversity brings to our practice;
- we are aware of the diverse nature of the world in which we live and the implications for children and young people.

This chapter, therefore, explores key concepts in diversity and equality and introduces a number of models and frameworks that challenge the reader to engage with complex issues in their practice and to consider creative approaches to developing and sustaining inclusive working environments.

A number of activities are introduced to enable the reader to critically reflect on their experience in practice settings. The chapter begins with an introduction to diversity and equality including an exploration of the legal and policy contexts that impact on services for children and young people. The activities in the first section are designed to assist practitioners to take a critical look at their own perceptions, knowledge and understanding of issues relating to diversity and equality. The activities in the second section, based on a practice scenario, are designed to enable the reader to begin to explore possible strategies towards developing and sustaining an inclusive working environment. In the final section, the activities engage the reader to take a more reflective and critical look at their own work environment in terms of the extent to which it is driven by inclusive practices, and identify potential solutions to some of the challenges encountered.

Defining and understanding concepts and terminology

Diversity

Diversity is a contested concept. It is one of those terms about which we all have an opinion and yet it continues to challenge us in terms of having a shared understanding. The Collins Paperback English Dictionary (2000) defines diversity as *the quality of being different and varied; a point of difference*. This definition is useful to start our thinking about diversity. However, diversity, as far as our practice is concerned, is a complex issue and requires a more informed exploration of the concept. The Department of Health (DH) defines diversity as:

> *the recognition and valuing of difference in its broadest sense. It is about creating a working culture and practices that recognise, respect, value and harness difference for the benefit of the organisation and the individual. Equality and diversity are not inter-changeable but are inter-dependent. There is no equality of opportunity if difference is not recognised and valued.*

(DH, 2003, page 8)

This definition is important to practitioners as it acknowledges the link between diversity and equality.

Pincus (2006) provides a useful overview of diversity as conceptualised within the social sciences and this is summarised below:

Counting diversity

One can conceptualise diversity purely in terms of such characteristics as age, race, gender, ethnicity and religion. As an example, this could entail counting the number of individuals in each of the above categories within a particular group or community and making comparison on how these are distributed within the wider society.

Culture diversity

Diversity can also be viewed in terms of cultural differences within society and between groups. Greater appreciation of different cultures can be seen as contributing to greater accommodation and tolerance of differences.

Good for business diversity

The business case for having diversity within a particular workforce is seen as good economic sense. Diversity, in this sense, is seen as benefitting business and employers by making the organisation more responsive, effective and efficient.

Conflict diversity

The focus here is on how the unequal distribution of 'power, privilege and wealth' within a community or society impact on individuals or groups contributing to difference and inequality.

More often than not we tend to conceptualise diversity in terms of a combination of all the above. However, our attempts to define and understand diversity often tend to emphasise the differences that exist within groups and communities. Viewing diversity in terms of differences and as 'business sense' tends to minimise the importance of the similarities between individuals and groups. What we have in common and what we share as individual human beings need to be celebrated just as much as the differences and the diversity we bring. Diversity needs to be viewed beyond just numbers, facts and as being 'good for business'; it needs to be valued and celebrated in terms of the richness and rewards it brings to the human experience. Inability to do so can lead us to perceive difference as sources of conflict and problems. When this is the case we begin to categorise people in terms of those who are privileged and those who are disadvantaged; those seen as oppressors and those seen as oppressed; those who discriminate and those who are discriminated against.

Where differences do exist these need not be seen in negative terms. As human beings we share certain characteristics with each other whilst also having our differences. It is what makes each one of us unique. We expect our differences to be acknowledged and valued; it also implies that we would value these in others. In explaining diversity and difference Gaine (2010) advocates the need to move away from explanations that serve to confirm our prejudices. Instead, he advocates the use of a social model that emphasises that difference and inequality, as experienced by people, are socially determined. In other words it is the interpretations we attach to perceived differences that matter. These interpretations can impact positively or negatively on individuals. He adds that *there is no chronologically determined age when someone passes from not-old to old, there is no exact borderline where one becomes disabled, there is not an absolute boundary between feminine and masculine behaviour, and what matters about skin colour is the social significance it carries* (page 117).

Addressing and accommodating diversity, therefore, requires a mindset that values *difference* whilst also acknowledging the *common bond* between people (Pless and Maak, 2004). It is, they add, the recognition of people as *different but equal* that motivates individuals to maximise their potential and effectiveness. Viewing difference as negative can ignore the positive contributions diversity brings to human interaction and experience. Welcoming and valuing diversity and difference mean we are ready to harness the benefits they bring. Mulholland et al. (2006) would be a useful source for further reading on this.

As practitioners we need to respond with equal commitment to each child and young person whilst recognising their needs as individuals. It is important to recognise that individuals are complex beings with different needs and requirements. Gender, age, sexuality and ethnicity are examples of characteristics we more commonly use to express differences in human beings. These are not 'natural' or 'fixed' differences but are socially and culturally determined. An individual's identity is not limited to one dimension; gender, ethnicity and age may all be part of an individual's rich and changing range of experiences. This understanding of identity is sometimes referred to as *intersectionality* and alerts us to the multiple forms of disadvantage an individual can experience (Gaine, 2010). Failure by the practitioner to recognise this complexity can lead to a superficial engagement with children and young people leading to ineffective practice.

Diversity and self-awareness

Self-awareness is an important starting place for developing an understanding of diversity. Our own individual experiences and our sense of who we are impact directly on our identity and how, in turn, we perceive and interact with others. Self-awareness ensures we are informed and sensitive to our own emotions, experiences and prejudices. An understanding of these are paramount to how we perceive and interact with others; making it possible for us, as practitioners, to recognise the individual needs of others and make a difference to their lives.

Activity 8.1 is about your identity and the influences that shape you and impact on how you are perceived by others.

ACTIVITY 8.1

We are all individuals with individual identities. Our identities give us a sense of who we are. In this activity you are asked to reflect on your identity:

- Using words, drawings or other medium, make a description of yourself.
- From the description of yourself circle aspects that you think are unique to you.

- Identify those aspects of your identity that you believe are more visible to others and those that are less so.
- From your experiences at work identify those aspects of your identity that are most valued by others and those that are less so.

Some aspects of your self-description will be visible to others and some will not unless you decide to share that information. We call these *primary* and *secondary* types of difference (Wilson and Iles, 1999). Identify those aspects of your identity that you would consider to be primary and those that you consider to be secondary. Which of these would you feel comfortable and confident to share with colleagues and others at work and why?

Self-awareness is a continuous process as we continue to learn throughout life. It requires us to take a critical look at ourselves and the society, community and organisation of which we are a part. Dominant cultures within a society, community or organisation can shape how we see ourselves and, more significantly, how we see others. *Cultural imperialism* (Young, 2000) is a concept used to explain situations where dominant cultures portray some elements of a group or community as more important and set these as *norms* against which others are viewed. These *norms* can often become the benchmark against which individual or group *sameness* and *difference* are measured.

In dominant cultures the potential exists for individuals, groups or practices that do not meet these *norms* to be seen as marginal and less important. These *norms* can consequently shape our perceptions and, in some cases, become a tool for measuring what is important and what is not; what is visible and what is not; what is valued and what is not; who belongs and who does not. Ryde (2009) explains that *being white* became invisible in colonialism; it became the 'normal' category. Such norms still drive our experiences and perceptions and as practitioners may shape what we, in turn, value in others. In the absence of self-awareness these can impact negatively on our actions, language, feelings and emotions. The potential always exists for differences to gain precedence over similarities and in such cases one can exaggerate the differences leading to over generalisation. An emphasis on difference, particularly where these do not meet perceived norms, can lead to discriminating and oppressive practices. Therefore, it is important, when exploring issues concerned with diversity, that we do not only focus on individuals or groups experiencing disadvantage; rather, we also need to take account of the social, political and economic contexts that contribute to inequality (Cooper, 2004). To address inequality and enable effective change we need to focus on both the individuals concerned and the contexts that give rise to oppression and discrimination.

Oppression

It is important to distinguish between prejudice and discrimination. According to Pincus (2006, page 21), the former refers to what one *thinks, feels and believes* about another whilst the latter is about how one's actions can impact negatively on others; *prejudice is what people think, and discrimination is what people do*. In other words discrimination is likely to occur when our personal feelings and beliefs (our prejudices) shape our behaviour. Pincus refers to three types of discrimination: *individual discrimination, institutional discrimination and structural discrimination*. *Individual discrimination* occurs when the actions of one individual has a negative effect on another.

Institutional discrimination arises in situations when the policies and practices of dominant institutions and organisations are intended to disadvantage others. *Structural discrimination* refers to institutional and organisational policies and practices that, although intended to be *neutral*, can nevertheless have negative consequences for some individuals or groups.

Prejudice and discrimination are part of oppression. Young (2000) refers to *five faces of oppression* individuals can experience in society: *exploitation, marginalisation, powerlessness, cultural imperialism, and violence.* She explains that social groups may be based on shared experiences and differences. Groups also have different power relations that might mean that particular groups face a greater likelihood of inequality and exclusion. Young (2000) makes the point that in the past oppression has meant force and tyranny. The term is also used to describe injustices that happen through everyday practices in liberal societies. Oppression, she explains, is a *structural concept* and occurs through systematic constraints and assumptions that are embedded in ordinary interactions. The aim is for individuals and institutions to promote and respect group differences without oppression. Not all groups are oppressed. Oppression occurs when an individual, a group or community, is subject to one or more of the following five conditions:

Young's Five Faces of Oppression (2000)

- *Exploitation*: is often associated with menial work. Although primarily focused on unequal experiences of individuals or groups in the workplace, exploitation can also be experienced in other settings including personal relationships.
- *Marginalisation*: refers to the 'alienation' and 'isolation' experienced by some individuals affecting their ability to integrate within a wider group or community.
- *Powerlessness*: can be conceived as a lack of 'power' and 'authority' to influence decisions and outcomes even when these impact directly or indirectly on one's own experiences.
- *Cultural imperialism*: implies that the dominant culture within a society or organisation predominates at the expense of other less visible cultures and practices. In such situations some individuals or groups can be perceived as being 'separate' and 'different' from a main group.
- *Violence*: fear of real or perceived of violence (physical or psychological) can seriously limit the extent to which individuals and groups can interact and move within the wider organisation or society. Such fear can affect ones participation as a full member of a community or organisation.

ACTIVITY 8.2

Referring to Young's framework outlined above, think of a situation where you have experienced one or more of these forms of oppression:

- How did you feel at the time?
- How can Young's framework help you to explore the experiences of children and young people, those of your colleagues at work, and people in the wider community?

To make the link between concepts of diversity, oppression and practice, the next section sets out the relevant policy and legislation.

The policy and legislative context

In Britain, children's services are covered by The Equality Act (2010). The Act brings together pre-existing legislation and introduces some new requirements including detailing action we can and must do in order to promote socio-economic equality. The Act defines equality and states why it is important.

Equality

This means everyone having the same chances to do what they can. Some people may need extra help to get the same chances.

Equality is right for many reasons:

- people enjoy life more if they are treated fairly;
- the country is richer because each and every person can do what they are best at;
- it is easier for people to live side by side and get on with each other if everyone is treated fairly.

The Equality Act (2010) protects people with the following characteristics from *direct and indirect discrimination*, *harassment* and *victimisation*.

The 'protected characteristics' are:

- age;
- disability;
- gender reassignment;
- marriage and civil partnership;
- pregnancy and maternity;
- race;
- sex;
- sexual orientation.

Direct discrimination is when a person or group with the above characteristics is treated less favourably. It is not discrimination when there is a justifiable reason such as protection of a child due to their age or the need to achieve a legitimate aim.

Indirect discrimination is when a person or group with the above characteristics is disadvantaged without justifiable reason.

Harassment includes unwanted conduct relating to the above characteristics that has the purpose or effect of violation of dignity or creates an environment that is intimidating, degrading, humiliating or offensive for that person or people.

Victimisation is when a person or people subject a person to detriment when they are, for example, taking proceedings through the Act.

Policy and legislation relating to children's services in England are focused on outcomes for *all* children and young people. *Every Child Matters* (DfES, 2003) requires all organisations working with children to ensure that the provision of services addresses the need for every child to meet the *five outcomes* (see Chapter 1). However these outcomes need to be sensitive to individual children. This can only be achieved with an understanding of diversity and individual children's experiences. When working with disabled children, for example, practitioners need to know how to communicate effectively and understand each child's verbal and non-verbal expressions. As Sloper et al. (2007, page 4) remind us, practitioners need to find out what the child enjoys and aims to achieve and to know how to create opportunities accordingly: *Achievements need to be seen and celebrated within the context of the child's abilities and potential.*

Key messages from research into inequality inform the development of policy and strategies to improve services. The National Equality Panel report (Hills et al., 2010) into economic inequalities in the UK showed that these inequalities have a lasting effect on outcomes in education, health, income and wealth. The Marmot Review (Marmot, 2010, page 16) highlights the health inequalities experienced by poorer sections of the community and advocates six policy objectives:

- give every child the best start in life;
- enable all children young people and adults to maximise their capabilities and have control over their lives;
- create fair employment and good work for all;
- ensure healthy standard of living for all;
- create and develop healthy and sustainable places and communities;
- strengthen the role and impact of ill health prevention and advocates.

These principles are also reflected in the *Early Years Statutory Standards* (DCSF, 2008d, page 6) that advocate:

> *providing for equality of opportunity and anti-discriminatory practice and ensuring that every child is included and not disadvantaged because of ethnicity, culture or religion, home language, family background, learning difficulties or disabilities, gender or ability.*

Activity 8.3 aims to enable you to critically explore an example of an equality of opportunity policy or statement and its implementation in your own practice or organisation.

ACTIVITY 8.3

Read the following from the *Early Years Statutory Standards* (DCSF, 2008d):

Providing for equality of opportunity

Providers have a responsibility to ensure positive attitudes to diversity and difference – not only so that every child is included and not disadvantaged, but also so that they learn from the earliest age to value diversity in others and groups making a positive contribution to society. Practitioners should focus on each child's individual learning, development and care needs by:

- *Removing or helping to overcome barriers for children where these already exist;*
- *Being alert to the early signs of needs that could lead to later difficulties and responding quickly and appropriately, including other agencies as necessary;*
- *Stretching and challenging all children.*

All children, irrespective of ethnicity, culture or religion, home language, family background, learning difficulties or disabilities, gender or ability should have the opportunity to experience challenging and enjoyable programme of learning and development.

(DCSF, 2008d, page 6)

From your reading of the above extract, highlight what you think will be the key issues and challenges facing those working with children, young people and families when striving to provide for equality of opportunity.

You should now be able to engage with the next stage of the exercise:

- All organisations are required to have a statement about equality and diversity. Locate the statement of equality and diversity in your practice agency. Does the equality and diversity statement indicate who was involved in its production? Is there evidence of children's and young people's involvement in the development of the statement?
- Which of the principles identified in the extract above are visible in your agency statement? Which ones are missing?
- Review the images of children and young people that are visible in your agency and consider how well they reflect diversity. How are children and young people able to influence the images visible in this environment?
- If you were invited to participate in a review of the statement what suggestions would you make about how it needs to be revised and who needs to be involved?

It is important to note the contribution to our understanding of diversity of new theories of childhood, as discussed in Chapter 2. These theories stress the active part children and young people play in constructing their lives in contrast to earlier theories that discuss child development as a rather biological process in which differences are viewed in problematic terms (James et al., 1998; Lee, 2001). The earlier constructs of childhood were developed as 'universal truths', but more recent theories are interested in the local and global contexts of children's lives and promote the active involvement of children and young people. As Wells (2009) points out children and young people are involved and experience conflicts, persecution and threats to their survival in many contexts. If children and young people are regarded in uniform ways as either 'normal' or 'abnormal' or are excluded from our understanding of their lives they can become 'silenced' and made invisible or made visible as 'other' in adult terms (Jones, 2009).

We also need to recognise how children and young people contribute to society. Children and young people around the world have been acting in a political context, campaigning around issues such as peace, climate change and children's rights. Children and young people have acted as consultants, advocates and researchers supporting peers, informing local and national policy-making. Many local authorities now have advisory projects involving children and young people to inform and review targets. The contribution of disabled children and children growing up in local authority care are important examples (Davis and Hogan, 2004; Dalrymple and Oliver, 2008).

The following section provides further strategies to help you develop more inclusive practices.

Tools and techniques

The *Five Faces of Oppression* framework (Young, 2000), explored above, provides us with a tool for understanding the experiences of individuals or groups who encounter discrimination. The Social Oppression Matrix (Hardiman and Jackson, 1997) below helps us recognise the sources and manifestations of oppressive actions at all levels of society. It is also useful in helping us take a critical look at our own practice and in working towards implementing inclusive practices.

You may find it useful to view the matrix in Figure 8.1 as a three-dimensional model (context, application and psycho-social levels) that helps us understand how discrimination and oppression manifest themselves at individual, institutional and societal levels:

- at the contextual level oppressive practices can arise as a result of individual, institutional and societal actions or inactions;
- at the application level oppressive practices can be observed in the attitudes and behaviour of individuals and within institutions and society;
- at the psycho-social level oppressive attitudes and behaviours can be either conscious (witting) or unconscious (unwitting).

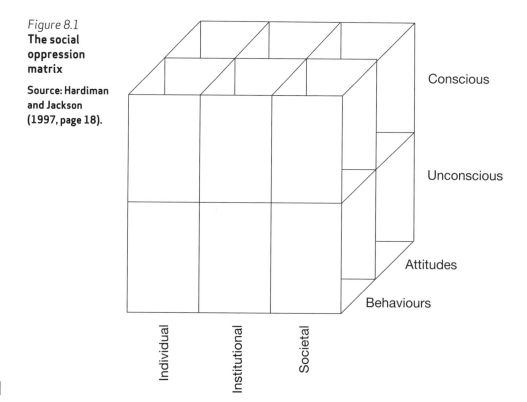

Figure 8.1
The social oppression matrix

Source: Hardiman and Jackson (1997, page 18).

As practitioners the matrix allows us to take a critical look at ourselves, the organisation in which we work and the society to which we belong. Issues, tensions and challenges exist at each of these levels. As practitioners we have to endeavour to address oppressive and discriminatory practices whenever these affect children and young people. In promoting anti-oppressive practice we need to conceptualise people as individuals who should be valued for who they are. As discussed in Chapter 5, it is about creating the environment where practitioners, children and young people collectively contribute as partners in shaping and developing services and practices designed to maximise individual potential. Practices are unlikely to be effective and meet the needs of individuals without meaningful participation and partnership.

Case Study 8.1 sets out a scenario and asks you to apply these frameworks to identify forms of oppression and to develop strategies to address this.

CASE STUDY 8.1   ARNI

When Mr Sol came to collect his son, Arni (aged 5) from the after-school club he told the manager that Arni does not want to come to the group any more as three other children tease him with homophobic words and push him around. Mr Sol explains that Arni speaks French confidently as he has recently moved from France. However when he is nervous, he tends not to say anything in case he is bullied for making mistakes in his English. The manager explains that the assistant practitioner will observe Arni in the group for a week. He says that he will tell Arni that this will happen and arranges to meet Mr Sol to discuss the situation the following week. The manager emails the plan to Mr Sol with a copy of the equality statement and anti-bullying policy that the governors produced the previous year.

- *Using Young's (2000) Five Faces of Oppression framework discussed earlier, identify the forms of oppression that Arni could have experienced.*
- *Using Hardiman and Jackson's (1997) Social Oppression Matrix in Figure 8.1 reflect on how the forms of oppression Arni experienced manifest themselves at individual, institutional and societal levels.*
- *Using Hardiman and Jackson's (1997) Social Oppression Matrix make a list of positive factors in the scenario that will support inclusive practices.*
- *Make a list of additional practices you would suggest to address each level of oppression that you have identified.*

The above case study situation is complex and you have limited information to work from. Some concerns will be immediate and others more long term for wider and more in-depth change. Here are some of the concerns and approaches we have identified. You might have others to suggest.

Manifestations of oppression

Some of the behaviour is violent and likely to be conscious, but are the three children conscious or unconscious of the attitudes towards sexual identity that they hold? The abusive terms used will impact on all the children and how safe and emotionally supported they feel in the after-school club environment and possibly at the school. Arni may be marginalised due to the dominant language of English and be seen by others as having a 'problem'. He may therefore feel that he does not belong in the group or community. Staff may not feel confident to challenge issues around sexual identity if they have not had any training in this area.

At an institutional level English is the dominant language. There may not be any references to France in the materials, books or resources provided. Similarly the heterosexual two-parent family norm may be dominant in play, toys and staff culture. The culture of the institution is likely to impact on how some aspects of diversity are more visible and valued than others. If the school equality statement and the anti-bullying policy were developed by governors without involvement of staff, they may feel unsupported to develop and implement inclusive strategies. In relation to community belonging, the norm within the organisation may be one that is based on residential stability. Staff may lack an understanding of the global context of childhood which can lead to greater geographical mobility, instability and insecurity. Garrett's (2009) critical analysis of the transformation of children's services programme suggests that practitioners need to understand how families move within and across countries and not limit practice to a bureaucratic form of exclusion. If children are separated from one or both of their parents and their communities, he explains, service providers need to respond to their needs and not consider a situation too temporary or bureaucratically complex.

At a societal level the media available to children may reflect dominant norms about 'the family' and present diversity and sexuality in problematic terms, if at all. Unless diversity in children and the wider community is acknowledged and given greater media coverage, dominant attitudes are likely to prevail, resulting in increased fear and anxiety among those who feel they do not belong. An understanding of the national legal framework regarding citizenship, asylum and migration status is also relevant to ensuring the needs of all children and young people are addressed (Garrett, 2009).

When looking at what can be done it helps to identify existing inclusive practices and the strengths in the scenario as a starting point.

Strengths and inclusive approaches

At an individual level it is important to recognise that many of the children are not engaged in the problematic behaviour reported by Mr Sol. It is also important to note that Arni can confide to his father who is prepared to take his experiences seriously and has the confidence to raise this with the after-school club manager. Arni brings a range of experiences that will be of value to the other children.

At the level of the institution, there is a policy to address equality and bullying and the manager is prepared to investigate and follow through the concern involving Mr Sol and informing Arni. Lefevre (2010) suggests observation is a good starting point to develop conditions for communication in terms of the location and environment. Planned observation over a period of time can illuminate what is happening and inform decisions. It also provides a method of learning how each child prefers to communicate and can be used to encourage children's communication skills. Observation can be the basis for deciding whether to see the children concerned individually, together or with another member of staff or their parents.

At the societal level there are legal and policy requirements and standards as outlined above. The children in the above scenario are five years old but will be aware of their own family and be developing their own attitudes towards the 'family'. At a societal level research and campaigns that promote equality can add to our understanding of the extent and nature of oppression. The following research, for example, would be useful in linking the equality and bullying policies in agencies working with young people.

Research shows that bullying is experienced by 65 per cent of young lesbian, gay and bisexual (LGB) people (Stonewall, 2007). Stonewall provides the following strategies for schools on their website and these are applicable to other settings. The above scenario is about children around five years old; however, the learning emerging from this is applicable to practitioners working with young people:

- Make sure there are clear anti-bullying rules at the school (or centre).
- Talk about LGB issues.
- Create an LGB friendly atmosphere using images, books, films.
- Make helpful resources available.
- Raise awareness with all students in large group events and activities.

Research shows that pupils who are disabled, or who are lesbian and gay, experience particularly high levels of bullying in and outside of school. It also shows that self-harm is linked to bullying and that young people's concerns are made invisible through a lack of response to both bullying and to self-harm (Jones, 2009).

So far, in this chapter, we have looked at oppression and what can be done to address this. Now we will turn the scenario around and ask *how can diversity be recognised, embraced and promoted?*

Promoting diversity and equality

In Case Study 8.1 the focus was on experiences of oppression and challenges encountered in one specific area of practice and we looked at potential strategies for addressing some of these. This final section addresses the need to actively promote equality and explores opportunities to celebrate diversity and community involvement. As we have seen the need to promote equality and to reduce inequality is now an important part of The Equality Act (2010).

The Equality Act (2010) requires us to take action to promote equality and to reduce inequalities through *reasonable adjustments*, *positive action* and the *equality duty*.

Reasonable adjustments are measures put in place (such as assistance or equipment) or removal of barriers that would otherwise disadvantage disabled people without justifiable reason. 'Justifiable' reason means that after consideration of the options available adjustments are not possible.

Positive action includes encouraging people with the protected characteristics to apply for jobs through such strategies as provision of training and open days.

Equality duty is a law for public bodies telling them that they must think about how they can make sure their work supports equality. For example, in their services, through their jobs, and through the money they spend.

Activity 8.4 follows on from Case Study 8.1 to consider how Arni and the other children can value each other and enjoy a sense of inclusion by gaining a greater understanding about each other.

ACTIVITY 8.4

You have been asked to plan a social event with children, young people, parents, carers and members of the community that aims to build a sense of community:

- Think about who you would involve in its planning and why?
- How would the involvement of children and young people help you to decide when and where you might hold this event?
- Make a list of activities you think would promote community involvement.
- Note the barriers and list some strategies to address them: how, for example, will you ensure that people on low incomes can participate and how will your publicity ensure that this is communicated effectively?
- How will you evaluate the event? What inclusive activities will you use with children and young people, staff and parents?

The activities above are designed to promote equality and diversity in working with children and young people as a continuing process. The involvement of children and young people and the involvement of practitioners are central to developing an inclusive culture and working environment. Kandola and Fullerton (1998, page 8) state that harnessing visible and non-visible differences *will create a productive environment in which everybody feels valued, where their talents are being utilised and in which organisational goals are met*. Opportunities such as the use of observation skills and team working, supervision and training are relevant sources of reflection, support and self-development. Evaluation activities, inspection and quality assurance information gathered within the organisation can show how inclusive practices have improved outcomes for children and young people when practitioners are involved and the data are made accessible.

The role of management is not explored in this chapter however practitioners familiar with the legislation and policy discussed above will have an understanding of the responsibilities of employers and the requirements towards employees. The discussion of oppression encourages practitioners to take a positive approach to greater involvement of marginalised groups within their own organisation. The use of a community event to promote diversity, for example, has the potential to harness and utilise practitioners' talents and may also inspire and provide a seed bed for further engagement through volunteering and work experience opportunities.

CHAPTER SUMMARY

In this chapter we have discussed issues and challenges we face, as practitioners working with children and young people, towards implementing inclusive practices. After reading this chapter you should have developed a sound understanding of concepts pertaining to diversity equality and inclusivity and how these are informed by recent changes in equality legislation. We have explored the impact of oppression and discrimination on those at the receiving end and also looked at strategies we can utilise to help prevent and address these.

We have encouraged you to reflect on your own experiences. The scenario we have discussed is a common situation illustrating dimensions of oppression that exist in more or less visible ways. We have offered some tools for analysis and strategies for building more inclusive practices. This approach recognises the need to understand:

- the variety of children's lives;
- the need to be flexible;
- the richness and challenges of difference;
- the need for support, reflection and research to review organisational routines and cultures;
- one's own role and responsibilities towards establishing inclusive practices.

This chapter has engaged with broad principles, challenges and opportunities to develop inclusive practices. Use the further reading and useful resources suggested below to explore how practice addresses diversity in different settings.

USEFUL RESOURCES

Disability services: an A–Z of what works
www.c4eo.org.uk/themes/disabledchildren/atozwebguide This guide contains evidence gathered by the Centre for Excellence and Outcomes in Children and Young People's Services (C4EO).

Early Childhood Forum – Celebrating difference
www.ncb.org.uk/pdf/cycr4.pdf The Early Childhood Forum campaign on addressing inequalities and valuing diversity and have produced this helpful leaflet to remind us why equality and a fair environment are fundamental to the well being of children and families and to provide information on the legislative framework. They offer examples of identifying and eroding discrimination.

C4EO
www.c4eo.org.uk/themes/disabledchildren/default.aspx?themeid=2& accesstypeid=1 This website contains useful good practice case examples as well as links to useful resources and research.

Free anti-bullying resources
www.anti-bullyingalliance.org.uk Anti-Bullying Alliance's free resources are filled with information about tackling bullying and practical ideas for activities to support children and young people.

Young Minds
www.youngminds.org.uk YoungMinds is the website that represents young people's mental health and well being.

FURTHER READING

McCartney, C and Lock, A (2007) *Diversity and Equality: Implementing Successful Strategies*. Horsham: Roffey Park Institute. Research published by Roffey Park looks specifically at how organisations can implement successful diversity and equality strategies.

Mulholland, G, Ozbilgin, MF and Worman, D (2006) *Managing Diversity: Words into Actions*. London: Chartered Institute of Personnel and Development.

www.ncb.org.uk/ecu_network/nqin/resources/engaging_families_principles.asp This new set of principles provides a framework for local authorities and national organisations to evaluate and improve engagement with families.

www.ofsted.gov.uk/Ofsted-home/Publications-and-research/Browse-all-by/Documents-by-type/Thematic-reports/The-special-educational-needs-and-disability-review The Special Educational Needs and Disability Review: A Statement Is Not Enough by Ofsted. This review was commissioned to evaluate how well the legislative framework and arrangements served children and young people who had SEN and/or disabilities. It considered the early years, compulsory education, education from 16 to 19, and the contribution of social care and health services.

9 THE CHILDREN'S WORKFORCE

NEW ROLES AND CAREER OPPORTUNITIES

Billie Oliver and Bob Pitt

COMMON CORE OF SKILLS AND KNOWLEDGE FOR THE CHILDREN'S WORKFORCE

- Draw upon personal experiences and other people's perspectives, to help you to reflect, challenge your thinking and to assess the impact of your actions.

- Have self-awareness and the ability to analyse objectively.

- Have the confidence to challenge the way you or others practise.

- Understand the value and expertise you bring to a team and that which is brought by your colleagues.

- Be aware of the roles and responsibilities of other professionals.

- Know how to work within your own and other organisational values, beliefs and cultures.

- Develop skills and knowledge with training from experts, to work with specialist services, enabling continuity for families, children or young people while enhancing your own skills and knowledge.

(CWDC, 2010a)

CHAPTER OBJECTIVES

By the end of this chapter you should have an understanding of:

- some background history and policy in relation to developing the children and young people's workforce;

- a range of recent government-initiated reviews relevant to the workforce;

- a variety of qualifications and training routes;

- different roles and responsibilities within the children and young people's workforce;

- where to find details on career and job opportunities;
- how to produce a personal development plan (PDP) setting out goals and aspirations.

Introduction

The Children's Workforce Development Council (CWDC) estimates that seven and a half million people work with children, which is one in five of all adults in England (www.cwdcouncil.org.uk/qualifications). While some work with children or young people every day, others have roles leading to intermittent contact, many as unpaid volunteers.

A government strategy document defined the children's workforce as *all those in England who work mainly with children, young people and their families* (DfES, 2005a) including those managing, planning and assisting frontline workers. It grouped main occupations or job titles under service headings such as *Social Care, Youth Work & Related, Childcare & Early Years, Education, Health*, and *Sport & Leisure*. It then estimated paid workers within the different occupation groups by sector: 1,572,800 in the public sector; 495,500 in the voluntary or community sector; and 683,600 in the private sector – a total of 2,751,900. The report acknowledged that it was difficult to know if this was an over- or under-estimate of the children's paid workforce, particularly due to gaps in the data used from the voluntary, community and private sectors.

A report on the children's social care workforce (CWDC, 2008) identified those working with children in day care, residential care, fieldwork (e.g. social workers), special needs establishments and fostering and adoption agencies. They estimated around 55,000 working in the public or statutory sector with local authorities and 32,500 in the private and voluntary sectors, predominantly women with a high proportion of part-time workers. The report referred to research by the National Centre for Social Research and the Institute of Volunteering Research that suggested around two million people volunteer each month in the children and young people's sector outside education settings although *it is not known how much of this is in social care* (CWDC, 2008, page 6).

A more recent report described a young people's workforce in England of about six million people (CWDC, 2009c) consisting of 775,150 paid staff and 5,272,600 volunteers. This report used data on those working with young people aged 13 to 19, or up to 25 for young people with learning difficulties or disability *either as their primary professional calling or as part of their profession*.

These reports highlight difficulties in putting exact numbers on the current children and young people's workforce other than to say it is large and diverse. One report just counts paid workers while the others are only looking at those working in the social care sector or with young people. Research studies may use different definitions of who or what counts as being a member of the workforce, which makes it difficult to compare and interpret whether a workforce may be contracting or expanding.

What is interesting in these studies is the detail on job titles. For example the 2005 report lists the following titles under *Youth Work & Related Roles: Youth Worker, Personal Adviser, Learning Mentor, Education Welfare Officer, Key Worker.* The 2009 report identifies *Youth Work* as only one component of a complex and fragmented young people's workforce. Within each component it lists a number of occupations that show how new professional roles are emerging, for example, *extended schools workers; family support advisors; play ranger; play or sport development worker; leaving-care workers; substance use workers; youth support workers; information, advice and guidance workers.* The picture emerging is based on data about the workforce in England. Activity 9.1 suggests finding out more about the workforce in the UK as a whole.

This chapter explores ongoing changes and developments in the children and young people's workforce, as described in government policy, and strategies to develop a more skilled and confident workforce that works effectively together. It outlines a selection of job roles and responsibilities including some of the emergent job titles. A range of qualifications and career opportunities are covered and readers are invited to reflect on their own personal and professional development. For example, you are encouraged to reflect on what skills, knowledge, experience and qualifications you are able to present in order to join or achieve your aspirations within the children and young people's workforce.

ACTIVITY 9.1

Find out more detail within the reports outlined above in order to get ideas about the range of jobs covered.

For example, in which sector do they appear (public, private, voluntary, community)? What are the pay scales that are offered? What are the demographic characteristics of the current workforce such as gender, age, educational qualifications and ethnicity?

Find the latest figures and details about paid or unpaid workers in the UK's children and young people's workforce, including England, Northern Ireland, Scotland and Wales.

Policy and legislation

The *2020 Children and Young People's Workforce Strategy* (DCSF, 2008b) identified a number of challenges encountered by front-line youth and children's workers. These included inadequate initial training and poor-quality leadership and management. It also highlighted concerns that not everyone in the children and young people's workforce is equipped with the necessary skills to work effectively with the most vulnerable children. The strategy set the agenda for the workforce to be well trained *throughout their careers* in order to improve their practice and advance their career prospects.

The UK general election in May 2010 produced no overall party majority and a Conservative–Liberal Democrat coalition government was established. A key idea of the new government is to create a *Big Society* (Cameron, 2009) where communities take more responsibility for delivering the services they receive. At the same time a worldwide financial crisis and recession has led to children's services across England having to make radical funding cuts and restructuring proposals.

Soon after coming to power the new government revoked the requirement for Children's Trusts to publish local children and young people's plans and announced a flurry of reviews on children and young people's policy. These included the following.

Childhood and Families Taskforce: Led by Prime Minister David Cameron this taskforce aims to make Britain *more family-friendly* (Clegg, 2010) and to look at the barriers to a happy childhood and successful family life. Among its areas of work it is exploring how the government can deliver on its commitment to promote a system of flexible parental leave. The taskforce is examining the support offered to parents of disabled children and the system of offering direct payments to carers. Further aims are to *look at how we can protect children in the event of family breakdown* and to find new solutions to creating secure spaces for children to play (Clegg, 2010). Responding to a consultation programme as part of this review, the Department for Education (DFE) noted public comments on the role of family in building cohesive societies. It recognised concerns about children growing up too early, teenagers not having enough to do, and difficulties for parents to balance family and working lives. It sees health visitors as playing a major role and restated the government commitment to providing an extra 4,200 health visitors. Free entitlement to nursery provision was extended to 15 hours per week for all three- and four-year-olds from September 2010. The coalition government has also expressed a commitment to take Sure Start back to its original purpose of early intervention with an increased focus on families in most need. It sees Sure Start Children's Centres as helping to address inequalities rooted in the start of a child's life.

Child poverty: In the *21st Century Welfare* paper launched in July 2010 the coalition government outlined its commitment to tackle child poverty through a system developed to help those trapped in a cycle of dependency where children are growing up in households in which neither parent works leading to a future stuck on benefits. The coalition government has stated it will maintain the goal set by the previous Labour government, which in 1999 pledged to eradicate child poverty in the UK by 2020.

A government-commissioned review of child poverty (Field, 2010) looked at life chances of children in the UK and set out to test the validity of the most commonly used definition of poverty. That threshold is a household income with 60 per cent or less of the average (median) UK household income in that year. The review concluded that the UK needs to address the issue of child poverty *in a fundamentally different way if it is to make a real change to children's life chances as adults.* It argued that a *shift of focus is needed* towards providing high-quality, integrated services aimed at supporting parents and improving the abilities of our poorest children during the first five years of a child's life.

There were two main recommendations in the report. First it proposed establishing a set of *Life Chances Indicators* that measure equality in life's outcomes for all children. Second it proposed establishing a new *Foundation Years status* covering the period from conception to age five. The Foundation Years, it is proposed, should become the first pillar of a new tripartite education system.

Child protection: The Munro review of children's social work and front-line child protection practice in England is looking at how communication between social work teams and universal children's services can be strengthened to improve early intervention processes. The team is also looking at how regulation can be simplified and bureaucracy reduced. Professor Munro's initial analysis of the child protection system (Munro, 2010) found that social workers are more focused on complying with processes and procedures, which is taking them away from spending time with vulnerable children and families. She said:

> A dominant theme in the criticisms of current practice is the skew in priorities that has developed between the demands of the management and inspection processes and professionals' ability to exercise their professional judgement and act in the best interests of the child. This has led to an over-standardised system that cannot respond adequately to the varied range of children's needs.
>
> (Munro, 2010, page 7)

The interim report also noted that serious case reviews, for example the case of Peter Connelly (Baby P), concentrate on errors when things go wrong rather than looking at ongoing good practice. It acknowledges other problems created by delays in the family courts impacting on the welfare of children, and professionals becoming demoralised by the failure of organisations to recognise the emotional impact of their work and to provide the support needed.

Children's Commissioner: The role of Children's Commissioner for England was created under the Children Act 2004 with the remit to promote awareness of the views and interests of children in England. The independent review of the role acknowledged that the Children's Commissioner has had *a significant impact on the lives of some children and young people*, but that overall the impact has been *disappointing* (Dunford, 2010, page 4). The government has subsequently welcomed the recommendations of the review to introduce legislation to strengthen the remit, powers and independence of the role (Dunford, 2010). Specifically the Office of the Children's Commissioner will merge with the Children's Rights Director in Ofsted to create the new Office of the Children's Commissioner for England. This strengthens the remit of the role by making it *rights-based*. The Commissioner will have greater independence from government by reporting directly to Parliament rather than the DfE. Increased powers include advising government on new policies, assessing the impact of new policies on children's rights, and making it the duty of government and local services to respond to concerns raised by the Commissioner. To improve the credibility of the post Dunford recommends that advice be always based on evidence and not on opinion. The post will be for a seven-year term.

Early intervention: This review (Allen, 2011) set out to examine how best models of early intervention schemes could be expanded across the country and how they can be funded by innovative and inventive means. The coalition government sees early intervention as the most appropriate means to tackle the root causes of some social problems. Intervening earlier with families, it is argued, can prevent children and parents falling into a cycle of deprivation, anti-social behaviour and poverty, thereby saving money in the long term. The *Early Intervention* review (Allen, 2011) stressed the need for a cultural shift towards stronger early intervention in children's services. It recommended the creation of an Early Intervention Foundation that would include central and local government, ethical and philanthropic trusts, foundations, charities and private investors. The foundation would be responsible for establishing *demonstrable improvements in the social and emotional bedrock of children* and would provide greater flexibility to innovate and to evaluate early intervention programmes throughout the country.

Early Years Foundation Stage (EYFS): The EYFS was introduced in 2008 to set standards in learning and welfare for those working and caring for children aged 0 to 5. It was in response to research highlighting how good quality childcare can support children's learning and development. The framework was split into two parts: first, learning and development requirements, and second, welfare requirements. The latter set out what providers must do to keep children safe, promote their welfare and ensure suitability of workers, premises, environment and equipment. The review of the EYFS (Tickell, 2011) aims to make it less bureaucratic and more focused on young children's learning and development so that the early years workforce will be spending more time with children and less time ticking boxes. Based on best and latest research evidence the review is considering if there should be one single framework for all early years providers, what is needed to give children the best start at school, whether young children's development should be formally assessed at a certain age and what standards are needed to keep children safe. Following the review, the subsequent report's recommended changes are expected to take effect in September 2012 after further consultation.

Special educational needs (SEN): This review aims to improve the SEN system to give parents of children with SEN or disabilities a choice of educational settings (mainstream, academy or special school); to make funding, including use of personal budgets for children and families, more transparent and cost-effective; to prevent unnecessary closure of special schools and involve parents in decisions about the future of special schools; to support young people with SEN and disabilities post-16 to succeed after education; and identify children with additional needs earlier through improved diagnosis and assessment. The coalition government believes that parents should be in control of their child's education and future, and wants all parents to have opportunities to get involved in the design and delivery of local services. A green paper making proposals for reform was published in 2011 (DfE, 2011).

Public health strategy: The white paper *Healthy Lives, Healthy People* (DH, 2010) sets out government plans for structural changes to the delivery of public health services and the proposed range of measures to improve the health and well being of children and young people. Key proposals included a *Public Health Responsibility Deal* to create partnerships with the corporate and voluntary sectors around food, alcohol, physical activity, health at work and behaviour change, and a child health promotion programme.

ACTIVITY 9.2

Choose one of the areas for review listed above and look for an update on progress with the recommendations using useful websites such as www.education.gov.uk or www.cypnow.co.uk. Write a few notes on the key findings, proposals and priorities of any report (an 'executive summary' of a report is a useful starting point). Find some of the responses to the report from organisations working in that area. Magazines such as *Children & Young People Now* or *Community Care* could be helpful.

The words in policy texts are used and positioned to present a case for change to the public and to influence the policy agenda (Scott, 2000). Policy texts may be found in government reports and documents, ministerial statements, departmental press releases, green and white papers. In August 2010, the magazine *Children & Young People Now* published details of an internal DfE memo revealing changes in government terminology since the coalition government took charge. The memo revealed words used before 11 May 2010 (when the coalition took office) and those with which they should be replaced. Key changes to phrases in the children's sector included the replacement of *Safeguarding* with *Child protection*; *Children's Trusts* with *Local areas, better, fairer services*; and using the term *Help children achieve more* in place of *Every Child Matters* or the *Five outcomes*. The government denied that the changes in the use of words indicated a change of policy direction and re-affirmed its commitment to *Every Child Matters* (DfES, 2003).

ACTIVITY 9.3

Here we look at interpreting the language of the coalition government. The memo referred to above suggested replacing the previous Labour government's aim that *England will be the best place in the world for children to grow up* with the coalition government aim to *make Britain the most family-friendly place in Europe*.

Think about your own practice area. What sorts of changes could you make to practice to make your organisation more *family-friendly*?

Training to work with children and young people

On its website CWDC refer to *a huge variety of qualifications available* to those wanting to join or progress in work with children, young people and families. In recent years different professions have demanded higher levels of entry qualification. For example social work, nursing, and youth work now look for university graduates with honours degrees. More recently the government has stated the aim that by 2015 all early years services will be graduate-led, with a requirement that all staff have a minimum Level 3 qualification that demonstrates their ability to work on their own initiative, plan and organise their work, and supervise others. A new standardised Level 3 Diploma for the children and young people's workforce was made available from September 2010, replacing previously existing diplomas in early years, social care and learning development support services. The aim of the Diploma is to simplify and rationalise the qualifications on offer and achieve a universal skills base across the workforce.

A range of training is available from colleges, universities, local authorities and independent providers that are full or part time, or work-based. Qualifications are offered at levels to suit all stages of career development. Specific professional qualifications in working with children and young people are available, for example within the early years workforce there are Early Years Professional Status (EYPS), National Professional Qualification in Integrated Centre Leadership, or Qualified Teacher Status (QTS).

The Skills Development Framework (SDF) was launched in 2010 by CWDC to support and inform the whole of the young people's workforce. It is intended to set out clear study progression pathways for those wishing to enter or develop new qualifications within the workforce. The SDF aims to support employers across the workforce to cultivate integrated working skills within their organisations. It informs employees, training providers, workforce development managers and national standard-setting bodies as they introduce and develop the skills and competences required for effective joined-up working. The framework provides a focus on the shared skills that underpin integrated working practice and that complement the important professional and specialist skills that workers already have. It provides a model that local employers can use to help improve support for young people. The SDF was reviewed in autumn 2010 to test its usefulness to employers, employees, volunteers and workforce development managers. You can access updated information about the framework at www.cwd council.org.uk/young-peoples-workforce/common-platform-of-skills-and-competences/sdf.

Roles within the children and young people's workforce

This section presents an overview of some of the roles within a large and diverse children and young people's workforce. A few illustrative examples of particular job roles are presented while indicating where you can get further information about the full range of career opportunities.

The children's workforce

Many jobs working with children are found within local authority, community, voluntary and private sector children and family services, including childcare, play work, residential work and work in educational settings. For example those without a relevant qualification can begin a career in early years work as an unqualified or apprentice childcare assistant, nursery assistant or assistant early years practitioner.

ACTIVITY 9.4

Make a list of practitioner roles involved in supporting a child or young person within an area of practice known to you.

Childcare or nursery assistants work with children aged 0 to 5 years in a range of settings such as pre-school, playgroups, crèches, day nurseries and children's centres. They work as part of a team that plans and organises stimulating educational and fun activities, while taking care of the children's personal needs such as food, washing and sleep. Unqualified assistants may need to have Maths and English GCSE at grade A–C and demonstrate motivation to work with children and families, as well as commitment to further study and training. Qualified assistants are likely to require at least a relevant Level 2 qualification and experience of working in a childcare environment.

ACTIVITY 9.5

Search the website www.direct.gov.uk for *Qualifications explained* under *Education and learning* for details on what the different levels mean (e.g. Level 2 or 3 qualifications).

Teaching or classroom assistants provide support to teachers in the classroom for children with learning or behavioural difficulties. They also offer general classroom or specific subject support such as preparing materials or covering literacy and numeracy. There are no set entry requirements although applicants are encouraged to have nationally recognised qualifications and previous relevant experience including nursery, play or youth work. Teaching assistants with Level 2 qualifications such as NVQ in Early Years Care and Education can work towards the

Level 3 Certificate for Teaching Assistants. Further progression could be to an Early Years Foundation Degree and EYPS, or to achieve the higher level teaching assistant (HLTA) status. HLTAs have higher levels of responsibility and may be required to supervise a class in the absence of the teacher. With this status teaching assistants can progress to teacher training by taking a degree leading to QTS.

Residential support workers, or care officers, are responsible for the safety and physical, social, emotional and educational well being of children in their care. They may take the lead role in co-ordinating the care planning process by working with the child, their family and other professional workers to meet that child's needs. Residential staff work to a rota system that enables the living unit to operate 24 hours a day, seven days a week. To work in this role requires paid or voluntary experience in the social care sector gained by working, for example, in a youth club, care home, nursery or with a relevant charity. Some may have experience of caring for a family member.

On starting the job the employer should provide induction training to approved national care standards known as the Common Induction Standards endorsed by Skills for Care (www.skillsforcare.org.uk/cis/). There is likely to be ongoing training throughout one's career. The General Social Care Council (GSCC) runs a register of qualified and student social workers in England. All social care workers, including support workers need to join the register and follow the GSCC Code of Practice (www.gscc.org.uk).

Social pedagogues (see Chapter 5 for a fuller discussion of this approach) are practitioners who work in a holistic way with children (or adults) embracing both social work and education. The roots of social pedagogy can be found in European countries such as Germany, Holland and Norway. The principles of social pedagogy have been increasingly observed in UK policy and practice. In 2007 the government announced a pilot programme to determine the impact of social pedagogic practice in children's residential care (Cameron et al., 2010). Social pedagogy is an integrated approach to care and education that does not recognise separate fields of disciplinary specialisation. It views the child or young person in a social context, where well being is a central concern. Social pedagogues are normally educated to degree level. You can read more about opportunities to train as a social pedagogue on the website www.socialpedagogyuk.com.

Case study 9.1 presents an example of how new job roles are emerging with responsibilities across different services. It is illustrative of the sort of workforce response that the coalition government is encouraging as it demonstrates a commitment to integration and to early intervention.

CASE STUDY 9.1   SOCIAL CARE WORKER

In one local authority there was an acknowledgement of tensions due to misunderstandings and lack of knowledge about roles between education and social care services. This was addressed by creating a social care worker post operating without a caseload. The social care worker works with schools, children's centres and social care services in a specific locality to improve working relationships between education and social care colleagues; to increase support and capacity for dealing with safeguarding and child protection issues within schools; and to pass on examples of good practice.

In one example the social care worker dealt with a mother and her child being harassed by an ex-partner who threatened potential abduction of the child. The mother told a member of staff at the nursery. On the day of the disclosure the social care worker met with the mother and member of the nursery staff. The worker then checked background information on the social care database and spoke to an appropriate colleague within the social care office. Informed and specific advice was given to the mother and nursery staff member. The harassment stopped within a few days and the mother felt more confident and knew what to do due to the advice received.

One head teacher acknowledged the usefulness of such interventions:

> [The social care worker]'s knowledge of social care process and procedure has supported and extended our working practice in school. In the past we could possibly have missed important pieces of information when supporting children and families. We have looked again at policies and procedures and updated and amended them. This has resulted in increased knowledge across the whole staff team and ultimately a higher level of safeguarding for our children and families.

The young people's workforce

A Picture Worth Millions (CWDC, 2009c) gives an overview of the numbers of people in the young people's workforce (see Figure 9.1). The research identified 775,150 paid workers and 5,272,600 volunteers. The largest sectors of paid workers were in sport and recreation (363,000), health (153,000), play work (110,000) and youth work (77,000). The largest numbers of volunteers were in sport and recreation and voluntary youth services such as the Scouts. The young people's workforce includes education welfare officers, learning mentors, Connexions personal advisers and those working in similar support roles.

Education welfare officers (EWOs) (or education social workers) work with young people whose education is being affected by poor attendance at school caused by family problems, health and psychological problems, bullying, inability to cope with schoolwork, poor relationships with teachers or lack of family support. EWOs work with parents and carers and in partnership with other staff to support children and young people. They are often employed directly by schools or special projects. EWOs are likely to have studied for a degree in social work or a related profession such as teaching or youth work.

Learning mentors usually work in schools or colleges with pupils of all abilities who need help to overcome difficulties that affect their learning. Learning mentors develop one to one supportive relationships and also work in group settings. The work of a learning mentor focuses on identifying the difficulties preventing the child or young person from reaching their full potential; helping pupils with study skills; developing anti-bullying strategies or personal skills to improve self-confidence, self-esteem and resilience; and helping pupils to modify their behaviours using techniques such as anger management. Minimum entry requirements of local education authorities or schools expect a good standard of general education including literacy and numeracy, as well as experience of working paid or unpaid with children or young people. Some employers expect a qualification or experience in areas such as teaching, learning support, social work, education welfare, youth work or counselling. You can get experience as a volunteer mentor by visiting the Mentoring and Befriending Foundation website at www.mandbf.org.uk/.

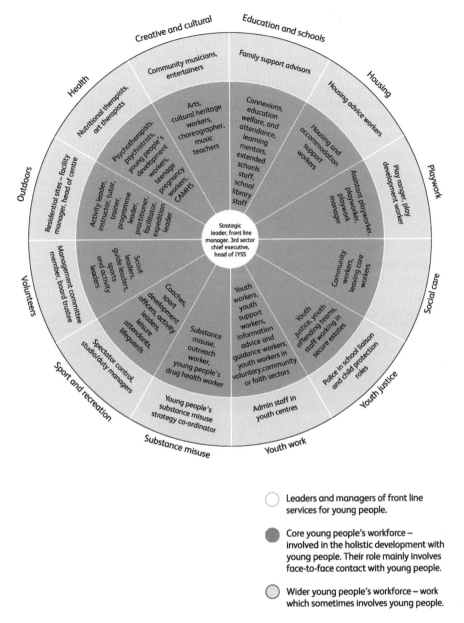

Figure 9.1 **Overview of the young people's workforce**
Source: CWDC (2009c, page 6).

New learning mentors can complete a National Learning Mentor Induction Training Programme followed by further in-service training.

Connexions personal advisers were introduced when the Connexions Service was established in 2001 with the aim of providing a comprehensive service to meet young people's need for impartial information, advice and support. Personal advisers access opportunities to help the young person's learning and progression and to ensure a smooth transition into adulthood and working life. Connexions Services aim to help all young people aged 13 to 19, and those aged up to 24 with a learning difficulty or disability. There is a particular focus on those at risk of being not in education, employment or training (NEET) and becoming socially excluded.

To become a personal adviser you need experience of working with young people and a professional qualification equivalent to at least NVQ Level 4 in Advice and Guidance or in Learning, Development and Support Services for Children, Young People and Those Who Care for Them; or the Qualification in Careers Guidance (QCG). A qualification in social work, youth work or education may also be accepted.

ACTIVITY 9.6

Read some of the stories of people who work in roles such as the ones described above by visiting the CWDC website at www.cwdcouncil.org.uk/ldss.

Youth housing support workers work with young people moving from hostel or temporary accommodation to their own flat. They will support young people to keep their tenancy by helping them to get into education, training or employment, or in practical tasks such as shopping for furniture, getting them registered with a doctor and dentist, or developing budgeting and other life skills. The Chartered Institute of Housing (www.cih.org/services/careers) accredits a range of housing-related qualifications. Shelter, *a charity working to alleviate the distress caused by homelessness and bad housing*, also provides training courses for people working in the housing sector (http://england.shelter.org.uk). Since 2009 a new qualification, the Award or Certificate in Working with Vulnerable Young People at Levels 3 or 4, has been available.

Youth justice workers work with different agencies and professionals to engage and enthuse young people in order to prevent offending and address youth crime. You can get involved as a professional practitioner or as a volunteer. Gaining relevant qualifications such as the Foundation Degree in Youth Justice as outlined in the Youth Justice National Qualifications Framework, can lead to employment with a Youth Offending Team (YOT). Within the YOT you may develop a specialist area such as substance misuse, accommodation, education and training. You might work within a secure establishment, such as a young offender institution, as an educator, custody officer or care officer. As a volunteer within the youth justice system you could volunteer as a *mentor, youth offender panel member* or *appropriate adult*.

ACTIVITY 9.7

Use the suggestions below, or any in the useful resources section at the end of this chapter, to identify job adverts and information about job roles working with children, young people and families that might interest you:

- www.barnardos.org.uk/work_with_us.htm
- www.cypnowjobs.co.uk
- www.lgcareers.com/
- https://nextstep.direct.gov.uk/Pages/Home.aspx
- www.publicjobsdirect.com/

List some of the job roles advertised under the following headings:

- *Working with young people* (e.g. learning mentor; youth adviser).
- *School age* (e.g. pupil support worker; learning support assistant).
- *Pre-school* (e.g. early years assistant; child support worker).
- *Specialist settings* (e.g. residential project worker; children's centre outreach worker).
- *Play* (e.g. community play worker; play ranger).
- *Parents/families* (e.g. parent outreach worker; family support worker).

Find out more about the roles by accessing general career information on the work, hours, salary, entry requirements, further training and development:

- Select two jobs of interest – one to apply for with your current experience and qualifications; and one for an aspirational application in the future.
- Access the job and person specifications online, by post, phone or email.
- Prepare/update your CV (enter *cv writing* in the search site of www.direct.gov.uk/ to access useful information).
- Devise a PDP or action plan of what qualifications, experience, skills and knowledge you need, and how you will get these through courses, further training and staff development.

Personal Development Planning (PDP)

According to Knott and Scragg (2010, page 18) *all university students are being encouraged/ required to undertake some form of PDP self-evaluation*. A PDP can be a map to guide you to develop your career by using the following steps:

- **Step 1: Describe and analyse your skills and personal qualities.** Draw up a list of your current skills and personal qualities that are relevant to working with children, young people and their families. Analyse these skills and qualities – what do you notice? Which seem particularly useful in current practice? Evaluate strengths and areas to improve. From this assessment, you can identify the skills or personal qualities you wish to grow, develop your goals and consider ways to accomplish them.
- **Step 2: Refine and develop your personal goals.** Think about your short-, mid- and long-term goals for between six months to five years. Your goals should be written down as SMART so that each is: Specific– what will you do? Measurable – what evidence will show if and how well you have done it? Achievable – is it possible? Relevant or Realistic – why is it important? Time-bound – by when will it be done? For example, a short-term goal might be to give a brief presentation at your next staff meeting about recent training you attended. This is an opportunity to develop skills and confidence in communicating with other professionals and to share information relevant to the workplace setting. Seek feedback on the presentation from your line manager/supervisor and others at the meeting as further evidence of what you did and how well.
- **Step 3: Action plan to reach goals.** Now that you have set your goals, what will you do to achieve them all? Devise an action plan that sets out what you will do, when and how in order to reach your goals.

- **Step 4: Review and update action plan.** Constant review of your personal development plan is the key to successful career development. It is important to regularly review and update your plan and CV.

A changing landscape

The picture presented by this chapter is one of ongoing change for those currently working in, or preparing to join, the children and young people's workforce. That change is seen not just in the job titles, roles and responsibilities but also in the wider landscape of policy. As we finish writing this chapter the reviews and policy changes continue to create uncertainty.

In October 2010 the government announced its decision to abolish the Youth Justice Board (YJB) in what has become known as the *bonfire of the quangos* (www.guardian.co.uk/politics/ 2011/jan/07/mps-committee-bonfire-quangos-botched). The YJB function of overseeing youth offending teams, spreading good practice and commissioning custody places is to be transferred to the Ministry of Justice raising concerns that management of youth justice *switches from experts with frontline practical experience of working with young offenders to civil servants* (Chandiramani, 2010).

In November 2010 the government declared its intention to withdraw funding from CWDC in order to direct money to front-line services. The sector skills council for the children's workforce will cease being a separate public body from government and see its functions taken over by the DfE. Those responsibilities will be transferred by 2012 although it is envisaged that CWDC will continue in some form (Higgs, 2010).

Whatever change and uncertainty lies ahead, it remains the case that the current children and young people's workforce of paid workers and unpaid volunteers is a significant proportion of the overall UK workforce. Governments, departmental structures, policies, agencies and job roles may change. However the knowledge and practical skills set out in the Common Core and presented at the beginning of each chapter in this book provide a stable foundation. It is this knowledge and those practical skills that will be required by employers to develop a skilled, qualified, flexible, competent, reflexive and confident workforce capable of delivering the best possible outcomes for children and young people in the UK.

CHAPTER SUMMARY

This chapter has presented the background history and policy context to developing the children and young people's workforce with reference to recent changes, reports and reviews. It has identified a variety of qualifications and training routes while indicating where the reader can find further useful information. The chapter has outlined some job roles and responsibilities within a large and diverse workforce. Activities have been included to encourage the reader to find out details on these and other roles. The chapter has concluded by inviting the reader to identify their own career and job opportunities, and to produce a PDP to set out their goals and aspirations for working with children, young people and their families.

USEFUL RESOURCES

www.barnardos.org.uk Barnardo's is a charity running projects throughout the UK working directly with families to provide services for children in poverty, young carers or children who have been sexually exploited.

www.cwdcouncil.org.uk/assets/0000/4335/LDSS_Brochure_Jan09.pdf A helpful brochure explaining the range of roles within Learning Development and Support Services for young people.

www.cwdcouncil.org.uk/workforce-data/occupational-summaries CWDC produces a series of summary sheets of occupations within the children and young people's workforce that cover job role, details of the workforce, pay and rewards, qualification levels, entry requirements, progression routes, training providers, and representational associations, trade bodies or unions.

www.cypnowjobs.co.uk This is a valuable source for looking for jobs across the children and young people's sector.

www.direct.gov.uk The official website of the UK government that includes information about all public services.

www.justice.gov.uk This web site is aimed at all practitioners working with young offenders. It encompasses online content from the Youth Justice Board, Ministry of Justice, Her Majesty's Courts Service, the Prison Service, the Legal Services Commission and many other justice agencies

www.ncma.org.uk The National Childminding Association (NCMA) is a charity and professional association working with registered childminders, nannies and other individuals or organisations in the area of home-based childcare, play, learning and family support.

www.ncvys.org.uk The National Council for Voluntary Youth Services (NCVYS) website contains information on how to find a volunteer placement, careers advice and funding sources to pay for training courses. Click on *Training* from the homepage menu.

www.teachingexpertise.com Use this website to search for *youth justice worker*. This will take you to an article about *a day in the life of a youth justice worker*.

www.yjb.gov.uk The YJB has information about working in the youth justice system. Click on *Get involved* from the *Public* section to find out more about the different roles as a volunteer or as a practitioner.

FURTHER READING

Brotherton, G, Davies, H and McGillivray, G (eds) (2010) *Working With Children Young People and Families*. London: Sage. This book is an introduction to the policy, theory and practice of working with children, young people and families.

Cottrell, S (2010) *Skills for Success: The Personal Development Planning Handbook* (2nd edition). Basingstoke: Palgrave Macmillan. This presents creative and constructive ways for students to think about their personal, academic and career goals.

National Centre for Social Research/Institute of Volunteering Research (2007) *Helping Out: A National Survey of Volunteering and Charitable Giving*. London: National Centre for Social Research/Institute of Volunteering Research. This national survey of volunteering and charitable giving was carried out in 2007, following on from the 1997 National Survey of Volunteering and the 2005 Citizenship Survey.

Pearson, I (2006) *Working with Young People: Real Life Guides*. Richmond: Trotman Publishing. Contains information, tips and case studies from people who work with young people as well as practical advice on what qualifications you need to succeed.

References

Action for Children (2009) *Stuck in the Middle: The Importance of Supporting Six to 13 Year Olds.* London: Action for Children.

Aldgate, J (2001) *The Children Act 1989 Now: Messages from Research.* London: DH.

Allat, P and Keil, T (1987) *Women and the Life Cycle: Transitions and Turning-Points. Explorations in Sociology.* Basingstoke: Macmillan Press.

Alexander, R (ed) (2009) *Children, their World, their Education: Final Report and Recommendations of the Cambridge Primary Review.* London: Routledge.

Allen, G (2011) *Early Intervention: Next Steps.* London: Cabinet Office.

Anning, A, Cottrell, D, Frost, N, Green, J and Robinson, M (2010) *Developing Multi-Professional Teamwork for Integrated Children's Services* (2nd edition). Maidenhead: Open University Press.

Ariès, P (1962) *Centuries of Childhood.* London: Penguin.

Arnstein, S (1969) A ladder of citizen participation. *Journal of the American Planning Association,* 35(4): 216–224.

Artaraz, K (2005) New Labour's 0 to 19 agenda: Social inclusion in an age of change. Paper presented at International Conference: 'Community, Work and Family: Change and Transformation', Manchester Metropolitan University, 16 March 2005. Available at: www.did.stu.mmu.ac.uk/cwf/index.shtml (last accessed 2 March 2011).

Atkinson, D (1999) *Advocacy: A Review.* Brighton: Pavilion Publishing/Joseph Rowntree Foundation.

Audit Commission (1994) *Seen But Not Heard: Detailed Evidence and Guidelines for Managers and Practitioners: Co-ordinating Community Child Health and Social Services for Children in Need.* London: Audit Commission.

Audit Commission (2007) *Changing Lanes: Evolving Roles in Road Safety.* London: Audit Commission.

Badham, B and Wade, H (2005) *Hear By Right: Standards for the Active Involvement of Children and Young People.* Leicester/London: NYA/LGA.

BANES (Bath and North East Somerset) (2008) *Early Years Transition Toolkit.* Available at: www.c4eo.org.uk/themes/general/resources.aspx?tab=tools&dm_i=7SL,4XOA,12Q33V, FC8F,1 (last accessed 2 March 2011).

Barker, R (2009) *Making Sense of Every Child Matters.* Bristol: The Policy Press.

Barnes, J, Leach, P, Malmberg, L, Stein, A and Sylva, K (2010) Experiences of childcare in England and socio-emotional development at 36 months. *Early Child Development & Care*, 180(9): 1215–1229.

Barrett, G and Keeping, C (2005) The processes required for effective interprofessional working, in Barrett, G, Sellman, D and Thomas, J (eds) *Interprofessional Working in Health and Social Care*. Basingstoke: Palgrave.

BBC News (2009) *Young 'Resent' Negative Images*. Available at: http://news.bbc.co.uk/1/hi/education/7820245.stm (last accessed 1 September 2010).

BBC News (2010) *BBC Survey of Young Carers*. Available at: www.bbc.co.uk/news/education-11757907 (last accessed 9 January 2011).

Beck, AT (1976) *Cognitive Therapy and the Emotional Disorders*. New York: International Universities Press.

Beckett, C (2006) *Essential Theory for Social Work Practice*. London: Sage.

Bee, H and Boyd, D (2009) *Developing Child* (12th edition). London: Allyn & Bacon.

Beinart, S, Anderson, B, Lee, S and Utting, D (2002) *A National Survey of Problem Behaviour and Associated Risk and Protective Factors among Young People*. York: Joseph Rowntree Foundation Publications.

Belsky, J, Lowe Vandell, D, Burchinal, M, Clarke-Stewart, K, McCartney, K and Tresch Owen, M (2007) Are there long-term effects of early child care? *Child Development*, 78(2): 681–701.

Bichard, M. (2004) *The Bichard Inquiry Report*. London: The Stationery Office.

Black, S, Devereux, P. and Salvanes, K (2005) The more the merrier? The effect of family size and birth order of children's education. *The Quarterly Journal of Economics*, 120(2): 669–700.

Bowlby, J (1953) *Childcare and the Growth of Love*. London: Penguin.

Bowlby, J (1957) *Maternal Care and Mental Health: A Report on Behalf of the World Health Organisation*. Geneva: World Health Organisation Monographs.

Bowlby, J (1969) *Attachment & Loss*. London: Hogarth Press.

Bowlby, J (1988) *A Secure Base: Clinical Applications of Attachment Theory*. London: Tavistock.

Bowlby, J, Fry, M and Ainsworth, M (1965) *Child Care and Growth of Love*. London: Penguin.

Boylan, J and Dalrymple, J (2009) *Understanding Advocacy for Children and Young People*. Maidenhead: McGraw-Hill.

Bradley, H and Hickman, P (2004) In and out of work? The changing fortunes of young people in contemporary labour markets, in Roche, J, Tucker, S, Thomson, R and Flynn, R (eds) *Youth In Society* (2nd edition). London: Sage.

Braye, S (2000) Participation and involvement in social care, in Kemshall, H and Littlechild, R (eds) *User Involvement and Participation in Social Care*. London: Jessica Kingsley Publishing.

Bredekamp, S and Copple, C (1997) *Developmentally Appropriate Practice*. Washington DC: National Association for the Education of Young Children.

Broadhead, P and Martin, D (2009) Education and *Every Child Matters*, in Barker, R (ed) *Making Sense of Every Child Matters*. Bristol: Policy Press.

Brown, C (1993) Blair targets 'family values' as a platform for Labour. *The Independent*, 26 June 1993. Available at: www.independent.co.uk/news/uk/politics/blair-targets-family-values-as-a-platform-for-labour-1493951.html (last accessed 1 July 2010).

Bruce, T (1991) *Time to Play in Early Childhood Education*. Sevenoaks: Hodder & Stoughton.

Bruner, J (1977) *The Process of Education* (2nd edition). Cambridge, MA: Harvard University Press.

Bryant, L. (2009) The art of active listening. *Practice Nurse*, 37(6): 49–52.

Butler-Schloss, E (1988) *Report of the Committee of Inquiry into Child Sexual Abuse in Cleveland 1987*. London: HMSO.

Bynner, J (2001) British youth transitions in comparative perspective. *Journal of Youth Studies*, 4(1): 5–23.

Byron, T (2008) *Safer Children in a Digital World: The Report of the Byron Review*. Nottingham: DCSF Publications.

Byron, T (2010) *The State of Play: Back to Basics.* Paris: Disneyland.

Cabinet Office (1999) *Modernising Government*, Cm 4310, March. London: The Stationery Office.

Cabinet Office (2010) *Prime Minister to Launch National Citizen Service Pilots for Young People.* Available at: www.cabinetoffice.gov.uk/news/prime-minister-launch-national-citizen-service-pilots-young-people (last accessed 2 March 2011).

Cairns S. (2000) Coming of age – the travel of young adults. *Town and Country Planning*, 69(4): 106–107.

Cameron, C, Jasper, A, Kleipoedszus, S, Petrie, P and Wigfall, V (2010) *Implementing the DCSF Pilot Programme: The Work of the First Year, Social Pedagogy Briefing Paper.* London: Thomas Coram Research Unit, Institute of Education.

Cameron, D (2009) *David Cameron: The Big Society.* Available at: www.conservatives.com/News/Speeches/2009/11/David_Cameron_The_Big_Society.aspx (last accessed 1 October 2010).

Cameron, D (2010) *Mending our Broken Society: Conservative Speech.* Available at: www.conservatives.com/News/Speeches/2010/01/David_Cameron_Mending_our_Broken_Society.aspx (last accessed 1 July 2010).

Case, S (2000) Refocusing on the parent: what are the social issues of concern for parents of disabled children? *Disability and Society*, 15(2): 271–292.

Chandiramani, R (2010) Abolition of YJB is difficult to justify. *Children & Young People Now*, 19 October.

Chawla, L and Malone, K (2003) Neighbourhood quality in children's eyes, in Christensen, P and O'Brian, M (eds) *Children in the City: Home, Neighbourhood and Community.* London: Routledge.

Child Abuse – A History (nd) Available at: http://www.libraryindex.com/pages/1361/Child-Abuse-History-ABUSE-DURING-INDUSTRIAL-REVOLUTION.html">Child Abuse—A History – Abuse During The Industrial Revolution (last accessed 10 March 2011).

Children and Young People Now (2010) National Citizen Service is a costly error. Available at: www.cypnow.co.uk/news/1031068/National-Citizen-Service-costly-error/ (last accessed 1 October 2010).

Children's Rights Alliance for England (2005) *Ready, Steady, Go: Participation Training Pack.* London: CRAE.

Claridge, J (2008) *At What Age Can I . . .?* London: The Children's Legal Centre.

Clarke, J and Newman, J (1997) *The Managerial State.* London: Sage.

Claxton, RP (1994) Empirical relationships between birth order and two types of parental feedback. *Psychological Record*, 44: 475–487.

Clegg, N (2010) *Deputy PM's Speech on Children and Families.* Available at: www.dpm.cabinetoffice.gov.uk/news/deputy-pms-speech-children-and-families (last accessed 10 March 2011).

Cohen, S (1978) *Folk Devils & Moral Panics: The Creation of the Mods and Rockers.* Oxford: Blackwell.

Coleman, J and Hagell, A (eds) (2007) *Adolescence, Risk and Resilience: Against the Odds.* Chichester: John Wiley.

Coleman, J, Catan, L and Dennison, C (2004) 'You're the last person I'd talk to', in Roche J, Tucker, S, Thomson, R and Flynn, R (eds) *Youth in Society* (2nd edition). London: Sage.

Coles, B (2004) Welfare services for young people, in Roche J, Tucker, S, Thomson, R and Flynn, R (eds) *Youth in Society* (2nd edition). London: Sage.

Cooper, D (2004) *Challenging Diversity: Rethinking Equality and the Value of Difference.* Cambridge: Cambridge University Press.

Cowen, A (2010) *Personalised Transition: Innovations in Health Education and Support.* Sheffield: The Centre for Welfare Reform.

Crick, B (1998) *Education for Citizenship and the Teaching of Democracy in Schools: The Crick Report.* London: QCA.

Cronin, M and Smith, C (2010) From safeguarding to Safeguarding, in Brotherton, G, Davies, H and McGillivray, G (eds) *Working with Children, Young People and Families.* London: Sage.

Crosby, D and Hawkes, D (2007) Cross-national research using contemporary birth cohort studies: a look at early maternal employment in the UK and USA. *International Journal of Social Research Methodology*, 10(5): 379–404.

Crosby, M (2005) Working with people as an informal educator, in Harrison, R and Wise, C (eds) *Working with Young People.* London: Sage.

Cumming, GS, Barnes, G, Perz, S, Schmink, M, Sieving, KE, Southworth, J, Binford, M, Holt, RD, Stickler, C and Van Holt, T (2005) An exploratory framework for empirical measurement of resilience. *Ecosystems*, 8: 975–987.

CWDC (2008) *The State of the Children's Social Care Workforce 2008.* Leeds: CWDC.

CWDC (2009a) *The Common Assessment Framework for Children and Young People.* Leeds: CWDC.

CWDC (2009b) *Social Pedagogy and its Implications for the Youth Workforce.* Leeds: CWDC.

CWDC (2009c) *A Picture Worth Millions: State of the Young People's Workforce.* Leeds: CWDC.

CWDC (2010a) *The Common Core of Skills and Knowledge: At the Heart of What You Do.* Leeds: CWDC.

CWDC (2010b) *Skills Development Framework: A Model to Support Local Employers Develop Integrated Working within the Young People's Workforce.* Leeds: CWDC.

Dahl, R (2003) Beyond raging hormones: the tinderbox in the teenage brain. *Cerebrum: The Dana Forum on Brain Science*, 5(3): 7–22.

Dalrymple, J and Oliver, CM (2008) Advocacy, participation and voice, in Oliver, CM and Dalrymple, J (eds) *Developing Advocacy for Children and Young People: Current Issues in Research, Policy and Practice.* London: Jessica Kingsley.

Daly, G (2004) Understanding the barriers to multiprofessional collaboration. *Nursing Times*, 100(9): 78.

Daniel, B and Wassell, S (2002) *Assessing and Promoting Resilience In Vulnerable Children.* London: Jessica Kingsley.

Daniel, B, Wassell, S and Gilligan, R (1999) *Child Development for Child Care and Protection Workers.* London: Jessica Kingsley.

Davis, JM and Hogan, J (2004) Research with children: ethnography, participation, disability and self empowerment, in Barnes, C and Mercer, G (eds) *Implementing the Social Model of Disability: Theory and Research.* Leeds: The Disability Press.

DCSF (2007a) *Extended Schools: Building on Experience.* Nottingham: DCSF Publications.

DCSF (2007b) *The Children's Plan: Building Brighter Futures.* London: HMSO.

DCSF (2008a) *Building Brighter Futures: Next Steps for the Children's Workforce*, DCSF-00292-2008. Nottingham: DCSF Publications.

DCSF (2008b) *2020 Children and Young People's Workforce Strategy*, DCSF-01052-2008. Nottingham: DCSF Publications.

DCSF (2008c) *Care Matters: Time to Deliver for Children in Care.* Nottingham: DCSF Publications.

DCSF (2008d) *Statutory Framework for the Early Years Foundation Stage.* Nottingham: DCSF Publications

DCSF (2009a) *The Children's Plan Two Years On*, DCSF-01162-2009. Nottingham: DCSF Publications.

DCSF (2009b) *Learning, Playing and Interacting: Good Practice in the Early Years Foundation Stage.* Nottingham: DCSF Publications.

DCSF (2010) *Working Together to Safeguard Children: A Guide to Inter-Agency Working to Safeguard and Promote the Welfare of Children.* Nottingham: DCFS Publications.

De Mause, L (ed) (1974) *History of Childhood.* London: Souvenir Press.

DfE (2010a) *Practitioners Experiences of the Early Years Foundation Stage*, ref: DFE-RR029. London: DfE.

DfE (2010b) *The Importance of Teaching – The Schools White Paper 2010*, Cm 7980. London: The Stationery Office.

DfE (2011) *Support and Aspiration: A new approach to special educational needs and disability*, Cm 8027, London: The Stationery Office.

DfEE (2000) *The Connexions Service: Professional Framework for Personal Advisers: Proposals for Consultation.* Nottingham: DfEE.

DfES (1998) *Quality Protects.* London: DfES.

DfES (2003) *Every Child Matters*, Cm 5860. London: The Stationery Office.

DfES (2004a) *Choice for Parents, The Best Start for Children: A Ten Year Strategy for Childcare.* Norwich: HMSO.

DfES (2004b) *Every Child Matters: Change for Children*, ref: 1081/2004. Nottingham: DfES Publications.

DfES (2004c) *Working Together: Giving Children and Young People a Say for Schools and Local Education Authorities.* Nottingham: DfES Publications.

DfES (2005a) *The Children's Workforce Strategy: A Strategy to Build a World-Class Workforce for Children and Young People.* Nottingham: DfES Publications.

DfES (2005b) *Extended Schools: Access to Opportunities and Services for All.* Nottingham: DfES Publications.

DfES (2006a) *Making it Happen: Working Together for Children, Young People and Families.* Nottingham: DfES Publications.

DfES (2006b) *The Lead Professional: Every Child Matters Fact Sheet, April 2006.* Nottingham: DfES Publications.

DfES (2008) *Practice Guidance for the Early Years Foundation Stage*, ref: 00266-2008BKT-EN. Nottingham: DfES Publications.

DH (1995) *Child Protection and Child Abuse: Messages from Research.* London: The Stationery Office.

DH (1999) *Quality Protects.* London: The Stationery Office.

DH (2000) *Framework for Assessment of Children in Need.* London: DH/DfEE.

DH (2001) *Valuing People: A Strategy for Learning Disability for the 21st Century*, Cm 5086. London: The Stationery Office.

DH (2003) *Equalities and Diversity: Strategy and Delivery Plan to Support the NHS.* London: The Stationery Office.

DH (2010) *Healthy Lives, Healthy People: Our Strategy for Public Health in England*, Cm 7985. London: The Stationery Office.

Doherty, J and Hughes, M (2009) *Child Development: Theory and Practice 0–11.* Harlow: Pearson.

Dunford, J (2010) *Children and Young People's Guide: Review of the Children's Commissioner in England*. London: DfE.

Dunn, J (1988) *The Beginnings of Social Understanding*. Oxford: Blackwell.

Dyhouse, C (1977) Good wives and little mothers: social anxieties and the schoolgirl's curriculum, 1890–1920. *Oxford Review of Education*, 3(1): 21–35.

Edwards, R, Hadfield, L and Mauthner, M (2005) *Children's Understanding of their Sibling Relationships: Summary of the Full Report*. Available at: http://www.jrf.org.uk/publications/childrens-understanding-their-sibling-relationships (last accessed 13 November 2010).

Egan, G (1998) *The Skilled Helper: A Problem-Management Approach to Helping* (6th edition). Pacific Grove, CA: Brooks/Cole Publishing.

Field, F (2010) *The Foundation Years: Preventing Poor Children Becoming Poor Adults: The Report of the Independent Review on Poverty and Life Chances*. London: Cabinet Office.

Fisher, T (1974) *Report of the Committee of Inquiry into the Care and Supervision Provided in Relation to Maria Colwell*. London: HMSO.

Furlong, A and Cartmel, F (1997) *Young People and Social Change*. Buckingham: Open University Press.

Gaine, C (ed) (2010) *Equality and Diversity in Social Work Practice*. Exeter: Learning Matters.

Gamble, A (1996) *Hayek: The Iron Cage of Liberty*. London: Westview Press.

Gardner, R (2009) 'Hoodies, louts, scum': how media demonises teenagers. *The Independent*, 9 June. Available at: www.independent.co.uk/news/uk/home-news/hoodies-louts-scum-how-media-demonises-teenagers-1643964.html (last accessed 1 September 2010).

Garrett, PM (2009) *Transforming Children's Services: Social Work, Neoliberalism and the 'Modern' World*. Maidenhead: Open University Press.

Gaventa, J (2006) *Triumph, Deficit or Contestation? Deepening the 'Deepening Democracy' Debate*. Brighton: Institute of Development Studies.

Gilligan, R (2000) Adversity, resilience and young people: the protective value of positive school and spare time experiences. *Children & Society*, 14: 37–47.

Gittins, D (1993) *The Family in Question: Changing Households & Familiar Ideologies* (2nd edition). London: Macmillan.

Goldschmied, E and Jackson, S (1994) *People under Three: Young Children in Daycare*. London: Routledge.

Goodman, A (2009) *Social Work with Drug and Substance Misusers* (2nd edition). Exeter: Learning Matters.

Gordon, T (1974) *Teacher Effectiveness Training*. New York: Peter Wyden.

Gordon, T (2000) *Parent Effectiveness Training: The Proven Program for Raising Responsible Children*. New York: Three Rivers Press.

Gordon-Rouse, KA (2001) Resilient students' goals and motivation. *Journal of Adolescence*, 24(4): 461–472.

Gough, D (1996) Defining the problem. *Child Abuse and Neglect*, 20(11): 993–1002.

Gove, M (2010) *Letter to Eileen Munro*. Available at: www.education.gov.uk/munroreview (last accessed 3 March 2011).

Grant, A (ed) (2010) *Cognitive Behavioural Interventions for Mental Health Practitioners*. Exeter: Learning Matters.

Green, J and Hert, L (1998) Children's views of accident risks and prevention: a qualitative study. *Injury Prevention*, 4: 14–21.

Gregg, P, Washbrook, E, Propper, C and Burgess, S (2005) The effects of a mother's return to work decision on child development in the UK. *The Economic Journal*, 115: 48–80.

Halpern, D (2005) *Social Capital.* Cambridge: Polity Press.

Hanawalt, BA (2002) Medievalists and the study of childhood. *Speculum*, 77(2): 440–460.

Hansen, K and Hawkes, D (2009) Early childcare and child development. *Journal of Social Policy*, 38(2): 211–219.

Hardiman, R and Jackson, BW (1997) Conceptual foundations for social justice courses, in Adams, MA, Bell, LA and Griffin, P (eds) *Teaching for Diversity and Social Justice: A Sourcebook.* New York: Routledge.

Harnett, R (2004) Doing peer advocacy: insights from the field. *Representing Children*, 17(2): 131–141.

Hart, R (1992) *Children's Participation: From Tokenism to Citizenship.* Florence: UNICEF.

Hassan, J, Grogan, S, Clark-Carter, D, Richards, H and Yates, V (2009) The individual health burden of acne: appearance-related distress in male and female adolescents and adults with back, chest and facial acne. *Journal of Health Psychology*, 14: 1105–1118.

Heafford, M (1967) *Pestalozzi: His Thought and its Relevance Today.* London: Methuen.

Healey, M and Ellis, B (2007) Birth order, conscientiousness, and openness to experience tests of the family-niche model of personality using a within-family methodology. *Evolution and Human Behaviour*, 28: 55–59.

Henderson, S, Holland, J, McGrellis, S, Sharpe, S, and Thomson, R (2007) *Inventing Adulthoods: A Biographical Approach to Youth Transitions.* London: Sage.

Henricson, C (2003) *Resolving the Tensions in Parenting Policy.* York: Joseph Rowntree Foundation. Available at: www.jrf.org.uk/publications/resolving-tensions-parenting-policy (last accessed 3 March 2011).

Hetherington, R, Cooper, A, Smith, P and Wilford, G (1997) *Protecting Children: Messages from Europe.* Lyme Regis: Russell House Publishing.

Higgs, L (2010) CWDC to lose government funding. *Children & Young People Now*, 16 November 2010.

Hills, J, Brewer, M, Jenkins, S, Lister, S, Lupton, R, Machin, S, Mills, C, Modood, T, Rees, T and Riddell, S (2010) *The Anatomy of Economic Inequality in UK: Report of the National Equality Panel.* London: Government Equalities Office.

Hockey, J and James, A (1993) *Growing Up and Growing Old: Ageing and Dependency in the Life Course.* London: Sage.

Holt, N (2007) *Bringing the High/Scope Approach to Your Early Years Practice.* Abingdon: Routledge.

Horwath, J and Morrison, T (2007) Collaboration, integration and change in children's services: critical issues and key ingredients. *Child Abuse & Neglect*, 31: 55–69.

Houston, S (2010) Building resilience in a children's home: results from an action research project. *Child and Family Social Work*, 15(3): 357–368.

Howe, N and Recchia, H (2006) Sibling relations and their impact on children's development, in Tremblay, RE, Barr, RG and Peters, RDeV (eds) *Encyclopedia on Early Childhood Development* [online]. Montreal: Centre of Excellence for Early Childhood Development. Available at: http://www.child-encyclopedia.com/documents/Howe-RecchiaANGxp.pdf (last accessed 3 March 2011).

Hughes, G (1998) *Unsettling Welfare: The Reconstruction of Social Policy.* London: Routledge.

Hutt, SJ (1989) *Play Exploration and Learning: A Natural History of the Pre-School.* London: Routledge.

Jackson, S and Sachdev, D (2001) *Better Education, Better Futures: Research, Practice and the Views of Young People in Public Care.* Ilford: Barnardo's.

James, A, Jenks, C and Prout, A (1998) *Theorizing Childhood.* Cambridge: Polity Press.

Jefferson, T, Herbst, J and McCrae, R (1998) Associations between birth order and personality traits: evidence from self-reports and observer ratings. *Journal of Research in Personality*, 32: 498–509.

Jeffs, T and Smith, M (2006) Where is 'Youth Matters' taking us? *Youth and Policy*, 91: 23–41.

Jeffs, T and Smith, M (2010) *Youth Work Practice.* Hampshire: Palgrave.

Jenks, C (1996) *Childhood.* London: Routledge.

John, M (2003) *Children's Rights and Power: Charging Up for a New Century* London: Jessica Kingsley Publications.

Johnson, F, Wardle, J and Griffith, J (2002) The adolescent food habits checklist: reliability and validity of a measure of health eating behaviour in adolescents. *European Journal of Clinical Nutrition*, 56(70): 644–649.

Jones, J (2002) 'It's antisocial, but who cares?', in *New Statesman*, 25 November.

Jones, P (2009) *Rethinking Childhood Attitudes in Contemporary Society.* London: New Continuum.

Joseph, D and Sterling, A (2010) The psychological effects of acne in teenagers. *British Journal of School Nursing*, 5(3): 122–126.

Kandola, R and Fullerton, J (1998) *Diversity in Action: Managing the Mosaic.* London: Institute of Personnel and Development.

Kennet and North Wilts Advocacy Project for People with Learning Difficulties (2002) *Policy Guidelines: A Guide to Advocacy.* Devizes: Kennet and North Wilts Advocacy Project for People with Learning Difficulties.

Kerpelman, JL and Pittman, JF (2001) The instability of possible selves: identity processes within late adolescents' close peer relationships. *Journal of Adolescence*, 24: 491–512.

Kimberlee, R (1998) Young people, the Labour Party and the 1997 General Election, a reply to Leonard and Katawala. *Renewal*, 6(2): April.

Kimberlee, R (2009) Streets Ahead on Safety: young people's participation in decision making to address the European road injury 'epidemic'. *Journal of Health and Social Care in the Community*, 16 (3): 322–328.

Kipping, R, Jago, R and Lawlor, D (2008) Obesity in children. Part 1: Epidemiology, measurement, risk factors, and screening. *British Medical Journal*, 337: 922–927.

Kirby, P and Bryson, S (2002) *Measuring the Magic? Evaluating and Researching Young People's Participation in Public Decision Making.* London: Carnegie Young People Initiative.

Klass, D, Silverman, P and Nickman, S (eds) (1996) *Continuing Bonds – New Understanding of Grief.* Levittown, PA: Taylor and Francis.

Knott, C and Scragg, T (eds) (2010) *Reflective Practice in Social Work* (2nd edition). Exeter: Learning Matters.

Kooiman, J (2003) *Governing as Governance.* London: Sage.

Kottler, JA and Kottler, E (1993) *Teacher as Counselor – Developing the Helping Skills You Need.* Thousand Oaks, CA: Corwin Press.

Kramer, L (2010) The essential ingredients of successful siblings relationships: an emerging framework for advancing theory and practice. *Child Development Perspectives*, 4(2): 80–86.

Kwaitek, E, McKenzie K and Loads, D (2005) Self-awareness and reflection: exploring the 'therapeutic use of self'. *Learning Disability Practice*, 8(3): 27–31.

Laberge, L, Petit, D, Simard, C, Vitaro, F and Tremblay, R (2001) Development of sleep patterns in early adolescence. *Journal of Sleep Research*, 10(1): 59–67.

Laming, H (2003) *Report of an Inquiry into the Death of Victoria Climbié*, Cm 5730. London: The Stationery Office.

Laming, H (2009) *The Protection of Children in England: A Progress Report.* London: The Stationery Office.

Lansdown, G (2000) The realisation of children's participation rights, in Percy-Smith, B and Thomas, N (eds) *A Handbook of Children's and Young People's Participation: Perspectives from Theory and Practice.* London: Routledge.

LARSOA (2006) Qwizdom helps get road safety message across. Available at: http://www. larsoa.org.uk/larsoa_archive/news_feb05/news02_qwizdom.htm (last accessed 8 March 2011).

Laslett, P and Wall, R (eds) (1972) *Household and Family in Past Time.* Cambridge: Cambridge University Press.

Leach, P, Barnes, J, Malmberg, L, Sylva, K and Stein, A (2007) The quality of different types of child care at 10 and 18 months: a comparison between types and factors related to quality. *Early Child Development and Care,* 178(2): 177–209.

Lee, N (2001) *Childhood and Society.* Maidenhead: Open University Press.

Lefevre, M (2010) *Communicating with Children and Young People: Making a Difference.* Bristol: Policy Press.

Lepper, J (2010) Old step in to stop youth offending. *Children & Young People Now,* 15 June 2010. Available at: www.cypnow.co.uk/Archive/1009778/News-Insight-Old-step-stop-youth-offending/ (last accessed 3 March 2011).

Le Riche, P and Taylor, I (2008) *The Learning Teaching and Assessment of Partnership Working in Social Work Education.* London: Social Care Institute for Excellence.

Lupton, K and Bayley, M (2006) Children's views on the road environment and safety. *Transport,* 159(TR1): 9–14.

Lyons, C (2004) *Breaking Down Walls – An Evaluation of the Work of Liverpool Children's Fund 2001–2004.* Liverpool: Centre for the Study of the Child and the Law, University of Liverpool.

Macgregor, J (2008) *Introduction to the Anatomy and Physiology of Children A Guide for Students of Nursing, Child Care and Health* (2nd edition). London: Routledge.

McNaughton, D, Hamlin, D, McCarthy, J, Head-Reeves, D and Schreiner, M (2007) Learning to listen: teaching an active listening strategy to pre-service education professionals. *Topics in Early Childhood Special Education,* 27(4): 223–231.

Madge, N (2006) *Children These Days.* Bristol: The Policy Press.

Magin, P, Pond, D, Smith, W and Watson, A (2005) A systematic review of the evidence for 'myths and misconceptions' in acne management: diet, face-washing and sunlight. *Family Practice,* 22: 62–70.

Makrinioti, D (1994) Conceptualisation of childhood in a welfare state, in Qvortrup, J et al. (eds) *Childhood Matters.* Aldershot: Avebury.

Mallon, E, Newton, J, Klassen, A, Stewart-Brown, S, Ryan, T and Finlay, A (1999) The quality of life in acne: a comparison with general medical conditions using generic questionnaires. *British Journal of Dermatology,* 140: 672–676.

Markus, H and Nurius, P (1986) Possible selves. *American Psychologist,* 41: 954–969.

Marmot, M. (2010) *Fair Society, Healthy Lives: A Strategic Review of Health Inequalities in England Post-2010* (The Marmot Review). Available at: www.marmotreview.org (last accessed 3 March 2011).

Mayall, B (2002) *Towards a Sociology for Childhood: Thinking from Children's Lives.* Buckingham: Open University Press.

Milbourne, L, Macrae, S and Maguire, M (2003) Collaborative solutions or new policy problems: exploring multi-agency partnerships in education and health work. *Journal of Education Policy,* 18(1): 19–35.

Miles, S (2000) *Youth Lifestyles in a Changing World*. Buckingham: Open University Press.

Miller, C (2004) *Producing Welfare: A Modern Agenda*. Basingstoke: Palgrave Macmillan.

Miller, W and Rollnick, S (2002) *Motivational Interviewing: Preparing People for Change* (2nd edition). New York: Guildford Press.

Mizen, P (2004) *The Changing State of Youth*. Houndmills: Palgrave Macmillan.

Moyles, J (1998) To play or not to play? That is the question, in Smidt, S (ed) *The Early Years: A Reader*. London: Routledge.

Mulholland, G, Ozbilin, M and Worman, D (2006) *Managing Diversity: Words into Actions, Executive Briefing*. London: Chartered Institute of Personnel and Development.

Munro, E (2007) *Child Protection*. London: Sage.

Munro, E (2010) *The Munro Review of Child Protection: Part 1 A Systems Analysis*. London: DFE.

National Assembly for Wales (2000) *Extending Entitlement: Supporting Young People 11–25 in Wales*. Cardiff: National Assembly for Wales.

NCB (2010) *Understanding Why*. London: NCB.

Netmums (2010) Gender survey: sugar and spice and not so nice? Mums are more critical of their daughters. Available at: www.netmums.com/homelife/Netmums_Gender_Survey. 5486/ (last accessed 15 November 2010).

Newman, J, Barnes, M, Sullivan, H and Knops, A (2004) Public participation and collaborative governance. *Journal of Social Policy*, 33(2): 203–223.

Noland, H, Price, JH, Dake, J and Telljohann, SK (2009) Adolescents' sleep behaviours and perceptions of sleep. *The Journal of School Health*, 79(5): 224–230.

NSPCC (2007) *Procedures and Core Standards: 3. Confidentiality and Information Sharing*. London: NSPCC.

Office for National Statistics (2010) *Social Trends, No. 40*. Newport: Office for National Statistics.

Ofsted (2001) *Raising the Achievement of Children in Public Care*. London: Ofsted.

Ofsted (2010) *The Special Educational Needs and Disability Review: A Statement is not Enough*. Manchester: Ofsted.

Oliver, B (2006) Identity and change: youth working in transition. *Youth & Policy*, 93: 5–19.

Oliver, B (2008) Reforming the children's workforce: a higher education response. *Learning in Health & Social Care*, 7(4): 209–218.

Osgerby, B (1998) *Youth in Britain since 1945*. London: Blackwell.

Owen-Blakemore, J and Centers, R (2005) Characteristics of boys' and girls' toys. *Sex Roles*, 53(9/10): 619–633.

Pateman, C (1970) *Participation and Democratic Theory*. Cambridge: Cambridge University Press.

Percy-Smith, B (2005) 'I've had my say, but nothing's changed!': Where to now? Critical reflections on children's participation. Paper presented at *Emerging Issues in the Geographies of Children and Youth* conference, Brunel University, 23–24 June.

Petrie, P, Boddy, J, Cameron, C, Heptinstall, E, McQuail S, Simon, A and Wigfall, V (2005) *Pedagogy – A Holistic, Personal Approach to Work with Children and Young People across Services*, briefing paper, June. London: Thomas Coram Research Unit.

Philip, K (2000) Mentoring: pitfalls and potential for young people. *Youth and Policy*, 67: 1–15.

Philip, K and Hendry, LB (1996) Young people and mentoring: towards a typology? *Journal of Adolescence*, 19: 189–201.

Pike, A, Kretschemner, T and Dunn, J (2009) Siblings – friends or foes? *The Psychologist*, 22(6): 494–496.

Pincus, FL (2006) *Understanding Diversity: An Introduction to Class, Race, Gender & Sexual Orientation*. London: Rienner Publishers.

Pless, NM and Maak, T (2004) Building an inclusive diversity culture: principles, processes and practice. *Journal of Business Ethics*, 54: 129–147.

Plummer, K (2001) *Documents of Life 2: An Invitation to a Critical Humanism.* London: Sage.

Pollard, K, Sellman, D and Senior, B (2005) The need for interprofessional working, in Barrett, G, Sellman, D and Thomas, J (eds) *Interprofessional Working in Health and Social Care: Professional Perspectives.* Basingstoke: Palgrave.

Pollet, TV and Nettle, D (2007) Birth order and face to face contact with a sibling: firstborns have more contact than laterborns. *Personality and Individual Differences*, 43: 1786–1806.

Pollock, L (1983) *Forgotten Children: Parent–Child Relations in England from 1500 to 1900.* Cambridge: Cambridge University Press.

Prince, R (2009) David Cameron: family values the key to responsible society. *The Telegraph*, 29 March. Available at: www.telegraph.co.uk/news/newstopics/politics/5070968/David-Cameron-family-values-the-key-to-responsible-society.html (last accessed 1 July 2010).

Rhodes, R (1997) *Understanding Governance: Policy Networks, Governance, Reflexivity and Accountability.* Buckingham: Open University Press.

Richards, D and Smith, M (2002) *Governance and Public Policy in the UK.* Oxford: Oxford University Press.

Roche, J, Tucker, S, Thomson, R and Flynn, R (eds) (2004) *Youth in Society* (2nd edition). London: Sage.

Rogers, CR (1957) The necessary and sufficient conditions of therapeutic personality change. *Journal of Consulting Psychology*, 21: 95–103.

Rossiter, M (2003) Constructing the possible: a study of educational relationships and possible selves, in *Proceedings of the 44th Annual Adult Education Research Conference.* San Francisco: San Francisco State University.

Rutter, M (1972) *Maternal Deprivation Reassessed.* Harmondsworth: Penguin.

Rutter, M (2002) Nature, nurture, and development: from evangelism through science toward policy and practice. *Child Development*, 73(1): 1–21.

Ryde, J (2009) *Being White in the Helping Professions: Developing Effective Intercultural Awareness.* London: Jessica Kingsley.

Salmon, C (1999) Birth order and relationships, friends, family, sexual partners. *Human Nature*, 14: 73–81.

Salmon, C and Daly, M (1998) Birth order and familial sentiment: middleborns are different. *Evolution and Human Behaviour*, 19: 299–312.

Sanders, D, White, G, Burge, B, Sharp, C, Eames, A, McEune, R and Grayson, H (2005) *A Study of the Transition from the Foundation Stage to Key Stage 1.* London: DfES.

Save the Children (2010) *£15,000 Cost of UK After-School Activities Threatens Social Mobility.* London: Save the Children.

Scott, D (2000) *Reading Education Research and Policy.* London: Routledge Falmer.

Shahar, S (1990) *Childhood in the Middle Ages.* London: Routledge.

Shaw, L and Kennedy, C (2008) The treatment of acne. *Paediatrics and Child Health*, 17(10): 385–389.

Sinclair, R and Franklin, A (2000) *Young People's Participation: Quality Protects Research Briefing No. 3.* London: DH.

Sloper, P, Rabiee, P and Beresford, B (2007) *Outcomes for Disabled Children*, Research Works No. 2. York: SPRU University of York.

Smidt, S (2006) *The Developing Child in the 21st Century.* Abingdon: Routledge.

Smith, M (2009) *Introducing Informal Education* [online]. Available at: www.infed.org.uk/i-intro.htm (last accessed 3 March 2011).

Spencer, J, Blumberg, M, McMurray, B, Robinson, S, Samuelson, L and Tomblin, B (2009) Short arms and talking eggs: why we should no longer abide the nativist–empiricist debate. *Child Development Perspectives*, 3(2): 79–87.

Stets, JE and Burke, PJ (2000) Identity theory and social identity theory. *Social Psychology Quarterly*, 63(3): 224–237.

Stewart, A, Petch, A and Curtice, L (2003) Moving towards integrated working in health and social care in Scotland: from maze to matrix. *Journal of Interprofessional Care*, 17(4): 335–350.

Stone, L (1977) *The Family, Sex and Marriage in England 1500–1800.* London: Weidenfeld & Nicholson.

Stonewall (2007) The School Report. Available at: aww.stonewall.org.uk/at_school/education_ resources/4121.asp (last accessed 10 March 2011).

Strohm, K (2002) *Siblings Coming Unstuck and Putting Back the Pieces. Stories of Everyday Life with Children Who Are Different.* London: David Fulton Publishers.

Sulloway, FJ (1996) *Born to Rebel: Birth Order, Family Dynamics and Creative Lives.* New York: Pantheon.

Sutter, G (2003) Penny dreadfuls and perverse domains: Victorian and modern moral panics, in Rowbotham, J and Stevenson, K (eds) *Behaving Badly: Social Panic and Moral Outrage – Victorian and Modern Parallels.* Hampshire: Ashgate.

Tarr, J (2005) Education, in Barrett, G, Sellman, D and Thomas, J (eds) *Interprofessional Working in Health and Social Care.* Basingstoke: Palgrave Macmillan.

Tarr, J (with Lloyd Smith, M) (2000) Researching children's perspectives: a sociological dimension, in Lewis, A and Lindsey, G (eds) *Researching Children's Perspectives.* Milton Keynes: Open University Press.

Taylor, I (2004) Multi-professional teams and the learning organisation, in Gould, N and Baldwin, M (eds) *Social Work, Critical Reflection and the Learning Organisation.* Aldershot: Ashgate Publishing.

Teather, S (2010) Speech to Daycare Trust annual conference, 16 November 2010.

Thomson, R, Flynn, R, Roche, J and Tucker, S (2004) Introduction to the second edition, in Roche, J, Tucker, S, Thomson, R and Flynn, R (eds) *Youth in Society* (2nd edition). London: Sage.

Thompson, P (1998) *Moral Panics.* London: Routledge.

Tickell, C (2011) *The Early Years: Foundations for life, health and learning. An Independent Report on the Early Years Foundation Stage.* London: HMSO.

Timms, C (ed) (2010) *Born Creative.* London: Demos Publications

Towner, E, Dowswell, T, Errington, G, Burkes, M and Towner, J (2002) *Injuries in children aged 0–14 years: A Report Prepared for the Health Development Agency.* Newcastle: University of Newcastle.

UNCRC (1989) *Convention on the Rights of the Child.* Available at: www.un.org/millennium/law/iv-10.htm (last accessed 9 January 2011).

UNESCO (2009) *Policy Guidelines on Inclusion in Education.* Paris: UNESCO.

van Beers, H, Chau, V, Ennew, J, Khan, P, Long, T, Milne, B, Nguyet, T and Son, V (2006) *Creating an Enabling Environment: Capacity Building in Children's Participation.* Stockholm: Save the Children.

Vincenten, J (2006) The time is right to invest in saving children's lives in Europe. *EuroSafe Alert*, 1(1): 5–6.

Warnock, H (1978) *The Warnock Report: Special Educational Needs.* Report of the Committee of Enquiry into the Education of Handicapped Children and Young People. London: HMSO.

Wells, K (2009) *Childhood in Global Perspective.* Cambridge: Polity Press.

Wenham-Clarke, P (2006) *When Lives Collide.* London: Wenham-Clarke Photography/Road Peace.

Wetz, J (2010) Schools need a nurturing culture. *Community Care,* 20 May: 26.

White, L (2001) Sibling relationship over the life course: a panel analysis. *Journal of Marriage and Family*, 63: 555–568.

Williamson, H (2009) European youth policy and the place of the United Kingdom, in Wood, J and Hine, J (eds) *Work with Young People: Theory and Policy for Practice.* London: Sage.

Willow, C (1997) *Hear! Hear!: Promoting Children and Young People's Democratic Participation in Local Government.* London: Local Government Information Unit.

Wilmott, P and Young, M (1962) *Family and Kinship in East London.* Harmondsworth: Penguin.

Wilson, EM and Iles, PA (1999) Managing diversity – an employers and managers challenge. *Journal of Public Sector Management*, 12(1): 27–48.

Wolfson, A and Carskadon, M (1998) Sleep schedules and daytime functioning in adolescence. *Child Development*, 69(4): 875–887.

Woman's Own Magazine (1987) Aids, education and the year 2000. *Woman's Own*, 3 October: 8–10.

Woodhead, M and Montgomery, H (2003) *Understanding Childhood: An Interdisciplinary Approach.* Chichester: Wiley.

Worden, W (1996) *Children and Grief: When a Parent Dies.* London: Guildford Press.

Young, IM (2000) Five faces of oppression, in Adams, M, Blumenfeld, WJ, Castaneda, R, Peters, HW and Zuniga, X (eds) *Readings for Diversity and Social Justice.* New York: Routledge.

Zwozdiak-Myers, P (ed) (2007) *Childhood and Youth Studies.* Exeter: Learning Matters.

Index